Patriots, Traitors and Empires

Stephen Gowans

PATRIOTS, TRAITORS AND EMPIRES

The Story of Korea's Fight for Freedom

Baraka Books
Montréal

ISBN 978-1-77186-135-9 pbk; 978-1-77186-141-0 epub; 978-1-77186-142-7 pdf; 978-1-77186-143-4 mobi/pocket

Book Design and Cover by Folio infographie
Editing and proofreading: Bronwyn Averett and Robin Philpot
Index: Sergey Lobachev
Maps on page 10 and 11: Julie Benoît
Back cover photo: Alamy Stock

Legal Deposit, 2nd quarter 2018

Bibliothèque et Archives nationales du Québec
Library and Archives Canada

Published by Baraka Books of Montreal
6977, rue Lacroix
Montréal, Québec H4E 2V4
Telephone: 514 808-8504
info@barakabooks.com

Printed and bound in Quebec

Trade Distribution & Returns
Canada and the United States
Independent Publishers Group
1-800-888-4741 (IPG1);
orders@ipgbook.com

We acknowledge the support from the Société de développement des entreprises culturelles (SODEC) and the Government of Quebec tax credit for book publishing administered by SODEC.

Société de développement des entreprises culturelles
Québec

Funded by the Government of Canada
Financé par le gouvernement du Canada
Canada

The Koreans have as little use for an American Korea as they had for a Japanese one. They want a Korean Korea.

CONTENTS

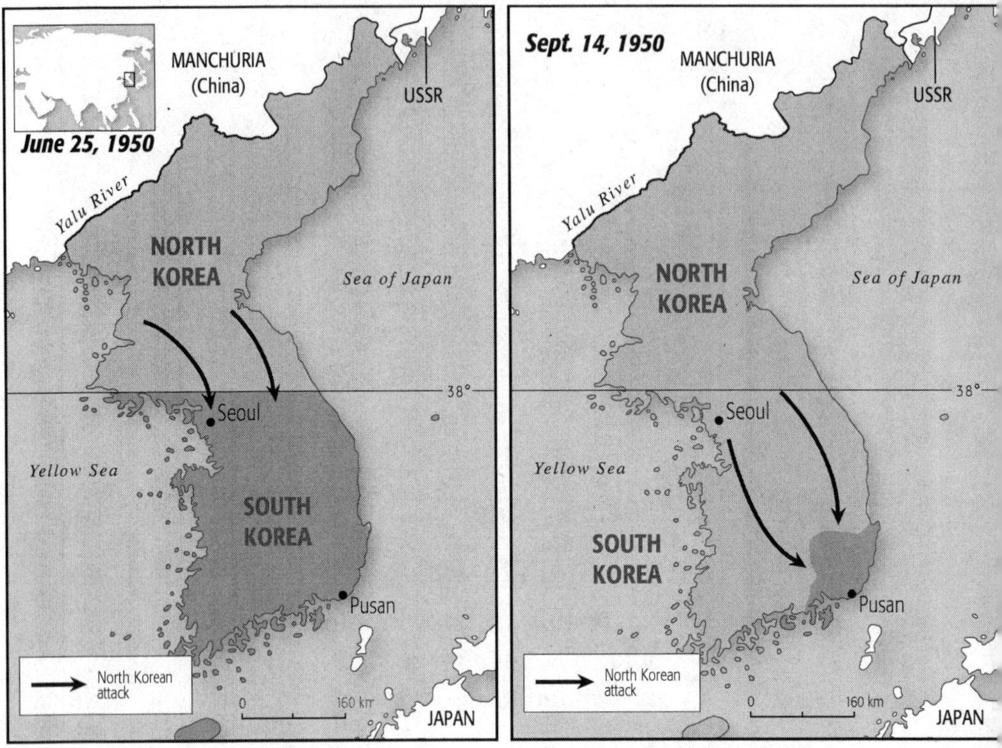

June 25, 1950
MANCHURIA
(China)
USSR
Yalu River
NORTH
KOREA
Sea of Japan
38°
Seoul
Yellow Sea
SOUTH
KOREA
Pusan
North Korean
attack
0
160 km
JAPAN
Sept. 14, 1950
MANCHURIA
(China)
USSR
Yalu River
NORTH
KOREA
Sea of Japan
38°
Seoul
Yellow Sea
SOUTH
KOREA
Pusan
North Korean
attack
0
160 km
JAPAN

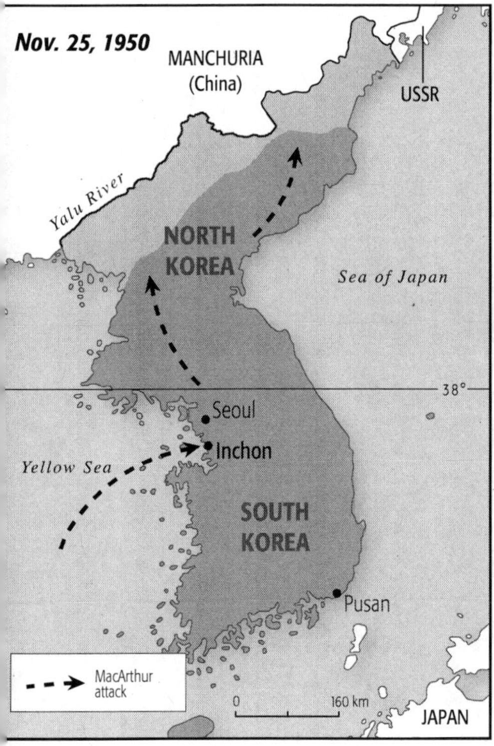

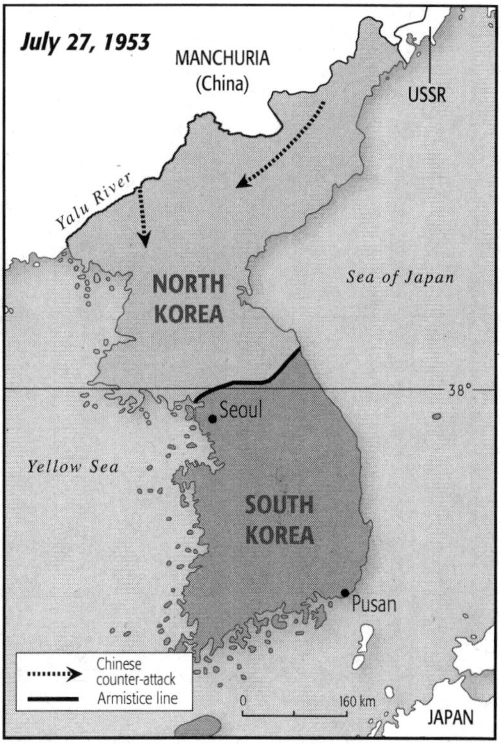

Attacks and troop movements during the Korean War 1950-53. The maps show the 38th Parallel. That line was drawn at midnight on August 10, 1945, by two US army colonels, Dean Rusk and Charles Bonesteel, the day after an atomic bomb was dropped on Nagasaki. Assistant Secretary of War John J. McCloy ordered them to "find a place to divide Korea" to *temporarily* partition the peninsula into separate US and Soviet occupation zones to accept the Japanese surrender. (See Chapter 4.)

INTRODUCTION

One Country—Two States

There are "not two but three Koreas: North, South and the American military bases."—William R. Polk[1]

There is only one Korea, but there are two Korean states. One, the Democratic People's Republic of Korea (DPRK), or North Korea, controls territory in the northern part of the peninsular country. The other state, the Republic of Korea (ROK), or South Korea, controls territory in the southern part. Both states claim sovereignty over all of the country and regard the other as illegitimately occupying territory over which it has jurisdiction by right. Neither state, then, regards the *de facto* border that separates them as an international frontier. On the contrary, they see the border, the so-called demilitarized zone, or DMZ, as a cease-fire line only, marking the dividing line between the two states at the end of the Korean War.

To signal that there is only one Korea, the DPRK is sometimes referred to as north Korea, with "north" in lower case, and its rival the ROK as lowercase "south" Korea. While I'm sympathetic to this protocol, I've opted to use the names North Korea and South Korea as informal synonyms of the DPRK and the ROK respectively, in keeping with conventional usage in the Western world. At the same time, I use these informal names to denote states within a single country, and not to designate two separate nations. While this may seem pedantic to some, the distinction is a useful one in understanding the intra-Korean conflict of 1950 to 1953 which has become known, outside of Korea, as the Korean War, but inside the country either as the 6.25 War or the Great Fatherland Liberation War, depending on which side of the DMZ you're on.

The two states can also be distinguished by two politically descriptive appellations: the patriot state, in the case of the DPRK, and the traitor state, in the case of the ROK. The DPRK was founded by Korean patriots who spent over a decade fighting for the liberation of Korea from Japanese domination. Japan's colonial rule over Korea began formally in 1910, and informally five years earlier, when Tokyo declared Korea a protectorate. When the Japanese empire collapsed at the end of the Pacific War in 1945, the DPRK's future founders insisted that Koreans organize their own affairs, without foreign interference. In other words, they demanded independence after four decades of foreign rule. The demand for liberty, no different from that of any other colonial people, represented the sentiment of virtually every Korean, and has lived on from generation to generation in the political program of the DPRK, which seeks to free Korea from domination by Japan's successor as foreign hegemon, the United States.

For the first two decades of its existence, the South Korean state was staffed at its highest levels by quislings—Koreans who had collaborated with the Japanese, including serving in the Japanese military and the colonial police. Some even took Japanese names. One quisling, who would later become president, beamed at the memory of receiving a gold watch from Japan's Emperor Hirohito, for services to the empire—services which included suppressing the guerrilla war waged by his compatriots to win manumission from Japanese domination. When US forces arrived on the peninsula in 1945, they recruited every Japanese hireling they could find to run their new anti-communist state on the Korean peninsula.

At the conclusion of the Pacific War, the war in the Pacific theater within the larger global conflict that was World War II, Koreans looked to the Soviet Union for inspiration. The Bolshevik Revolution in 1917 had inaugurated the anti-colonial movement, and the Bolsheviks inspired the "wretched of the earth" to emancipate themselves, a project to which the Soviet Union contributed admirably. Across the globe, communism resonated with oppressed peoples. It no less resonated with Kim Il-sung, the founder of the DPRK, a charismatic anti-Japanese guerrilla leader who would very likely have won the national elections planned by the United States and Soviet Union for post-World War II Korea had Washington not scuttled them in favor of elections held within its own occupation zone, whose outcome it could control. The United States blocked the creation of an independent, unified (and very likely communist) Korean state, by creating an alternative state every bit as deserving of the obloquy "puppet state" as was Manchukuo, the state created by Japan in neighboring Manchuria in 1932 under the nominal leadership of the Chinese and actual leadership of the Japanese. The traitors Washington recruited to staff its puppet state served as the public face of the Republic of Korea. They were "advised" behind the scenes by a coterie of US officials, the most important of which were the US ambassador, the CIA station chief, and the top US military official in Korea, the latter of whom had (and continues to have) operational control of the ROK military. The quislings participated in the political partition of Korea to thwart the achievement of their compatriots' left-wing political aspirations, fought an anti-insurgency war in the south to crush left-wing guerrillas, accepted the occupation of the Korean peninsula by US troops, and acceded to their own military's subordination to US command.

Korea has long struggled for freedom, from Japanese control in the first half of the twentieth century, and subsequently from US domination from 1945 to today. This is the story of the patriots who have fought for independence and of the empire-builders and traitors who have opposed them.

As a nation, Korea has existed for over a thousand years, within clearly delineated and recognized borders.[2] Koreans, however, have had the great misfortune to live on geostrategically significant territory which has been contested by powerful states that have used Koreans as pawns in their rivalries. Korea has been subjected to countless foreign invasions; few other countries have suffered as many.[3] As the newspaper of North Korea's lead political party put it in 2017, the "Korean peninsula has historically been the biggest hotbed in the world where [the] strategic interests of big powers sharply collide [owing to Korea's] geopolitical position."[4] That observation was made in connection with the reasons North Korea believed it needed nuclear weapons, namely, to defend itself against the depredations of great powers, in particular, against the greatest power of all, the United States.

Geographically attached to China, Korea was a tributary of the much larger country. It became the object of the First Sino-Japanese War—a conflict fought in the waning years of the nineteenth century between the dominant East Asian power and an emerging one, Japan, for influence in Korea. Japan emerged victorious, and soon after fought Russia, a Eurasian juggernaut, for control of Korea and the contiguous Chinese province of Manchuria, a war occasionally referred to as World War 0. Japan emerged victorious from its contest with the Tsar's empire, to the consternation of Europe, for a non-white race had defeated for the first time a great power, in a global international order that theretofore had been characterized by unalloyed white supremacy. (East Asia would soon be menaced by another sort of racial supremacy—that of the Yamato, or ethnic Japanese, who would seek to lead a great Asian family, in which Koreans would be reduced to the status of adolescents to be taken in hand and guided by the *soi-disant* superior Japanese.) Soon after, Japan abolished Korea as an independent country, renamed it Chosen, and integrated it into its rapidly expanding Empire of the Rising Sun. By the close of the First World War, Japan had built an empire which, apart from Korea, included Taiwan, a chain of Pacific islands, the southern half of Sakhalin, and privileges in the semi-colony of China.[5]

With the Japanese empire's defeat in the Pacific War in 1945, the United States, newly emerged as the world's greatest power, and an empire itself (if undeclared), established its own presence on the Korean peninsula, bisecting Korea into separate US and Soviet occupation zones, as a temporary measure (it was said) to accept the Japanese surrender. However, by 1947, the growing strength of communist forces in East Asia convinced US officials that withdrawal from Korea would allow emancipatory movements in the region to flourish. US officials had no interest in encouraging movements which fought to overthrow colonial oppression and to bring an end to the exploitation of man by man. On the contrary, they were more interested in replacing the chains of European and Japanese colonialism with the fetters of US imperialism.

Koreans, US military officials on the ground had observed, aspired to a communist future, and the industrial assets built in Korea by the Japanese would provide fertile soil in which Korean communism could blossom. At the same time, the victory of Mao's national liberation forces in China was imminent, and that suggested that communism had momentum.

Meanwhile, in Japan, there was an economic crisis, which was proving to be a catalyst for the growth of communism, as post-war Japan looked to a brighter future than the one capitalism, with its frequent downturns, incessant threats of joblessness, growing inequality, omnipresent insecurity, and wars of industrial extermination, had delivered. To counter the communist threat to US financial, industrial and commercial interests, and the geostrategic and military interests with which they were entangled, Washington decided to engineer the political partition of the Korean peninsula. This would offer a number of advantages. Control over Korea south of the 38th parallel, the dividing line US officials had unilaterally drawn in the dying days of the Pacific War, would allow Washington to restore Korea's economic linkages to Japan. This would facilitate the renewal of Japan's capitalism, restart the engine of the country's economic growth, and make the Japanese forget about the attractions of communism. Secondly, Korea's gravitation to a communist future could be immediately eclipsed in the south, and its expansion from the north contained, if not rolled backed altogether. And finally, the United States would have a permanent perch on the doorstep of China, to contain the Reds in the giant

East Asian country. US forces would also be within close range of the Soviet Union, which shared a border with Korea.

The Republic of Korea was established in 1948 at the instigation of the United States, over the objections of most Koreans, who opposed the political partition of their country. Koreans had expected that before 1950, elections would be held for a pan-Korean government. At least, that's what they had been promised. The proclamation of the ROK on August 15, 1948, left Koreans in the south aggrieved. Most had opposed the elections that led to the formation of the government. Koreans in the north were also incensed. Like their southern compatriots, they aspired to a single, democratically-elected Korean government, but with this desideratum at least temporarily foreclosed, they proclaimed their own state, the Democratic People's Republic of Korea, three weeks later, on September 9. The US-created state in the south would refuse to recognize the DPRK, just as Washington had refused to recognize the Korean People's Republic, the republic Koreans had proclaimed for themselves on September 6, 1945, before US forces arrived in Korea.

The United States obtruded its military onto Korea three weeks *after* the Japanese surrender, having spilled not a single drop of blood for Korea's liberation. In contrast, Soviet forces had fought their way into Korea a full month before US forces arrived. The Soviet push into Manchuria and contiguous Korea—and the spilled blood of Soviet soldiers in the campaign–was one of the principal causes of Japan's surrender. The Japanese had hoped that the Soviets—neutral in the Pacific War until August 8, 1945—would broker a peace. But when the Soviets declared war on Japan, and crossed the frontier into Japan's empire, Tokyo knew its cause was hopeless. It surrendered one week later.

The Korean state that would be established in the Soviet occupation zone, the DPRK, was founded by anti-Japanese guerrillas who, like Soviet soldiers, had spilled their blood to liberate Korea. Korean guerrillas had fought the Japanese and their Korean collaborators for years, both within Korea, and from contiguous Manchuria. For 13 long years, Kim Il-sung had been a principal figure in the guerrilla struggle against Japanese imperialism. If anyone deserved to lead a newly independent Korea it was Kim, or Koreans like him, who had devoted their lives to achieving Korea's freedom from foreign domination, and fought long, arduous battles against the country's Japanese tormentors. In contrast, Washington installed Syngman Rhee as the head of its new Korean state, a man who had spent nearly four decades in the United States collecting degrees from Ivy League universities, including a Ph.D. from Princeton. When he was finally driven out of Seoul by exasperated Koreans, he returned to the bosom of his imperial master's embrace, accepting a comfortable retirement in Hawaii. The new South Korean government designated the DPRK not as a state, but as an anti-state organization, deemed to be illegally occupying territory north of the 38th parallel, a designation that remains to this day.

The Soviets withdrew from Korea on December 25, 1948, three and a half months after the founding of the DPRK, leaving North Koreans free to manage their own affairs (which Soviet occupation forces had largely allowed them to do anyway), and the peninsula free from at least one occupying power. The other occupying power, the United States, declined to quit the country, making a brief show of exiting the peninsula in the summer of 1949 by withdrawing combat troops, but leaving hundreds of military advisers behind and secret protocols in place to keep Korean forces under US operational control. US combat forces in large numbers returned a year later. The US military, then, has had a continuous presence on the Korean peninsula since the summer of 1945. Astonishingly, a US general continues to exercise wartime operational control over the South Korean military, an uncomfortable reality that disproves the comforting myth (for South Koreans and US citizens) that the ROK is a sovereign country and not—what the North Korean media never grow tired of pointing out—a puppet of Washington.

South Korea's status as a colony of one empire, the Japanese, and a puppet state of another, the United States, is illustrated by a telling spatial continuity pointed out by Bruce Cumings, a University of Chicago historian who has written widely and compellingly on modern Korean history and whose work I have drawn on extensively to tell the story of Korea's fight for freedom. Cumings observed that in "1894 the Japanese army established its main base at Yongsan, on the outskirts of old Seoul; it [later became] an American military base—a gigantic complex smack in the middle of an enormous, sprawling, bustling city—contemporary Seoul." Cumings wrote that he couldn't "think of another capital city quite like it, where you turn a corner and suddenly see a mammoth swatch of land given over to a foreign army."[6]

Critics would say that the presence of a huge US military base in the middle of the country's capital is only a reflection of South Korea's need to defend itself against a belligerent and aggressive North Korea, and of Seoul's decision to seek US assistance as a security partner. The argument is flawed. First, South Korea is far more deserving of the descriptions "belligerent" and "aggressive" than is North Korea. The ROK has fought unprovoked wars in Vietnam, Afghanistan and Iraq, in all three cases under US command, which is to say, as a "puppet," or, in the preferred vernacular, as an "allied" military force of the United States. The DPRK, in contrast, has never fought an unprovoked war or deployed military forces beyond the Korean peninsula. Second, despite South Korea's alleged vulnerability to North Korean attack, its leaders felt secure enough from the mid-1960s to the mid-1970s to deploy more than 300,000 troops to Vietnam. Surely, a country which professes to be under imminent threat of attack from its northern neighbor could ill-afford to spare even a single solider to fight a war of choice two-thousand miles away. Third, the US-commanded South Korean military has fabricated a wholly implausible story that it is incapable of defending the ROK without US assistance, despite its overwhelming military superiority over the DPRK. In 2013, the ROK's defense intelligence director, Cho Bo-geun, said improbably that despite spending many times more than North Korea on defense, the ROK would lose in a one-on-one fight with its northern neighbor. "If South Korea fights alone," said Cho, "South Korea would lose." But if "we fight as an alliance with the US under the current operational plan, [we will] win by an overwhelming margin."[7] At a meeting with top military officials in the summer of 2017, newly elected South

Korean president Moon Jae-in expressed frustration that his top military advisers insisted that South Korean troops were unable to independently defend the state against North Korea. The ROK is larger than the DPRK in population, GDP, military budget, and the sophistication of its weaponry. How could it be the case, Moon demanded, that the ROK armed forces were incapable of defending South Korea "when our economy has been stronger [than North Korea's] since the 1970s and our military expenditures have topped theirs for decades now?"[8] A previous South Korean president, Roh Moo-hyun, had asked the same question, expressing annoyance over his top generals insisting that a US military presence on the peninsula was indispensable to the ROK's defense. It's significant that despite the protests of the country's highest elected officials, nothing has changed. South Korea remains a base of operations for the Pentagon, its military under US operational control.

CHAPTER I

The Empire of Japan

Our masters fight to have you, lovely creature
They race to seize you in their headlong course.
Each feels most fit to bleed you white in the future
Most justified in taking you by force. —Bertolt Brecht[1]

"[In] Korea, Japanese gendarmes and officers are in charge, shooting and hanging anybody who dares so much as think of freedom."
—Congress of the Peoples of the East, Baku, September 1920

Japan's empire builders "first trained their guns on Korea,"[2] wrote Louise Young, a US historian of modern Japan. The decision to build an empire was multifactorial, driven by a network of mutually reinforcing causes that led Japanese leaders to set their sights on the Korean peninsula, the gateway to the Asian continent, with its abundant raw materials, alluring markets, cheap labor, and potential enemies, a short distance, just one thousand kilometers (600 miles) from Japan across the body of water the Japanese call the Sea of Japan and the Koreans call the East Sea.

As an emerging industrial power, Japan required access to vital raw materials necessary for its industrial development. Unlike the United States and Russia, whose expansive continental empires contained almost all the raw materials a modern industrial economy needed, or France and Britain, whose vast overseas empires teemed with vital natural resources, Japan lacked almost every input the country's industrialists required, with the exception of coal.[3] With Korea under its control, Japan could offer its manufacturers a guaranteed source of raw materials, as well as cheap labor. What's more, Korea could furnish Japan with a secure supply of agricultural goods. The need for an alternative source of foodstuffs had become increasingly pressing. By the early twentieth century, Japan's food production was no longer self-sufficient,[4] owing to the tensions between its growing population and its mountainous topography, which left little room for farming.[5] Japan was also deficient in oil, which would become important later on, as warships converted from coal to oil, and industrial economies increasingly depended on secure sources of petroleum. Securing supplies of oil was not a factor in Japan's integration of Korea into its empire, but it was significant in the subsequent expansion of the empire and its conflict with the United States. Industrial expansion, moreover, exacerbated Japan's dependency on foreign markets and raw materials, creating growing pressures to acquire foreign territory. The more Japan industrialized, the more dependent it became on foreign markets and sources of raw materials, and the more dependent it became, the more it was driven to expand its empire.[6]

Japan wasn't the only empire that had set its sights on Korea, and Japanese leaders, recognizing this, moved to pre-empt rival claims to the peninsula. The United States was aggressively expanding. Between 1776 and 1890, a period of 114 years, US territory grew by 3,357,000 square miles, an average of 29,535 square miles per year, or 81 square miles per day. Washington's acquisition of colonies in the Pacific—Hawaii in 1893, Cuba and the Philippines in 1898, and Samoa in 1899—enkindled fears in Tokyo that US statesmen and industrialists harbored ambitions to acquire Korea as a colony, and might even turn their imperial ambitions on Japan itself.[7]

Russia was another looming threat. According to the late US author, lawyer and historian David Fromkin, "Until the end of the decade before the First World War, the Russian Empire had been expanding at the expense of its neighbors at a prodigious rate and for a long time. It has been calculated that, at the time, the

Russian Empire had been conquering the territory of its neighbors at an average rate of 50 square miles a day for 400 years."[8] The Romanov Empire was building the Trans-Siberia Railway, which, once completed, would provide the Tsar a route to infiltrate Russian troops into Northeast Asia, where they could embark upon the project of enlarging the Tsar's domains.[9] Russia coveted the Korean peninsula for its warm-water ports, of which it was in short supply. And if Russia expanded its imperial demesne over Korea, how long would it be before the Tsar's imperial ambitions turned to Japan?

Japan's empire builders had seen how the great powers had humiliated China, making it into a colony, not of one great power, but of all of them, as Sun Yat-sen, the founder of modern China, had lamented.[10] Japan resolved that it would not fall prey to the same fate. "In an international order where the 'strong devour the weak,' the Japanese concluded they could either join the West as a 'guest at the table' or be served up with China and Korea as part of the feast,"[11] wrote Louise Young. They would, then, emulate the great powers. Japan would build its own empire by devouring as much of its surrounding territory as it could, before the great powers arrived on the scene. "Just as U.S. president James Monroe had informed the great powers that they better stay clear of Latin America," observed Sarah Paine, a professor of strategy and policy at the US Naval College, "likewise increasing numbers of Japanese favored making East Asia their exclusive preserve." Marshal of the Imperial Japanese Army, Terauchi Hisaichi believed that eventually all of Asia would fall under Japanese control.[12]

The first step in building Japan's empire would be to wrest Korea from China's orbit. On July 25, 1894, Japan went to war with China over the question of who would control Korea. The Japanese government resolved to unilaterally impose reforms on Korea, which Tokyo promised would benefit Koreans by lifting them out of poverty through expanded trade. Using language that anticipated the rhetoric Washington would employ more than a century later to justify its leadership of a new global economic order, Japan promised to create a win-win solution for both countries by opening Korea to the global economy.[13]

Unsurprisingly, Koreans rejected Japan's self-proclaimed leadership[14] and greeted the First Sino-Japanese War, not as the beginning of a period of Korean efflorescence, but as the commencement of a painful period of imperial Japanese rule[15] marked by, among other things, a foreign military base in the middle of Seoul, which would become a seat for ongoing foreign domination of the peninsula that would last through the twentieth century and into the twenty-first. The war incubated an intense animus among Koreans toward the Japanese. To counter Tokyo's imperial ambitions, the Korean monarchy sought out the protection of other great powers. Queen Min, the royal consort, looked to St. Petersburg as a counterpoise to Japan and purged the government of ministers whose sympathies lay with the Japanese. The Japanese government responded by arranging to have her eliminated. She was murdered on October 8, 1895, "to the enduring outrage of the Korean people."[16]

Less than a decade later, Japan fought Russia over the question of which empire would control Korea and the contiguous Chinese province of Manchuria. The war was preceded by a series of negotiations in which the two countries proposed to divide the two territories. In 1896, Tokyo offered to bisect Korea along the 38th parallel, anticipating the United States' partition of the peninsula along the same parallel 49 years later. Japan proposed to establish a sphere of influence south of the parallel, while Russia's sphere would lie to the north. The Russians declined, their ambitions set on the warm-water ports of the south, and insisted that all of Korea fall within Russia's ambit.[17] The Japanese tried again in 1903, this time proposing to let Russia have Manchuria in exchange for Japan taking all of Korea. Again, the Tsar balked, demanding an exclusive sphere of influence in Manchuria and a shared sphere in Korea.[18] Soon, negotiations between the two empires collapsed, and by 1904 the rivalry escalated into war. Japan launched a surprise attack on the Russian fleet, stationed at what was then called Port Arthur (now Lushunkou District), causing incalculable damage and Russia's defeat. Japan's vanquishing Russia stirred all of Asia and horrified Europe. For the first time ever, a non-white nation had defeated a great power in battle.[19] A seismic event which shook the Western world, the war touched off the 1905 revolution in Russia, but inaugurated Korea's enslavement by Japan.

With Japan now in control of Korea, the United States sought to consolidate its own imperial assets in the Far East. In 1905, US Secretary of War William Howard Taft and Japanese prime minister Count Katsura Taro signed a memorandum in which the United States would recognize Japanese domination of Korea in return for Japan recognizing US control of the Philippines.[20] The agreement rankled Kim Il-sung, who would point out years later how the United States had connived with Japan to sell Korea into colonial slavery, in return for Japan recognizing Washington's own imperial ambitions, a hard truth lost on his Korean compatriots who placed their hope in the United States winning Korea's manumission from Japanese rule at the Paris Peace Conference following World War I. The widely held but erroneous belief that US President Woodrow Wilson had promised a post-war world of self-determination, and the hostility of the great powers to the colonial peoples' demands for it, confirmed Kim in the belief, which would play no small role in North Korea's official philosophy of self-reliance, or *Juche*, that it "is a tragic lesson that Korea should not count on other nations for independence, because they [do] not care."[21] Instead, Koreans would have to emancipate themselves, in accordance with the communist theory to which Kim subscribed. That theory held that any group that is oppressed can count on none but itself to bring about its liberation. Other people wouldn't free Koreans; Koreans would have to free themselves.

The result of Japan's victory over Russia was that Tokyo established a protectorate over Korea in 1905. Japan would now run Korea's foreign affairs, its police, and its communications systems, and station Japanese troops on Korean soil.[22] The US-supported affront to Korean sovereignty touched off a major insurgency, of such large scope that as many as 15,000 insurgents were killed and up to 10,000 jailed in uprisings between 1905 and 1907, the first martyrs in Korea's long and enduring war for freedom.[23] On August 1, 1907, the Japanese resident general ordered the Korean army disbanded, touching off a new round of riots and intensifying an anti-Japanese insurgency. Between July 1907 and October 1908, 14,000 Koreans were killed fighting to liberate Korea from the Japanese yoke.[24] From 1907 through 1910, guerrilla bands numbering nearly 10,000 came close to evicting the Japanese colonizers from Seoul. By Japanese accounts, in 1908, nearly 70,000 Korean guerillas had engaged Japanese troops in almost 1,500 confrontations. This was hardly a war of minor skirmishes, but a determined military effort to expel the Japanese invaders. The Japanese occupation forces, however, proved formidable, and gradually overcame the insurgency. The number of guerrillas dropped to about 25,000 in 1909 and then plummeted to below 2,000, as insurgents fled to the safety of neighboring Manchuria.[25] Kim Il-sung would later take up the insurgent cause in the frozen mountains of the Chinese region, forming the core of the future Korean People's Army (KPA), North Korea's military force.

Korea was formally absorbed into the Japanese empire on August 22, 1910, ceasing to exist as a country, and re-named Chosen by the Japanese. That day would become "the darkest day of any subsequent year in Korean history," observed Bruce Cumings[26] and would mark the beginning of what historian Frank Baldwin termed a 35-year period of "particularly intense colonial control compared to other colonial areas, like India and Indochina, which were far from their metropolitan centers."[27]

During the Japanese colonial period, Korean culture was outlawed. All Korean political organizations were disbanded.[28] Korean newspapers and public gatherings were prohibited. The education system was Japanized.[29] Koreans were forced to speak Japanese, take Japanese names, and worship at Shinto shrines, even though Shintoism, the traditional religion of Japan, was foreign to Korea.[30]

The Empire of the Rising Sun built up Korea economically, developing mines, industry, railways, and electric power plants. But the development was geared to the needs of Japan's empire and its financiers, industrialists, and militarists. Koreans became Japan's peripatetic, super-exploited workforce, the coerced labor on which the wealth of the empire would be built. In pursuit of Japan's imperial project, Koreans were reduced to the status of subhumans, dehumanized as machines and beasts of burden, denied the dignity of self-determination, and alienated from their language and culture.

At the same time, Korea was transformed from a territory whose agricultural activity sustained a Korean population into a Japanese granary. Huge blocks of land were transferred into Japanese hands, and agriculture was steered away from Korean to Japanese needs.[31] In 1938, 60 percent of Korea's harvested rice was exported to Japan. According to the American journalist Anna Louise Strong, "The Japanese ate seven times as much rice per capita as the Koreans, condemning the latter to eat rice huskings and cheaper grains."[32] What land did remain in Korean hands was owned by local landlords whose oppressive rents made the Korean peasantry among the world's lowliest and most oppressed.[33] Korea's landed families would, after decades of collaboration with the Japanese, become the nucleus of a new post-Japanese South Korean state, and founders of the *chaebols*—literally "wealth clans"—the hydra-like family-owned conglomerates that dominate South Korea's economy, including Samsung, Hyundai, and LG.

Manufacturing and mining, like agriculture, were subordinated to Japan's needs. Almost all major industry north of the 38th parallel belonged to the Japanese,[34] and was engaged in producing semi-finished products which were shipped to Japan. Not a single plant produced finished goods for the Korean market.[35] Korean needs were simply not a consideration. On top of this, Korean workers were discriminated against in pay. According to Bruce Cumings, "Japanese workers in Korea got over 2 yen per day in 1937, a Formosan [Taiwanese] worker 1 yen, and a Korean worker .66 yen."[36] The pay was intolerably low, and working conditions were insufferably harsh. In the mines, Koreans were forced to work punishingly long hours, the women bare-breasted.[37]

As Japan took steps to expand its empire through military conquest, Koreans were impressed into service as conscripted laborers, sent to every corner of the empire to satisfy the requirements of Japan's military and economic expansion.[38] In 1941, about one of every 17 Koreans was in Japan, half working in Japanese industry. By 1944, one in eight had been relocated outside Korea, to other parts of the empire, where they were needed as laborers. Twenty percent were uprooted, either shipped beyond Korea's borders or living in Korea outside of areas in which they were born.[39] At the close of World War II, one third of the industrial labor force in Japan was made up of Koreans.[40] At least ten thousand Koreans were employed as conscripted laborers in Japanese war plants in Hiroshima and Nagasaki. They perished in the US atom bombing of the two cities.[41]

Echoes of past oppressions can be heard in the present. Those who descend from dominant groups which benefitted from race-, class-, or sex-based discriminations of the past enjoy advantages which have carried forward across generations to the present. Likewise, the disadvantages imposed on groups which suffered under past discriminations continue to be visited upon their descendants, even when the discriminations have formally come to an end.

Aso Taro, Japan's prime minister from September 2008 to September 2009, and later deputy prime minister and minister of finance in the government of Abe Shinzo (Abe is known as Shinzo Abe in the West), is an example of historical oppressions profiting contemporary figures through descent. Aso is the scion of a wealthy mining family whose wealth was built on the forced labor of Koreans.[42] His considerable advantages, in education, position, wealth, and connections, derive less from his personal qualities (however admirable they may be) than from the conscripted labor of the thousands of Koreans his forbears exploited in their mines. It is from the womb of coerced Korean labor that Aso's wealth—and all the advantages it confers—was born.

Aso is the grandson of another former Japanese prime minister, Yoshida Shigeru, who is related by marriage to two other former Japanese prime ministers, Sato Eisaku and Kishi Nobosuke. Kishi was the commerce and industry minister in Japan's puppet Manchurian state, and later the munitions ministry supremo. He oversaw the coerced labor of hundreds of thousands of Koreans and Chinese in Manchurian-based mines and factories.[43] Tojo Hideki, who would lead Japan's cabinet during the Pacific War, was

Manchukuo's head of military police. Both Kishi and Tojo, as members of the wartime Japanese cabinet, co-signed the declaration of war against the United States in 1941. After the war, Kishi was jailed on war crimes charges.[44]

Despite his war criminal status, geopolitical events conspired to transform Kishi into a US asset and esteemed politician. The end of the war brought opportunity to the United States, but also danger. The danger was that the people of the world, the bulk of whom were victims of colonialism and the failures of capitalism, would be inspired by the example of the Soviet Union and the communists who identified with it. Lenin had urged the colonial oppressed to rebel against their imperial masters, and Moscow had furnished national liberation movements with assistance. This inspired the colonial downtrodden, gave them hope, and persuaded them to look favorably on the communists. Moreover, while the rest of the world went backward during the capitalist crisis of the Great Depression, the Soviets forged ahead, building a great industrial economy with full employment. Hadn't the Soviets, in the space of a decade, turned an underdeveloped country into an industrial behemoth, a model that other underdeveloped countries could emulate? Additionally, the USSR had emerged victorious from the greatest colonial war ever waged, that of Nazi Germany against the Soviet Union, impelled by the German imperialist aim of winning *lebensraum* (living space) and enslaving the peoples of Eastern Europe. Almost all of the heavy lifting in the fight to crush Nazism was done by the Soviets. What's more, the Red Army had played a lead role in toppling the Empire of the Rising Sun, while communists led the resistance to Axis occupation forces throughout Europe and Asia. Communists worldwide were held in high esteem after World War II; they had been in the vanguard of every fight against all that was rotten, reactionary, and exploitative.

In China, in the years immediately following the Pacific War, communist forces, led by Mao Tse Tung, were advancing toward victory in a great anti-colonial and anti-feudal struggle, offering inspiration to other peoples of East Asia seeking liberation. At the same time, Europe and Japan were reeling from economic breakdown caused by the war. Washington worried that local communist forces would come to power in Germany and Japan, pushed by widespread hardship and pulled by the prestige the communists had won as the most dedicated of the anti-fascist forces. Top US State Department and Pentagon officials feared that if communists came to power in Berlin and Tokyo, German and Japanese industrial potential would be brought under local popular control, tilting the balance of world power away from US hegemony. Real security against the popular revolt against empire-building and the failures of capitalism required the restoration of faltering economies and a crackdown on communists. The solution, in the view of the US power elite, was a stimulus program to put Japan and Germany back to work and the recruitment of anti-communists to take up major posts in the new US-allied post-war states. Kishi—the war criminal who oversaw the use of coerced labor in Manchurian munitions factories—was identified as a promising candidate to lead a new post-war anti-communist Japan.[45] Kishi's reputation was instantly rehabilitated. He was exonerated for wartime opposition to the US empire, and served two terms as Japan's prime minister, becoming known in some circles as "America's favorite war criminal." Under the tutelage of Washington, the new Japan would not be much different from the old one. It would remain implacably opposed to forces of national liberation and hostile to a world of equality and democracy, its leaders chosen from among former enemies for their anti-communist credentials.

Kishi is held in the highest esteem by yet another Japanese prime minister, Abe Shinzo, Kishi's maternal grandson. While Kishi was in Manchuria organizing the conscripted labor of Koreans and Chinese, Kim Il-sung, the grandfather of Kim Jong-un, the current leader of North Korea, was in Manchuria leading a guerrilla war against Kishi and other Japanese empire-builders, war criminals and freebooters. Eight decades later, Kim Il-sung and Kishi would meet "again through their grandsons," observed Bruce Cumings,[46] as vectors of contending social forces: revolutionary nationalism vs. imperialism, labor vs. parasitism, emancipation vs. reaction.

The Japanese dragooned Koreans into another form of coerced labor—enslavement to satisfy the lust of Japanese soldiers. Possibly as many as 200,000 women were impressed into a system of sexual slavery. By the time the system was fully established, the vast majority of sexual slaves were Koreans.[47]

As Bruce Cumings relates, "Japanese historians had written about the sexual slavery system for decades, but were told time and again by the authorities that no archival documents existed on it." Then, in 1992, Japanese "historian Yoshiaki Yoshimi walked into a military library and found such documents just sitting on the shelf. His 1995 book, *Comfort Women: Sexual Slavery in the Japanese Military During World War II*, is now a standard source."[48]

The first documented comfort station, the anodyne term used to sanitize the description of what were *de facto* rape stations, was established in Japanese controlled Manchuria in 1932, the year Kim Il-sung launched his insurgency against the empire-builders under whose supervision this miserable institution flourished. By 1938 there were already approximately 30,000 to 40,000 women, mainly Koreans, subjected to regular sexual violence by Japanese soldiers.[49]

Sexual slavery carried on even after the fall of the Empire of the Rising Sun, resurrected by the South Korean army during the Korean War.[50] It is perhaps of some significance that the ROK Army was, at the time, dominated at its highest levels by Koreans who had served in the Japanese Imperial Army, some of whom had even served in army units tasked with hunting down Kim Il-sung. Is it any surprise, then, that this very same army, with its historical connections to the Japanese through its officer corps, should set up a Japanese-style system of sexual bondage? It's also of significance that at the time, the South Korean army was, as it has been throughout its history, under the operational control of a US commander. Hence, the United States was complicit in the sexual slavery practiced by the ROK Army.

The terms "comfort women" and "comfort station" evince a patriarchal bias. Whose comfort was involved? Certainly not that of the women who were kidnapped or otherwise coerced into sexual slavery. "Comfort" is presumably what the institution offered its male beneficiaries—either "comfort" in sexual release, or the "comfort" of domination. But importantly, the institution, and the women who were dragooned into it, are described in terms of what they offered men, as if the interests of men are primary, and those of the female victims, of little moment. The women coerced into sexual slavery weren't "comfort" women who worked at "comfort stations" but enslaved rape victims impressed into service in rape stations for the satisfaction of soldiers who were raping, both literally and figuratively, an entire nation.

While Japanese counter-insurgency efforts managed to quell the Korean struggle for freedom by 1910, resistance continued, and was never fully expunged at any point during Japan's colonial rule. In 1912, the insurgency was strong enough that the Japanese had arrested 50,000 Korean rebels. By 1918, 140,000 patriots were arrested by Japanese colonial security forces.[51] Koreans had no intention of capitulating to their Japanese conquerors.

In 1919, mass movements against colonialism swept across the colonial world, and on March 1, Korea erupted in anger. Over the next two months, at least 500,000 Koreans took part in street demonstrations in 600 different locations.[52] The police were unable to cope with the disturbances, and the Japanese garrison army was called in to crush the uprising. Clashes between protestors and the army led to hundreds, if not thousands, of deaths,[53] adding to the Golgotha of some 30,000 Koreans who had already been martyred in efforts to liberate their country dating from 1905.

"All the pent up angers and sorrows of living under the Japanese imperialists for ten long years exploded," wrote Kim Il-sung, many years later.

> Ten years after the annexation, Korea had become a gigantic dungeon, no better than those of the Middle Ages. The Japanese colonists used naked military power to suppress the Korean people's aspiration to become free again. The Japanese took away our freedom of press, freedom to hold meetings, freedom to form organizations, and freedom to march. They took away our human rights and properties. The Korean people formed secret organizations, independence fights, mass enlightenment activities, and had built up considerable potential energy against the decade of plunder and exploitation by the Japanese.[54]

Kim complained that some of the leaders of the movement against Japanese colonization "believed that Korea could be freed by sending petitions to other nations. They took and swallowed US President Woodrow Wilson's 'Doctrine of Self-Determination' and expected the United States and other Western powers to pressure Japan into freeing Korea," Kim recalled. "They wrote petition after petition, becoming laughing stocks of the imperialists."[55]

Syngman Rhee, whom Washington would recruit to lead South Korea, spent his days in Washington lobbying diplomats and State Department officials. A "gentleman" who spoke impeccable English, Rhee "begged and pleaded with representatives of the imperialist nations," wrote Kim Il-sung, but the imperialist countries "were more keen on grabbing more colonies for themselves than freeing any colony."[56]

"The end of World War I brought false and rapidly dashed hopes to those on the receiving end of imperialism," wrote Sarah Paine. US "president Woodrow Wilson's Fourteen Points nowhere promised (though many interpreted them to promise) national self-determination. The Versailles Peace Treaty did not make good on the promise that was never made and this failure deeply disappointed the colonized worldwide."[57]

Wilson did promise self-determination, though not universally, and only to the peoples of the defeated Hapsburg and Ottoman empires. Wilson's point 10 of his 14-point plan for the post-WWI order expressed the view that "the people of Austria-Hungary should be accorded the freest opportunity to autonomous development," while his point 12 recommended that "other nationalities under Turkish rule" be accorded the same opportunities. But Wilson failed to deliver a sweeping, universal call for the manumission of all colonial peoples.

To be sure, Wilson did dilate on the importance of self-determination, which he defined as the right of all people "to choose the sovereignty under which they shall live,"[58] but he implicitly invoked an exclusionary clause that proponents of liberalism have traditionally used to differentially assign rights and privileges within their ostensible system of equality. Wilson implicitly defined "people" as subjects of defeated rival empires, denying the charter of humanity to the subjects of allied empires, such as that of Great Britain, which held hundreds of millions of Indians in thrall, among others, and who would not be subsumed under Wilson's definition of those worthy of self-determination. Indians, Koreans, Africans—the subject peoples of the allied powers—were tacitly defined as non-people, or sub-humans—intellectually and culturally inferior beings for whom self-governance was impossible.

The same kind of exclusionary liberalism applied at home. Wilson believed in the supremacy of the white race. As Stephen Kinzer has pointed out, Wilson "removed African-Americans from government jobs, segregated the transit system in Washington, D.C., and had 'Birth of a Nation' screened in the White House—saying afterward that its portrayal of noble Klansmen repressing ape-like black thugs was 'a splendid production.'"[59]

In international affairs, Wilsonian liberalism meant equality for whites and the denial of a charter of humanity for non-whites. Self-determination would be the exclusive preserve of Europeans, denied to Koreans, Chinese, Indians, Egyptians, and Palestinians. The falsely labelled paladin of the equality of peoples favored a Jewish Palestine (i.e., a Palestine settled by white Europeans), or, to put it another way, the negation of the rights of (non-white Arab) Palestinians. Neither had Wilson any intention of conferring self-determination upon the people of Central America into whose countries he kept dispatching US Marines to install governments congenial to US business interests. In office, Wilson intervened militarily in Cuba, Haiti, the Dominican Republic, Mexico and

Russia, unwilling to grant the people of these countries the right of self-determination.[60]

"In 1916," recounts Kinzer, "Wilson drafted a speech to Congress declaring, 'It shall not lie with American people to dictate to another people what their government shall be.' He sent it to his secretary of state for review. It came back with this notation in the margin: 'Haiti, S. Domingo, Nicaragua, Panama.' Confronted with this inconvenient reminder, Wilson decided not to deliver the speech."[61]

Looking back on the March First movement, Kim Il-sung was scathing in his assessment of Koreans who believed that the United States would sincerely offer relief from Japanese imperialism. He recalled that it was the United States that had brokered the peace treaty between Russia and Japan in 1905 that handed Korea to the Japanese. And it was Washington, through the mechanism of the Taft-Katsura Treaty, that colluded with Tokyo to divide Korea and the Philippines between the two of them.

Kim thought Korean leaders equally naïve in assuming that demonstrations would move the Japanese to abandon their project of colonialism, a project in which they had invested significantly in time, resources, and manpower. "Many Koreans mistakenly assumed that the Japanese would get out if they marched for several months shouting slogans," wrote Kim. "They were sadly mistaken; the Japanese were not about to leave Korea on account of mere marches. Japan had fought three wars over Korea. ... In the nineteenth century, after the Meiji Reform, the Japanese formulated a plan to take Korea by force. It was asserted that Korea was essential for the Empire to expand. ... Japan fought wars with Russia and China over Korea. America and Great Britain supported Japan in these two wars."[62] Japan was not going to abandon its imperial project simply because Koreans expressed their objection in marches and slogans.

Kim likened Japan and the United States to armed robbers. "An armed robber in your house will not spare your life, just because you plead for your life. Other armed robbers standing outside will not rush inside to help you no matter how loud you scream. If you want to live, you must fight off the armed robber yourself. Armed robbers must be fought with arms."[63]

Instead of taking up arms, and freeing Korea by their own efforts, Koreans who resisted Japanese colonization "died shouting freedom and justice, appealing to the conscience of humanity and human rights advocates of the world, in vain,"[64] Kim wrote. It "is a tragic lesson," he lamented, but true nonetheless, "that Korea [could] not count on other nations for independence, because they did not care."[65] What the "failed March First Movement taught us," Kim concluded, was that we must "build up our strength on our own." Koreans "must unite and achieve independence on their own."[66]

As a model, Kim looked not to Wilson and his doctrine of self-determination limited to the subjects of defeated rival empires, nor to the United States, with its agreement to recognize Japanese imperial aims in Korea in exchange for Japan recognizing US imperial aims in the Philippines. Wilson's "so-called doctrine," scoffed Kim, "was nothing but an American ruse to counter the October Revolution in Russia."[67] Kim, instead, would look for inspiration to Russia and the Bolsheviks.

Lenin had called in March 1917 for "the liberation of *all* colonies and of *all* oppressed nations,"[68] (emphasis added) not just those of enemy countries. It would take a superhuman effort to fight the Japanese, Kim had concluded. "We must learn from the Russian revolution and arm the people of Korea, in order to free our nation and build a new Korea of equality, freedom, and justice for all."[69]

Ho Chi Minh, the revolutionary nationalist leader of Vietnam, had himself been seduced and betrayed by Wilson's faux-liberal rhetoric about self-determination. In fact, Ho had appealed directly to Wilson at the Paris Peace Conference, and to other delegates, to no avail.[70] But, Ho, like Kim Il-sung, discovered that the program of the Bolsheviks had the substance that Wilson's (exclusionary) doctrine of self-determination lacked.

Ho recalled, after World I, living in Paris, that he "would distribute leaflets denouncing the crimes committed by the French colonialists in Viet Nam." He was a member of the French Socialist Party, and while he attended meetings regularly, he struggled to follow the discussions, especially those concerning the split within the socialist movement, between the reformists and the communists. "What I wanted to know," he recalled, was which of the branches of socialism sided "with the peoples of colonial countries."[71]

Today, the split between reformists and communists is remembered to have originated in a disagreement over whether to achieve socialism gradually, through piecemeal reforms within the existing capitalist system, or all at once, through revolution. But there was another point of contention: colonialism. Eduard Bernstein, a leading figure in the reformist movement saw "the colonial enterprise" as desirable, and necessary to the attainment of socialist goals in Europe. Without "the colonial expansion of our economy," he wrote, "the poverty that still exists in Europe today, which we are trying to eradicate, would be much worse and we would have much less hope of eliminating it. Even when counterbalanced by the crimes of colonialism, the benefits from colonies always weigh more heavily on the scale."[72]

The communists, led by Lenin, had a different point of view. They were advocates of genuine, inclusive, self-determination—self-determination for all peoples, not just for white Europeans.

The future leader of the Indochinese struggle for independence was given a tract by Lenin, which had been published in *l'Humanité*, the newspaper of the French Communist Party. It was titled "Thesis on the National and Colonial Questions."

Lenin presented the following argument. The formal or legal equality between person A, who sells his labor, and person B, who buys it, conceals a profound inequality. Person B exploits and person A is exploited. Without redressing the inequality between persons A and B, no true equality exists. "The real meaning of the demand for equality," wrote Lenin, "consists in its being a demand for the abolition" of exploitation, or the abolition of what we might call "parasitism"—living off the labor of others. This, by itself, however, did not directly answer Ho's question. Ho insisted on knowing whether Lenin was on the side of the colonial peoples.

A narrow reading of Lenin would suggest that his concern was with the inequality between workers and capitalists, the principal focus of much of the socialist movement to that point. But Lenin argued that exploitation wasn't limited to the relationship between classes within countries. It also existed between countries. There exists, Lenin wrote, a "colonial and financial enslavement of the vast majority of the world's population by an insignificant minority of the richest advanced capitalist countries." In other words, the unequal relationship that exists between the bourgeoisie and the proletariat also exists between a minority of wealthy capitalist nations and the rest of humanity (much of which those in the wealthy capitalist nations regarded as either subhuman or intellectually, culturally, and morally inferior, incapable of self-government, and suitable only for lives of exploitation as beasts of burden.)

Democracy among nations, if it is to have any substantial meaning, cannot, Lenin wrote "be restricted to the bare, formal, purely declaratory and actually non-committal recognition of the equality of nations"; it must entail the abolition of the exploitation of one nation by another. To achieve the abolition of exploitation, both within the metropolitan countries and between nations, Lenin called for the exploited of the metropolitan countries to pursue with the exploited of the colonies a joint revolutionary struggle to overthrow the economic elites of the metropole.[73] In terms of France's domination of Vietnam, this meant that the Vietnamese as a people and French workers should pursue a joint revolutionary struggle to overthrow their common enemy, namely, the French shoguns of finance, industry and commerce who exploited both groups. The success of this strategy, of course, would depend on French workers recognizing that the affinity between themselves and the peoples of the French colonies was more significant than the linguistic and cultural affinity they had with the French elite. Nevertheless, in Lenin's words were found not only a sincere recognition of the colonial peoples' right to liberation, but a concrete program by which to achieve it.

Ho was ecstatic. "What emotion, enthusiasm, clear-sightedness and confidence it instilled into me!" he exclaimed. "I was overjoyed to tears. Though sitting alone in my room, I shouted out aloud as if addressing large crowds: 'Dear compatriots! This is what we need; this is the path to our liberation!'"[74]

Earlier, Lenin had expanded the definition of socialist revolution beyond what socialist leaders such as Bernstein understood socialism to mean. "The socialist revolution is by no means a single battle," Lenin wrote in his essay "The Revolutionary Proletariat and the Right of Nations to Self-Determination." Instead, it is "a whole series of battles around all problems of economic and democratic reforms" including "equal rights for women" and—importantly, from the perspective of people trying to free themselves from colonial subjugation— "self-determination." Socialism "would remain an idle phrase," Lenin insisted, "if it were not linked up with a revolutionary approach to all the questions of democracy, including the national question," by which he meant the right of peoples, including Koreans, to exercise sovereignty over their own affairs, rather than being enslaved by imperialist masters. Lenin envisaged what he termed "a truly democratic, truly internationalist" order, in which each nation is free to set its own course and freely join with other states in relationships of mutual benefit.

The prescriptive stress in Lenin's writings on what was called the national question was on *mutual* benefit *contra* relationships in which benefits are monopolized by a stronger nation at the expense of a weaker one, as they are, for example, in the free trade agreements that dominant economic powers have always insisted upon. The United States, which until the end of WWII had the highest tariff barriers in the world, and had relied on protectionist policies for economic development, from the days of Alexander Hamilton to 1945, now insists on a level playing field. When it was the dominant economic power, Britain, too, insisted on free trade, and the United States, then a developing country, balked. But today, poor, post-colonial countries, whose economic development has been historically stifled, distorted, and yoked to the requirements of their former colonial masters, are not supposed to emulate the development practices of the United States. They cannot possibly compete on a level playing field with empires that have amassed enormous wealth, and have done so not only through their own past protectionist measures, but also through their long histories of plundering the colonies and semi-colonies of their resources, land, and labor.

A direct line runs from Lenin's view that the international order ought to be based on the voluntary association of equal partners for mutual (and not coerced and unequal) benefit, to the official view espoused by such countries as the DPRK and the Republic of Cuba. This view, needless to say, runs completely counter to the US view. The US view unabashedly declares the intention of the United States to coerce states, by one means or another, into relationships of subordination to Washington.

Kim Il-sung's continuity with Lenin was evident in a speech he made to the 85th Inter-Parliamentary Conference in April 1991, just a few years before his death.

> In order to build the new world aspired to by mankind, it is necessary to abolish the unequal old international order in all fields of politics, the economy and culture and establish an equitable new international order. There are large and small countries in the world, but there cannot be major and minor countries; there are developed nations and less developed nations, but there cannot be nations destined to dominate other nations or those destined to be dominated. All countries and nations are equal members of the international community and as such have the right to independence and equality. No privilege and no arbitrariness should be tolerated in international relations; friendship and cooperation among countries must be fully developed on the principles of mutual respect, non-interference in the affairs of other countries, equality and mutual benefit.[75]

Seven months prior to Kim's statement, US president George H.W. Bush had proclaimed a New World Order, in which all countries would be subordinate to the United States. Washington would exercise "world leadership."[76] The implication of Bush's New World Order was that the planet would be divided between nations destined to be dominated and one nation, the United States, which would dominate. Only the United States would have the right to independence, and the Pentagon, CIA, and US state and treasury departments would exercise leadership over the affairs of other countries. The expression of Bush's declaration of US world leadership can be seen in the words of a Pentagon spokesman, Rear Admiral John Kirby, who, in 2015, declared that the United States retains the "right," the "responsibility," and "the resources" to intervene in any country unilaterally to achieve US foreign policy goals.[77]

Lenin made one other point in his essay which portended what the oppressed peoples of the world would construe as Wilson's betrayal of their aspirations for freedom. People struggling for manumission from colonial enslavement would find no allies among governments dominated by the proprietary classes of the great powers, the Bolshevik leader warned. The business class "always betrays the interest of the people and of democracy," and "is always ready for annexations and for oppressing other nations."

When the Bolsheviks formed the Communist International in 1919, an organization of communist parties from around the world, they established twenty-one conditions of membership. Condition number eight had enormous appeal to colonial peoples, who had been reduced to the status of *untermenschen* (subhumans) to be ruled by a *Herrenvolk* (master race.)

> A particularly marked and clear attitude on the question of the colonies and oppressed nations is necessary on the part of the communist parties of those countries whose bourgeoisies are in possession of colonies and oppresses other nations. Every party that wishes to belong to the Communist International has an obligation of exposing the dodges of its 'own' imperialists in the colonies, of supporting every liberation movement in the colonies not only in words but in deeds, of demanding that their imperialist compatriots should be thrown out of the colonies, of cultivating in the hearts of the workers in their own country a truly fraternal relationship to the working population in the colonies and to the oppressed nations, and of carrying out systematic propaganda among their own country's troops against oppression of colonial peoples.[78]

Communist ideology would resonate "globally among colonized and downtrodden peoples," noted the US Naval College's Sarah Paine[79], and the reason why—because it offered the world's oppressed people the charter of humanity they sought, to use a phrase Jean-Paul Sartre once eloquently crafted[80]—is evident in the yawning chasm that emerged between the new society of equality the Bolsheviks created and the societies of white supremacy the wealthy capitalist powers maintained.

In contrast to the *Herrenvolk* powers, in 1935, three years after Kim Il-sung embarked on his campaign of guerrilla insurgency against the Japanese, the British intellectuals Beatrice and Sidney Webb described the Soviet Union—Kim Il-sung's and Ho Chi Minh's model in contrast to Wilson's race-based pro-colonial liberalism—as the very antithesis of the imperialist countries' *Herrenvolk* polities. In their voluminous *Soviet Communism: A New Civilization*, the Webbs contrasted the racial policies of the great powers with those of the USSR, under the heading "The [USSR's] Insistence on Racial Equality." Beginning their survey with the British Empire, the couple noted that within this vast area, containing five hundred million inhabitants, only seventy million, or 14 percent, were accorded political rights. The "self-governing Dominions"—South Africa, Canada, Australia and New Zealand—were white supremacist settler states. South Africa differentially accorded rights, privileges, and duties on the basis of race, "while Canada and Australia ignored the native tribes (when they did not exterminate them) as possible citizens of the newly formed state." And 400 million Indians were denied any political rights at all, their country governed, not by themselves, but by the British civil service.

But the British Empire was hardly unique, the Webbs observed. In the United States, citizens of African origin, "though assumed to be entitled to vote and to represent voters, [were] by the electoral law and administrative practice of particular states excluded from fully-fledged citizenship with the right to vote and to become representatives." (In the 1930s, the United States was an anti-Jewish white supremacist country every bit as repressive, persecutory, harassing, menacing, and violent toward its citizens of African origin as was the contemporaneous, white supremacist, anti-Jewish Nazi state toward its Jewish citizens.)

In contrast, observed the Webbs, an outstanding feature of the Soviet Union was its "absolute refusal to regard racial characteristics" as a legitimate basis on which to assign rights, privileges and duties. Indeed, one "of the reasons for the Anti-Comintern

Axis, uniting Nazi Germany, Fascist Italy and Shintoist Japan in hostility to the Soviet Union, was this insistence by the Bolshevist government on racial equality throughout the USSR. These three Great Powers were all alike intent on extending by force of arms, the dominance of their own race over new territories inhabited by so-called inferior races, who [had] no right to self-determination and were to accept the social order imposed by the conqueror, or to risk extermination."[81]

Parenthetically, a comment made by Lenin in the statement of his thesis on the equality of nations reminds us of how, in some respects, little has changed since the Bolshevik leader wrote his tract in 1920. South Korea, a state established by Washington for reasons of US political, economic, and strategic aims, can without hyperbole be called a puppet state in the way Manchukuo, the state established by the Japanese in Manchuria in the 1930s, is often described. To most Americans and Europeans, South Korea is an independent, sovereign state, and at worse, a semi-sovereign state, but not a puppet. Yet a state which was conceived, midwifed, and suckled by Washington; which oversees an economy built by massive injections of financial and other aid from the United States and significant economic concessions accorded to it in order for it to develop economically to showcase the merits of the capitalist way of life in the Cold War competition with North Korea; which hosts "the largest overseas American military base in the world," described by the US Army as the largest US power projection platform in the Pacific[82]; whose military remains under the command of the Pentagon and has been deployed to suppress Koreans who have taken up arms to overthrow the uninvited US presence in their country; which has contributed troops to US wars of aggression in Vietnam, Afghanistan, and Iraq: such a state is hardly independent. Lenin thought it was necessary "constantly to explain and expose ... the deception systematically practiced by the imperialist powers, which, under the guise of politically independent states, set up states that are wholly dependent on them economically, financially and militarily." South Korea is a paradigmatic expression of the kind of dependent state Lenin had in mind.

CHAPTER 2

Imperialism

"[Unless] the economic essence of imperialism ... is studied, it will be impossible to understand and appraise modern war and modern politics."—Lenin[1]

Koreans were victims of Japanese colonialism, as well as of a higher-level process: imperialism. Imperialism is the activity, enterprise and methodology of building empires. There are a number of ways empires can be built. One is by establishing colonies. But there are other ways, as well.

Empires can be declared and formal, or undeclared and informal, or both. Whatever form they take, empires are structures predicated on systems of domination, of one country or nation over another. The British, French and Japanese empires were declared and formal but parts of them were also undeclared and informal. The US empire is mainly undeclared and informal, but there are declared parts as well. The US empire incorporates five inhabited "territories"—Puerto Rico, Guam, Northern Mariana Islands, United States Virgin Islands and American Samoa (and 11 uninhabited ones)—which are effectively colonies. The people who live on these territories have no meaningful political representation in Washington. But for the most part, the US empire is informal and undeclared.

There are multiple possible ways a metropole—the empire's home country—can incorporate other people into its empire. By stationing its troops on the soil of other countries, the United States can directly, though informally, dominate these countries. If the governments of countries that accept a US military presence enact policies the US government dislikes, Washington can use its military to either intimidate the foreign government into altering its policies, or directly intervene to overthrow it, or persuade the host country's military to do so. Typically, where US troops are deployed abroad, the Pentagon has (usually) decisive influence over the host country's armed forces. This is often achieved through the integration of the foreign military into the US command structure, either formally or informally, directly or indirectly. South Korea offers a good example. ROK forces are integrated as an auxiliary military force into the US command. Currently, there exists a formal agreement giving the United States operational control of the South Korean armed forces during war. But even if Seoul had formal control of its military, *de facto* control would remain with the United States, so long as the US military is present on the Korean peninsula. The Pentagon will never cede operational control of its forces to an allied military. Some in South Korea—embarrassed by the observation of North Korea that the ROK's military dependency on the United States reveals its status as a US puppet—have pressed for Seoul to assume formal wartime operational control of South Korean military forces. But it is unrealistic to believe that, in the event of war, the Pentagon, which has close to 30,000 troops permanently stationed in South Korea, would place its East Asian-based military assets under the control of a South Korean general. US national security strategy, as we'll see, is predicated on the notion of US leadership. The United States does not cede military leadership to subordinate parts of its empire.

A stark illustration of one of the ways in which the United States uses its military to enforce its domination may be conveyed in three points, related to a comment Alexander Haig made to United Press International in 2002 about the reasons why the United States stations tens of thousands of troops in Europe,[22] and continues to do so, long after their ostensible purpose for being there—to defend Europe against the (wholly unrealistic) threat that the Soviet Union would attempt to spread socialism to Western Europe by force—had dissolved.

The first point concerns the position Haig once held, before becoming secretary of state in the Reagan Administration. From 1975 to 1979 Haig was Supreme Commander of NATO forces in Europe—which is to say that he, as a US general, had under his command the combined military forces of NATO's European members. By design, a US flag officer always commands NATO's combined forces. Additionally, in "war NATO's Supreme Allied Commander has the power to suspend Europe's civilian rules"[3]—in other words, to exercise a dictatorship over the greater part of Europe. The second point is that Haig explained that the Pentagon had 70,000 US troops in Germany because US troops kept "European markets open to [the United States]. If those troops weren't there," explained Haig, "those markets would probably be more difficult to access."[4] The third point is that imperialism is a process of domination guided by economic interests (for example, keeping European markets open to US investment and exports.)

In 2015, the United States had 52,000 troops in Japan, 38,000 in Germany, nearly 30,000 in South Korea, 11,000 in Italy, and 9,000 in Britain.[5] Three of these countries, Germany, Japan, and Italy, are former Axis powers that, in the 1930s and early 1940s, established, or tried to establish, closed economic zones, which had the effect of excluding US foreign investment and exports. During the great global capitalist crisis of the 1930s (one of many economic crises in the history of perpetually crisis-prone capitalism), Great Britain also created a closed economic zone, through an imperial preference system of high tariff walls which encircled the empire. This had the effect of severely attenuating the global profit-making opportunities available to US (and other non-British Empire) businesses and investors. Today, the US military footprint is strongest in countries in which US fears of closed markets have historical resonance. Equally important, the significant US troop deployments to Great Britain and the former Axis countries are manifestations of a US commitment to safeguard the security of former imperial rivals. By taking on the role of guardian, the United States relieves its former competitors of the necessity and expense of building militaries which could be used to rebuild rival empires to challenge the United States. This benefits US foreign policy by eliminating former imperialist adversaries as potential military threats to US hegemony and keeps their markets open to US businesses.

While the *degree* of US military ubiquity is open to debate, there's no doubt that the US military *is* ubiquitous. The five countries named above aren't the only ones in which the United States has a military presence. Depending on how a military installation is defined, the United States has at least 662 bases in 36 foreign countries,[6] or as many as 800 bases in 160 foreign countries and territories.[7] By any measure, the Pentagon's tentacles reach far beyond the frontiers of the US "homeland" (a word which, itself, is redolent of the stench of empire). According to David Vine, the "United States probably has more foreign military bases than any other people, nation, or empire in history."[8] Such a nation could deny that it has built an empire, but to do so would require the construction of a special reality, a *folie en masse*, or the creation of something tantamount to the "epistemology of ignorance" Charles Mills argued was necessary, to fail to see that the "liberal" political system of the Western world is, and has always been, white supremacist (i.e., illiberal.)[9]

Mills' view, while related to liberalism and race, also illuminates the divergence between the idea of the equality of nations, codified in the United Nations Charter, and the reality of imperialism. The "officially sanctioned reality is divergent from actual reality." Therefore, one "has to learn to see the world wrongly, but with the assurance that this set of mistaken perceptions will be validated by" the official "epistemic authority,"[10] namely, corporate-funded think-tanks, corporate-endowed universities, corporate-owned mass media, and corporate-dominated governments. Thus, on matters related to foreign relations, the official ideology prescribes an inverted epistemology, an epistemology of ignorance, which produces the ironic outcome that the denizens of imperialist countries will in general be unable to understand the world their countries have made.[11]

The epistemology of ignorance relies on a lexicon of equivocation. Journalists who write for the US empire's most distinguished newspapers—the *New York Times*, the *Washington Post*, the *Wall Street Journal*—routinely employ language that acknowledges the United States' imperialist nature, while at the same time never directly acknowledging the existence of a US empire, and therefore, denying it. For example, the *Wall Street Journal*'s Michael M. Phillips has written about "new ways the U.S. projects power around the globe," pointing out that the "U.S. has come to rely on elite military units [special-operations forces] to maintain its global dominance," and that "America's special-operations forces have landed in 81 countries, most of them training local commandos to fight so American troops don't have to."[12] In a few brief sentences Phillips shows that the United States is globally dominant and that one of the ways it maintains its dominance is through special operations forces which project US power in over four score countries. He also reveals one of the indirect mechanisms by which the United States produces and reproduces its empire: by training local commandos to fight as US surrogates. Phillips nowhere uses the words "empire," "imperialism," or "system of domination," although the words British Empire, French Empire, German Empire, Russian Empire, Ottoman Empire, Austro-Hungarian Empire and even Soviet Empire are all considered acceptable constructions. The United States—which began as 13 former British colonies on the Atlantic coast of North America pursuing a "manifest destiny" of continental expansion, (the inspiration for Nazi Germany's *lebensraum* policy); which fought a war with Spain for colonies; which promulgated the Monroe Doctrine asserting a sphere of influence in the Americas; which stole Panama to create a canal; whose special operations forces project US power in 81 countries; whose generals control the militaries of the combined NATO members in Europe and the military forces of South Korea; whose military command stations one hundred thousand troops on the territories of former imperialist rivals, manifestly has an empire.

And yet this reality is denied, as assuredly as is the reality that the United States, built on the genocide of Native Americans and the slave labor of Africans, overtly white supremacist until the mid-1960s, and covertly white supremacist since, is unequivocally *not* a beacon of Enlightenment values, unless liberalism is defined as equality and liberty assigned exclusively to white men who own productive property. Indeed, so antithetical is the United States to the liberal values of the equality of all peoples and nations, freedom from exploitation and oppression, and the absence of discrimination on the bases of class, race, and sex, that it's difficult to apprehend in what sense the United States has ever been liberal or has in any way had a legitimate claim to being the repository of the values of the Enlightenment.

Zbigniew Brzezinski, US president Jimmy Carter's National Security Adviser, and a central figure in the US foreign policy establishment, could compare the United States to the Roman, Manchu, and European empires but could not bring himself to speak of a US empire. Instead, he spoke of a "hegemony of a new type" and described the United States as a "global power," which has "primacy," and exercises "supremacy."[13] The philosopher and historian Domenico Losurdo, eschewing euphemism and rejecting the epistemology of ignorance, uses a more fitting and descriptive term for Brzezinski's equivocations: the international dictatorship of the United States.[14]

Helpfully, however, Brzezinski enumerates some of the direct and indirect mechanisms by which the United States exercises "global power" with a "scope and pervasiveness" that is "unique" in world history[15]—that is, creates and reproduces its international dictatorship.

First, the United States has a "peerless military establishment, the only one with effective global reach," allowing it to "project forces over long distances in order to impose" its "political will."[16] Second, it "emphasizes the technique of co-optation (as in the case of defeated rivals—Germany, Japan ...) to a much greater extent than the earlier imperial systems did."[17] Third, graduates of US "universities are to be found in almost every Cabinet on every continent."[18] US universities recruit talented individuals from abroad, instill in them US imperialist ideology and values, and equip them with academic credentials and prestige which conduce to their landing important political positions at home. In this way, US imperial goals indirectly structure the political decision-making of other countries. Fourth, the "International Monetary Fund (IMF) and the World Bank can be said to represent 'global' interests, and their constituency may be construed as the world. In reality, however, they are heavily American dominated and their origins are traceable to American initiative."[19] Bruce Cumings describes the so-called Bretton Woods institutions in similar terms: the United States, he writes, has "a very active foreign economic policy seeking to enmesh developing countries in Asia and Latin America into a host of [US]-influenced multilateral organizations," including the World Bank and IMF, which are little more than instruments of the US Treasury Department.[20] Hence, through a mixture of military, economic, and ideological instruments, the United States has created a globe-spanning system of domination—an empire.

Before the Great War, the war now known as WWI, most of the world was partitioned among eight great powers. The very fact that the world was partitioned implied empire and imperialism, even if one of the great powers, the United States, shunned the terms. The most powerful of the great powers—those which controlled the greatest territory—were Britain, France, Russia and the United States. A second tier included Germany, Austria-Hungary, Japan, and Italy. Germany, Japan, and Italy would become known as "have not" powers, indicating that their colonial possessions were limited by comparison with the Big Four. The Big Four had colonies—continental and mainly internal in the case of Russia and the United States, and overseas in the case of Britain and France. The "have-not" powers were new industrial powers without the large continental expanse of the United States and Russia or the globe-girding network of colonies and protectorates of Britain and France. The Big Four could rely on their vast empires to furnish them with the raw materials they needed to run their factories, the crops they needed to feed their people, and the land they needed to settle their surplus populations.

As their industrial economies grew, the have-not powers found themselves pressed to secure sources of raw materials, as well as markets for their finished products. Land on which to settle their teeming populations also became important. Industrialization—including the mechanization of agriculture—had engendered sudden and massive population shifts, as displaced subsistence farmers migrated from the countryside to the city. Germany, for example, was in the early twentieth century a vast warren of urban slums, teeming with people without "living space." The inability of the industrial capitalist economies of the have-not powers to furnish all their citizens with employment meant that large parts of their populations were "surplus." This created a potential for unrest and possibly revolution.

The continual westward expansion of the United States through conquest of Native American territory defused potential revolutionary movements by providing immigrants of European origin with land (that of the indigenous peoples) to settle—a process of turning proletarians into landowners. Likewise, angry Britons without prospects who might take a militant revolutionary path could immigrate to Canada, Australia, New Zealand, or South Africa to settle on the land of the aboriginal peoples of the British dominions. Their French counterparts also had outlets in the French colonial domain, particularly Algeria. Hence, the problem (from the perspective of the great powers' ruling classes) of social revolution was solved through the dispossession of indigenous peoples. Cecil Rhodes, the notorious British imperialist—our Hitler, as one black South African aptly described him—told the British ruling class that "Empire, as I have always said, is a bread and butter question. If you want to avoid [social revolution], you must become imperialists."[21]

There were five important drivers of capitalist imperialism: the need for (1) raw materials, (2) markets, and (3) investment opportunities; the need (4) to hold territory for strategic reasons to protect supply and shipping routes; and the need for (5) outlets to settle surplus populations, made redundant by the mechanization-driven displacement of subsistence farming. Raw materials, markets, and investment opportunities could be freely obtained in an open international trade and investment system, but any great power could deny its rivals access to these necessities as a means of strengthening its own position. This made the up-and-coming powers—Germany, Japan, and Italy—extremely vulnerable. Without vast territorial possessions, they could thrive only in a global economic system that was open to international trade and investment.

But who, or what, was to guarantee it would remain open? There were obvious incentives for the Big Four to create advantages for their own financiers, industrialists, and commercial concerns by securing for them as much economic space as possible while restricting the space open to their international competitors. With the world already largely divided among the four great powers, Britain, France, the United States, and Russia were thus in a position to stifle the emerging powers by impeding their access to the world's raw materials, markets, and investment opportunities.

The Great War did nothing to ameliorate the situation of the three have-not powers. On the contrary, the war made Great Britain and France stronger. The two imperial behemoths divided up the defeated Ottoman Empire and helped themselves to the colonies of the vanquished Germany. Their wartime allies, Italy and Japan, who had been promised territorial gains, were denied them after the war.[22] The upshot of the great global conflagration, then, was that Britain and France enlarged their economic space, while Japan and Italy made no gains, and Germany fell behind.

Japan, whose mountainous topography afforded little room for agriculture, lacked almost all the natural resources a modern industrial economy needed. It was almost entirely dependent on imports of foodstuffs and raw materials, making it extremely vulnerable to naval blockade and placing it at the mercy of the countries and great powers that controlled its industrial economy's desiderata. Iron ore—necessary for the production of steel—had to be imported from China and Malaya. Japan had virtually no internal source of oil. It relied almost exclusively on foreign sources, and in the first decades of the twentieth century Britain and the United States controlled almost all the world's supply. The solution to Japan's vulnerability, as far as the country's rulers could figure, was to secure control of territory that would provide the inputs Japan's industrialists needed.[23]

Japan's delegate to the Versailles conference, at which matters pertaining to the settlement of the war were decided, urged a rejection of what he termed "the Anglo-American centered peace." "No doubt the condition before the war was satisfactory from the viewpoint of Great Britain and America," wrote Prince Konoe Fumimaro, a future prime minister (1940-1941), "but it cannot be said so, when considered from the viewpoint of justice and humanity. As may be seen in their history of colonization, England and France occupied most of the less civilized countries long ago and made them their colonies. In consequence, Germany and other latecomers could hardly find any land to secure for their expansion. This state of things was contrary to the fundamental principle of equal opportunity and a right to the equal existence of different countries."[24]

Echoing Konoe, the Japanese journalist Kiyoshi Kawakami observed:

> Here is Japan, struggling to resolve, partly at least, her population problem by becoming an industrial and trading nation, and yet harassed by a lack of three essential materials of industry—oil, iron, and coal. If she steps an inch out of her narrow precincts and tries to obtain, say in Siberia or China, the privilege of working such mineral resources, down comes the sword of Damocles in the shape of protest, official or otherwise, from the Western nations. ... [The] question is, is the existing world order right, allowing a few nations to monopolize vast territories and enormous resources, and compelling others to eke an existence out of their limited lands and scanty resources.[25]

The Great Depression spurred Britain, the United States, and France to step up protectionist measures. This intensified the dissatisfaction of the have-not powers, who wondered how they could flourish in a world in which their access to raw materials and markets was severely restricted. At the best of times, Germany, Japan, and Italy were dependent on the imperial titans to grant them access to the markets and territories the titans controlled. Now, with the global capitalist system in crisis, the doors to the economic spaces dominated by the great powers were slamming shut.

The problem facing the emerging industrial powers was now bigger than mere dependency; they could be starved of raw materials and export markets altogether. Thus, efforts to acquire economic space would have to be redoubled, and force used if necessary.[26]

Having already acquired Taiwan, Korea, the southern half of Sakhalin, and a string of Pacific islands, Japan now undertook to bring Manchuria and Mongolia into its empire, in order to solve the "critical problems of population and foodstuffs," as one Japanese officer put it in 1931.[27] Japan's captains of finance, industry, and commerce looked greedily upon China as a new frontier. Its size exercised a magnetic appeal to Japanese business people and investors spellbound by the East Asian giant's immense market,[28] an attraction that has lost none of its power since. Investors worldwide continue to lust after China as a vast reserve of potential customers. At the same time, Manchuria, like Palestine and the American West, was imagined by its colonizers as a *terra nullius*, that is, an empty space—an almost limitless frontier awaiting Japanese settlement,[29] or, making a slight alteration to the words with which white European Zionists justified their theft of Palestinian land for Jewish settlement, a land without people for a people with too little land.

In September 1931, conspirators in the Japanese army instigated a "false flag" operation in Manchuria to create a pretext to launch a military occupation of the territory. Six months later, a new state was created on the occupied territory.[30] Nominally under Chinese control, but actually under Japanese direction, the new state was called Manchukuo, literally "state of Manchuria." The state is almost invariably described as a puppet state for three reasons. First, it was created by Tokyo on foreign territory Japan occupied militarily. Without Japanese intervention, Manchukuo would never have existed. The state was not of Chinese origin, proclaimed by Chinese for Chinese reasons, but was of Japanese provenance, created for Japanese reasons. Second, while the heads of Manchukuo's government ministries and departments were Chinese, vice-ministers and advisers were Japanese. Third, Japan and Manchukuo signed a mutual defense treaty making the Kwantung Army, the

Japanese garrison in Manchuria, responsible for its national security.[31] For these reasons, Manchukuo is so routinely referred to as "the puppet state of Manchukuo" that one might think that "the puppet state of" should be capitalized and made part of Manchukuo's official name, as in The Japanese Puppet State of Manchukuo.

In the absence of a theory of the epistemology of ignorance it would be difficult to understand why South Korea isn't also called a puppet state (except by the North Korean media). There are striking parallels between South Korea and Manchukuo. Both states were created by empires on foreign territory which armies of the empires occupied for reasons related to imperial expansion. While the political offices of the empire-created states were occupied by local actors, fostering the appearance of local sovereignty, imperial advisers played a large role behind the scenes. And in both cases, responsibility for national security was ceded through "mutual agreement" to the empire, whose military remained as an occupying force on the states' territories.

Like Brzezinski, who could talk of the US empire, not as an empire, but as a hegemony of a new type, the furthest Western scholars, journalists, and commentators seem to be willing to go to acknowledge that there exists on the Korean peninsula an entity which ought to be rightfully called "the US puppet state of South Korea," is to acknowledge that South Korea exists "in the soft soil of semi-sovereignty," and that it has "a weak state vis-à-vis the United States."[32] These are the words of the leading US historian of modern Korea, an acknowledgement, without actually saying it, that the ROK has a status fundamentally equivalent to that of Manchukuo.

Emboldened by the example of Japan extending its economic space in the face of the imperial titans erecting protectionist walls around the vast territory they controlled, Italy invaded Abyssinia (today's Ethiopia) on the ground that it "needed the area for its economic survival"[33]—which is to say, it was driven by the expansionary logic its industrial capitalist economy created. Ethiopia occupied the intervening space between Somalia and Eritrea, which Italy already held as colonies. By acquiring Ethiopia, Italy could control a large contiguous space on the Horn of Africa, which it would call Italian East Africa.

> The Italian position was clear. Britain ... was to blame. Its empire spanned the world and hogged the lion's share of resources without regard to the rights of others. A propaganda leaflet showing John Bull bestriding the globe declared that "England has in its hands or controls almost all the raw materials produced in the world: from cotton to wool, from petroleum to diamonds, from coal to gold." Because it was aware that without its empire it would be a third-rate power, "England has used the great riches in its possession to impede in every way those who, less favored by nature, have attempted, as is their right, to find new sources of riches and work." This was not fair, and it could not be tolerated. "At the base of every war and especially those which are being fought nowadays, there is an economic claim. Peoples less rich in raw materials, or densely populated nations, need to procure all that is indispensable for their existence, or to seek in less inhabited territories an outlet for their always growing population. ... No one can deny to any people the right to life. ... We Italians in particular do not wish to be exposed forever to every possible form of economic suffocation because we lack oil or coal or iron or rubber or wool."[34]

For its part, Germany launched a series of aggressions in Europe in the late 1930s, beginning with the annexation of Austria in 1938, and culminating in Operation Barbarossa, the June 22, 1941 invasion of the Soviet Union, initiating the greatest war of colonial expansion in history. Hitler boasted that Germany's *Drang nach Osten*, its push to the east, an objective that had long characterized German foreign policy, would secure for the Reich the economic self-sufficiency Germany had craved. "We shall become the most self-supporting State, in every respect ... in the world," the Führer promised. "Timber we shall have in abundance, iron in limitless quantity, the greatest manganese-ore mines in the world." As for oil, Germany would "swim in it."[35] Under Hitler's direction, the Third Reich set out to build (by force) a *Grossraumwirtschaft*, a "greater economic zone," over most of Europe.

In a January 1937 article in *Foreign Affairs*, the journal of the Council on Foreign Relations, the Wall Street-funded and -directed foreign policy think-tank, Hjalmar Schacht, Hitler's minister of economics and president of the Reichsbank, adumbrated the causes of Germany's forthcoming aggressive expansion.[36] He titled his article "Germany's Colonial Demands."

Before WWI, Schacht explained, Germany bought industrial inputs all over the world. "The markets where raw materials were procured were completely free." Additionally, emigration and immigration "was open and was looked on with favor." But with the collapse of the world (capitalist) economy, all "these elementary principles of international trade and intercourse" had disappeared. Strict regulations governing "immigration into almost all countries where formerly immigrants were welcome" now impeded the outward migration of Germany's surplus population. In the place of free trade had arisen "quotas and restrictions, to say nothing of constant increases in the more effective tariffs. German investments abroad," Schacht complained, had "been taken away without compensation, and the markets where raw materials" had been previously obtained were now almost impossible to access.

For these reasons, and with no other choice, Germany had embarked on a project of autarky, that is, self-sufficiency. The great power critics of Germany's drive to economic self-sufficiency were hypocritical, Schacht said. "People entirely forget" that autarky has "long since been achieved by such countries as France and Great Britain, not to mention Russia and the United States." So "vast is the geographical expanse of the United States of America, so enormous its wealth, that it is much less dependent than other countries on an exchange of goods with the outside world." Similarly, Russia contains "all kinds of raw materials." What's more, the British Empire had "more than a quarter of the earth's surface at its disposal" containing "one-quarter of the world's wheat, one-half of the world's wool and rubber, one-quarter of the world's coal, one-third of the world's copper, and almost all of the world's nickel." Of twenty-five raw materials vital to a modern industrial economy, "the British Empire was amply supplied in its own territory with no less than eighteen, was supplied to a certain extent in two cases, and was deficient in only five." Germany, in contrast, "was sufficiently supplied by its own production in only four cases, was more or less adequately supplied in two, and was completely without supplies in nineteen." In Italy and Japan, wrote Schacht, "conditions are equally unfavorable."

Returning to the world economic crisis, Schacht pointed out that the quantity of raw materials Germany could procure on the world market was now "far below what Germany" needed "to keep her industries going and maintain the standard of living for her people." Ominously, he warned, "There will be no peace in Europe until this problem is solved. No great nation willingly allows its standard of life and culture to be lowered and no great nation accepts the risk that it will go hungry."

To strengthen his case, Schacht cited the analysis of Colonel Edward M. House, a US diplomat who had been an adviser to Woodrow Wilson. House had written in *Liberty* magazine that,

> Germany, Italy and Japan need reservoirs into which to pour their manpower and from which to draw those necessities and raw materials which nature denied them. But the greatest possessing nations—Great Britain, France, the United States and Russia—are unwilling to grant to their less fortunate fellows more than the crumbs that fall from their colonial table. ... Great Britain, France, Russia and the United States must receive Italy, Germany and Japan on terms adjusted to present world conditions and recognize their insistence upon being given their proper part of the colonial resources of the world. Chaos and catastrophe will be upon us unless those that have among the Powers are willing to share in some way with those that have not.

Here, then, was the situation that confronted the world: an "insignificant minority of the richest advanced capitalist countries" had divided up the globe into economic spheres. Central to the relations among these countries was conflict over "the territorial division of the world, of the struggle for colonies, of the 'struggle for economic territory.'" The world had been partitioned. In the future, only redivision was possible. Japan, Italy, and Germany could not meet the demand for raw materials, markets, and outlets for emigration that their industrial capitalist economies had created, except by conquering new territory. But there was no new territory to conquer. Therefore, only two possible outcomes remained: the great powers in possession of vast territorial extent would either have to voluntarily cede some of their territory to the have-not powers, or the have-not powers would have to take the territory by force.[37]

From the point of view of Japan, Italy, and Germany, the division of the world among the great powers was unfair. The emerging industrial nations were denied access to colonies and territory. But what of the overwhelming majority of the world's people who lived and worked in the territories the great powers coveted? Where were the voices of the people living in the colonies and semi-colonies, who vastly outnumbered the denizens of the industrialized world? The caterwauling of Japan, Italy, and Germany about the denial of their place in the sun was simply a plea to be brought into the club of a few powerful world marauders armed to the teeth, who would exploit the vast majority of humanity.[38] After all, "less than one-tenth of the inhabitants of the globe; less than one-fifth, if the most generous and liberal calculations were made, of very rich and very powerful states" were bickering over how much of the plunder of the remaining 80 percent of humanity they each should receive.[39]

Lenin had written in 1917 that rivalry among the advanced industrialized countries had "become very keen because Germany has only a restricted area and few colonies,"[40] an observation which could have been made with equal validity about Italy and Japan. Without recognizing the economic roots of empire-building, Lenin wrote, it would "be impossible to understand and appraise modern war and modern politics."[41] The cogency of Lenin's analysis was tacitly acknowledged at the end of World War II by the Allies. Their initial plan (subsequently abandoned) was to de-industrialize Germany and Japan. These two advanced capitalist industrialist powers, which had threatened the economic space of the United States, France, and Britain, in an effort to enlarge their own, would be transformed into agricultural societies, shorn of the drive and the means to launch aggressive wars. This was an acknowledgement that industrial capitalism reposed at the root of the Axis's aggressive, expansionary, foreign policies.

For Lenin, the solution to the problem of "powerful world marauders" embroiling "the whole world in their" wars "over the sharing of their booty," was neither more war nor bringing Germany, Italy, and Japan more fully into the world system of imperial domination as charter members. His solution was to eliminate the world system of imperial domination altogether, and with it, other relationships of domination as well, including those of class and gender.

Lenin had founded a new organization in 1919, the Third International, which dedicated itself to "the struggle of the working class and the oppressed nations of the whole world to free themselves."[42] The Bolshevik leader had denounced Japan's "savage tortures of the Korean patriots and barbaric exploitation of Korea."[43] This contrasted sharply with the US position of conniving with Japan to divide up the Philippines and Korea between the two empires. Where the United States and Britain had facilitated Japan's oppression of the Koreans, Lenin and the Bolsheviks denounced it, and urged Koreans to free themselves. This would inspire patriots in Korea, including Kim Il-sung.

CHAPTER 3

The Patriot

When "the leading scholar of Korean communism, Dae-sook Suh, was finally allowed to explain the real story to a large audience of young people in Seoul in 1989, upon hearing that Kim Il-sung was in fact a hero of the resistance, they all burst into applause."[1]

Kim Il-sung was born Kim Sung-ju in 1912. He adopted the name Kim Il-sung as a *nom de guerre*, in the same way Lenin (Ulyanov), Trotsky (Bronstein), Stalin (Jughashvili), and Ho Chi Minh (Nguyen Sinh Cung) and other revolutionaries had done. He was neither a puppet installed in a North Korean Soviet satellite state by Joseph Stalin, as US propagandists would have it, nor an imposter who stole the name of a famous anti-Japanese guerrilla, as South Korean propagandists would allege. Instead, he was a genuine Korean patriot who devoted his life to achieving Korea's freedom—"recognizably a hero," as Bruce Cumings would call him—who "fought for a decade in the harshest winter environment imaginable, with temperatures sometimes falling to 50 degrees below zero."[2] On top of 13 years leading an armed struggle against the Japanese, Kim spent over four decades building an independent Korean state on a US-divided peninsula, protecting it from the depredations of the United States, and trying to unify the peninsula as an independent Korean nation. "It is easy to lose a country," Kim once wrote, "but difficult to win it back."[3] In over six decades of struggle, Kim was never able to fully overcome the difficulties he encountered.

The guerrilla leader and state founder recognized that Korea's independence would be a long-term project, possibly beyond the span of any individual's lifetime. "India won its independence from England after 200 years of colonial enslavement," he wrote. "The Philippines and Indonesia won their independence after 300 years. Algeria after 130 years. Sri Lanka after 150 years and Vietnam after nearly 100 years."[4] Korea's freedom may take centuries, he believed. But he seemed to sense that independence was inevitable if Koreans struggled for it.

Kim Il-sung was born in a village close to Pyongyang in 1912. His father, a Korean patriot, participated in the 1919 uprising, when Koreans, and other oppressed peoples around the world, erupted in anger at Woodrow Wilson's failure to deliver self-determination to the colonial oppressed. For the senior Kim's opposition to Korea's colonial enslavement he was jailed by Japanese authorities. Released from prison in 1925, Kim's father followed the footsteps of other patriots, moving his family to Manchuria to escape Japan's control.[5]

As a high school student, Kim Il-sung joined an underground Marxist group and read the works of Marx and Lenin. This led, in 1929, to his arrest and incarceration for a number of months. After Japan created its puppet state in Manchuria in 1931, Kim joined the Chinese Communist Party, and went underground to organize guerilla opposition to the Japanese occupation.[6] He founded his first guerrilla unit in the spring of 1932,[7] with the long-term objective of liberating Korea.[8]

Owing to its freedom from Japanese control prior to 1931, Manchuria had become a refuge for many Koreans, who now formed the majority of resisters to the Japanese conquest of the Chinese province. Approximately eight of every ten anti-Japanese guerrillas in Manchuria were Koreans. And Koreans made up the vast majority of Chinese Communist Party members in the region.[9]

By February 1936, Kim was the Communist Party leader in eastern Manchuria, a man of considerable reputation and, while only 24 years of age, a major figure in the resistance movement. Kim's formal position was as commander of the 3rd Division of the

Kim Il-sung greets members of the Women's International Democratic Federation in 1951. (Photo: Alamy Stock).

Communist Party-led Northeast Anti-Japanese United Army. Under his command were several Chinese regimental commanders.[10]

So significant a figure was Kim that the Japanese army established a special division to hunt him down, headed by General Nozoe Shotoku.[11] One of Nozoe's top officers was a Korean traitor, Kim Sok-won, who had joined the Japanese Imperial Army and taken the Japanese name Kaneyama Shakugen. Kim Sok-won would later become the commander of South Korean forces on the 38th parallel, playing a signal role in the events surrounding the beginning of the Korean War in 1950.

Kim Sok-won wasn't the only traitor who worked to hunt down Kim Il-sung and the Korean *maquis* (rural guerrillas) led by him. Another was Park Chung-hee, who joined the Japanese Imperial Army, and adopted a Japanese name, Takagi Masao. As a Lieutenant in the emperor's military, he was assigned to a counter-insurgency unit to hunt down his countrymen.[12] Park later became South

Korea's president, and is the father of Park Geun-hye, the disgraced former ROK president, who was forced to resign in 2017 in a scandal. Her term in office overlapped that of North Korea's leader Kim Jong-un, Kim Il-sung's grandson.

By 1937, Kim Il-sung had become the commander of the 6th Division of the Northeast Anti-Japanese United Army, a unit informally known as the division of Kim Il-sung.[13] A Soviet journal, in 1937, reported that in "the course of combat with Japanese imperialists great and talented leaders have had the opportunity to distinguish themselves. ... Among them the detachment of [Kim Il-sung] stands out, especially." The article noted that Nozoe's Special Kim Division had failed to capture the talented guerrilla leader.[14]

Galvanized by their persistent failure to snare the elusive Kim and crush the guerillas, the Japanese decided to step up their efforts to eradicate the future North Korean leader and his m*aquis* army. In August 1939, Tokyo deployed approximately 24,000 troops and police officers to a six-month-long counterinsurgency operation.[15] Two Japanese colonels who participated in the hunt told US occupation forces in 1951 that "Kim was 'the most famous' of Korean guerrillas in the late 1930s. He was particularly popular among the Koreans in Manchuria, they said, adding that many Koreans praised him as a Korean hero and gave him, secretly, both spiritual and material support.'"[16]

As a new decade began, Kim, whose growing reputation would bring him even to the attention of the top US State Department Korean specialist in far-off Washington, was the guerrilla leader in Manchuria who the Japanese feared above all.[17] He had risen even higher in the ranks of the Communist-led anti-Japanese army, becoming the commander of the second operational region of its First Army.[18] But as the Japanese strengthened their counter-insurgency efforts, the guerilla army began to collapse. Aided by Korean hirelings, the Japanese army eventually whittled Kim's unit down to 12 fighters, at which point they were reorganized into a brigade of the Soviet Red Army.[19] Comprising between 1,000 and 1,700 troops, mainly Chinese with a few hundred Soviet advisers, the brigade was divided into four battalions, one of which Kim commanded.[20]

Bruce Cumings observed that as a guerrilla, Kim became "a classic Robin Hood figure," stealing across the Korean border, taking land from "landlords and Japanese puppets," giving it to poor peasants, and eliminating "remnants of 'feudalism'" and "discrimination against women."[21] Kim would build North Korea on the same principles of resisting foreign control, overcoming feudalism, and implementing democratic reforms.

While Kim was playing a lead role in the struggle to expel the Japanese invaders from Manchuria, Tokyo was expanding its empire, constructing what it called the Greater East Asia Co-Prosperity Sphere.

By 1939, Korea and Taiwan were supplying Japan with enough rice to make it self-sufficient. And Manchuria had become an important part of the Japanese economy as a source of coal and iron ore.[22] But the Greater East Asia Co-Prosperity Sphere presented two problems. First, it had to be imposed on other people, who were refractory to Japanese domination, necessitating significant military investments to suppress militant opposition. Second, the sphere contained the world's principal sources of tin and rubber, two vital raw materials other great powers, including Great Britain and the United States, imperatively needed, but lacked. The need of US and British industrialists for these raw materials and Japan's near monopoly over them could lead to war.[23]

With the rise of the automobile, British investors anticipated the importance of rubber as a lucrative natural resource and invested heavily in rubber plantations in Malaya. British investment would account for three quarters of the world's output of rubber by the early 1920s. Soon rubber plantations were springing up in the Dutch East Indies as well. Combined, the two areas produced 98 percent of the world's rubber crop. Rubber took on added importance for Britain as its single largest source of dollar earnings.[24]

For the United States, the region the Japanese aspired to fold into their co-prosperity sphere was also the source of one of the few industrial inputs the empire lacked: tin. One US economist forecast doom if US businesses were locked out of the region. The US economy, he wrote, and the US military "cannot be operated without rubber and tin, which at present cannot be obtained in adequate quantity except from the British and Dutch colonies in Southeast Asia. And Japan today commands the trade route connecting the west coast of the United States with the Malaysian Straits ... Here, ready to hand for Japan, is a safer and more powerful weapon against the United States than the folly of naval attack."[25]

When the *Wehrmacht* began its march across Europe in the late 1930s, the East Asian colonial possessions of the defeated European powers came up for grabs. Prostrated by the German juggernaut, Britain, France, and the Netherlands were too weak to defend their East Asian colonies. When the Netherlands and France fell, the Dutch East Indies and French Indochina became tasty morsels, ready to be picked off by a Japan hungry for empire-building opportunities. Focusing on defense of the home island, Britain was unable to commit sufficient forces to protect its East Asian possessions, leaving Hong Kong and Malaya virtually undefended. Japan struck. Alarm bells sounded in Washington, as well as in London, at Whitehall, and at Stratton House, where the Dutch government was in exile. Tokyo's imperialist impulses had been unleashed, and the Dutch, British, and US empires were in danger. Something had to be done. In response to the threat posed by their Japanese rivals for the plunder of the colonies, the three powers imposed sanctions, froze Japanese assets, and restricted Tokyo's access to oil, a resource over which the three governments combined had a near monopoly.[26]

Rather than bringing Japan to its knees, the oil embargo heightened the determination of the country's empire-builders to conquer territories rich in oil. The key was to incorporate the Dutch East Indies and British Borneo into the Japanese empire. Together, these two European colonial possessions produced nine million tons of oil annually, enough to satisfy Japan's requirements.[27] But how to accomplish this task, without inviting a blocking military response from Washington?

The answer, in the view of Japanese planners, was to launch a preventive military strike against the US Pacific fleet based at Hawaii. If the fleet could be sunk in a surprise attack, Japan could buy time to conquer the Western colonies of East Asia before the Americans could respond. While the United States rebuilt its Pacific fleet, Japan could integrate its neighborhood into a formidable self-sustaining empire, which would include all the resources necessary for self-defense and industrial growth, eclipsing the great powers' capability to block Japan's development by denying it access to critical resources.[28]

The plan worked—for a time. Japan's surprise attack at Pearl Harbor rendered the United States *hors de combat* in the Pacific for nearly half a year. During this period, the Japanese quickly undertook a series of wars for global redivision, seizing a number of US, British and Dutch colonies, which the Americans, British, and Dutch had themselves earlier captured, in some cases from other empires, and in all cases from the indigenous people. This string of annexations included the Philippines, British Malaya, Singapore, the Dutch East Indies, Borneo, and New Guinea, along with a string of Pacific Islands.[29] The Japanese hoped that by the time the United States had recovered sufficiently, it would recognize the construction of the Great East Asian Co-Prosperity Sphere as an accomplished fact. And if not, with access to a large empire from which vital industrial inputs could be obtained, including oil and rubber, Japan would be well-armored to withstand a US-British assault.

That gamble, however, failed to pay off. Because the United States procured nine-tenths of its tin and virtually all of its rubber from a region now under Japanese control—and because Britain relied heavily on sales of Malay rubber for its foreign exchange—the chances of Washington and London acceding to Tokyo's efforts to redivide the world were as great as the chances Tokyo would blithely accept being frozen out of the imperial contest.[30]

Ultimately, it was Japan's status as an island state and its failure to invest sufficiently in its navy which led to its undoing. The sources of the imports it needed to run its factories and feed its people reposed across open stretches of water. In order to fight a war against the United States, it would need to defend the sea lanes it depended on for transportation of vital supplies. But that proved to be far too challenging a task for the under-resourced Japanese navy. The United States navy blockaded its East Asian rival, starving Japan of inputs from its colonies.[31] As 1944 came to a close, the stream of rice shipments from Taiwan and Southeast Asia had become a trickle, while rice imports from Korea were reduced by half.[32] Oil was so scarce that Japanese pilots began to fly Kamikaze missions to preserve fuel. A suicide attack caused five to ten times the damage of a conventional attack, but used only half as much fuel, since there was no return trip.[33]

Once Japan's access to food and industrial inputs was choked off, surrender was only a matter of time. Acutely aware of its increasingly untenable position, Tokyo held out the hope that the Soviet Union—with which it had a non-aggression pact—would broker a peace agreement. But unbeknownst to the Japanese, Stalin had given his commitment to Roosevelt and Churchill at the Yalta conference of February 1945 to enter the war in the Pacific three months after the end of the war in Europe. The war in Europe ended on May 8, 1945. Exactly three months later, on August 8, Stalin sent Soviet forces sweeping into Manchuria and Korea, delivering the *coup de grace* which ended the war. In the US-dominated popular history of WWII, it was Washington's decision to unleash atomic devastation on two militarily insignificant Japanese cities that constituted the final blow against the Japanese. However, this chauvinist narrative completely elides the significance of the Soviet entry into the war. Even before the Soviets declared war on Japan, Japanese leaders recognized that defeat was only a matter of time, and that their only hope was to engage Soviet assistance to sue for peace. When that hope was dashed, Japanese leaders knew that all was lost. Their situation had deteriorated from desperate to hopeless. Within a week, Japan surrendered.

CHAPTER 4

The US Occupation

"The people's committees set up by the south Korean people immediately after liberation were not recognized and, worse still, they were dissolved and their functionaries were arrested and thrown into jail."—Kim Il-sung, 1946[1]

At midnight on August 10, 1945, two US army colonels, Dean Rusk and Charles Bonesteel, were ordered by John J. McCloy, Assistant Secretary of War, to "find a place to divide Korea" to *temporarily* partition the peninsula into separate US and Soviet occupation zones to accept the Japanese surrender. McCloy, a Wall Street lawyer, would later serve as president of the World Bank, chairman of Chase Manhattan Bank and chairman of the Council on Foreign Relations. Rusk, a future US secretary of state, and Bonesteel, who would command the combined US and ROK forces in Korea in the late 1960s, chose the 38th parallel as a dividing line because it would place Seoul, Korea's capital, within the US zone.[2]

Kim Il-sung, hearing of the planned division of the peninsula, expressed misgivings. Korea, he wrote, was an "ancient nation that" had "known a continuous existence within well-recognized boundaries" for over a millennium.[3] There was no internal reason to divide the country. Koreans hadn't asked for division. And Korea wasn't a defeated aggressor state, like Germany, to be divided into occupation zones to keep it down. On the contrary, Koreans had "contributed to destroying fascism through their long-drawn-out national-liberation struggle."[4]

"When we were in the Soviet Far East region, we heard the news that the US army would be stationed in Korea south of the 38th parallel," Kim recalled years later. "This meant that the troops of two big powers would be stationed in our country at the same time." It was a bad omen. A simultaneous occupation by Soviet and US forces "might turn our country into an area of confrontation between socialism and capitalism, and our national force was liable to be split into left and right, patriots and traitors to the nation."[5]

During the war, the Allies deliberated on what should be done with countries under Axis control, if the Axis was defeated. Washington favored a post-war arrangement for Korea, in which the peninsula would be jointly governed by the United States, Britain, and the Soviet Union during a transitional period leading to eventual Korean rule.[6] Korea would be granted independence at an appropriate time, determined by the Allies.[7] Washington considered Koreans incapable of governing themselves, at least straightaway. It was widely believed by people in the Western world that only white Europeans and North Americans were capable of self-government, and that non-whites would have to be brought under the white man's tutelage for some period of time to be equipped with the moral, intellectual, and cultural capabilities they were deemed to lack and that were considered necessary for self-government before they would be allowed to govern themselves.

Empire-builders, some of whom occasionally hypocritically sang paeans to the equality of humankind, viewed the social world as a hierarchy. At the top were the empire-builders themselves—males of the metropole who owned landed, industrial, or financial property. At the bottom lay the "savages"—aboriginal peoples whose existence could be extinguished and their lands expropriated without much concern. Above the savages were the barbarians, the peripheral people of empires, including Koreans, who bore a different culture and spoke different languages from the empire-builders. Interposed between the barbarians and lords of humanity were the *canaille,* the common people, of the metropolitan countries.

Koreans were clearly regarded by Japanese and US empire builders as barbarians. To the Japanese they were ethnic cousins, who lacked the cultural and moral equipment of the Japanese people, and so had to be taken in hand and guided. To the Americans, Koreans were adolescents, unschooled in self-government, who would need to be guided, through a long (and in the case of Koreans situated south of the 38th parallel, an indefinite) period of cultural, intellectual, and military development before they would be allowed to fully govern themselves.

The ideology of the empire-builders is articulated clearly by the French imperial theorist Jules Harmand (1845-1921).

> It is necessary ... to accept as a principle and point of departure the fact that there is a hierarchy of races and civilizations, and that we belong to the superior race and civilization. ... The basic legitimation of conquest over native peoples is the conviction of our superiority, not merely our mechanical, economic, and military superiority, but our moral superiority. Our dignity rests on that quality, and it underlies our right to direct the rest of humanity. ... [We] bring order, foresight, and security to a human society which, though ardently aspiring for these fundamental values without which no community can make progress, still lacks the aptitude to achieve these from within itself. ... With these mental and material instruments, which it lacked and now receives, it gains the idea and ambition for a better existence, and the means of achieving it.[8]

In contrast, those who belonged to the Leninist tradition, that is, communists, took equality seriously. In the communist view, the social world was not a hierarchy, but flat, egalitarian. The equality of humankind wasn't to be a matter of rhetoric, but of practice. Communists believed that all peoples were equal, and that social, political, and economic rights should be assigned without regard to social and national origin or gender. From the communist point of view, Koreans, as much as any other people, had a right to self-determination, to direct their own affairs and to associate with other people and nations on the basis of equality and mutual benefit. As far as the communists were concerned, Koreans were not adolescents, who needed to be guided through a period of nonage, as the Americans believed, but full human beings, with rights equal to those of any other human being, including the right to self-governance.

Communists were the authentic inheritors of the liberal movement of freedom and equality begun by the French Revolution. Communism, indeed, originated in the left wing of the great wave of democratization inaugurated in 1789 by French revolutionaries. Communists took to heart the Rights of Man and declarations of liberty, equality, and human solidarity, from which also originated Olympe de Gouges's 1791 Declaration of the Rights of Women and of the Female Citizen.

For white people in metropolitan countries who have no personal history of oppression based on their national origin and race, and who have been fed a steady diet of anti-communism from childhood, it is difficult, perhaps nearly impossible, to understand that people who had been assigned to the lowest rungs of humanity and had felt the sting of oppression flocked to communism with alacrity, as the route to their full incorporation into the community of human beings. Nelson Mandela said, "For many decades communists were the only political group in South Africa who were prepared to treat Africans as human beings. ... Because of this, there are many Africans today who tend to equate freedom with communism."[9] The sentiment was equally prevalent among Koreans. As a doctrine of liberation which granted all people the charter of humanity, communism was, and remains, what Hitler hated it for: "the final culmination and distillation of the Enlightenment."[10]

Empire-builders accepted the French Revolution's "goals of liberty, equality, and fraternity," wrote the father of fascism studies Robert Paxton, "but they applied them in ways suitable for" the empire-builders themselves.[11] Theirs was a truncated liberalism, inclusive of white male property owners, and excluding everyone else in proportion to their social, economic, and cultural distance from the minority the doctrine included. By contrast, communists followed the Enlightenment ideas of liberty, equality, and fraternity to their logical destination,[12] refusing to stop at a way station which granted rights to white male property owners of the imperial metropole alone. If all humans were equal, then *all* humans, male and female, white and non-white, rich and poor, were equal. Slavery, apartheid, racism, colonialism, patriarchy—all of these institutions were unthinkable in a country governed by communists, yet they were accommodated by, indeed, created, defended, and promoted by the self-proclaimed icons of liberal democracy—France, Britain, and the United States.

France and Britain denied hundreds of millions of colonial subjects their basic humanity, while proclaiming themselves champions of democracy (Britain) and *liberté, égalité, fraternité* (France). The United States—founded by slave owners who built a continental empire on a Golgotha of Native Americans; which practiced the vilest form of slavery known to humanity (racial, chattel slavery) for the first nine decades of its existence; which operated a regime of *de jure* white supremacy until the mid-1960s, and of *de facto* white supremacy thereafter; and whose persecution in the 1930s of descendants of former slaves matched the Nazi's contemporaneous persecution of Jews—unabashedly and quite incorrectly proclaims itself to be the beacon to the world of the Enlightenment values of freedom and democracy.

Thomas Metscher defines communism as "a theory of liberation" closely connected to the Enlightenment, concerned with the overthrow of all conditions in which human beings are debased, enslaved, and abandoned. Its goals are human equality[13] and the liberation of the downtrodden, the exploited, and the oppressed from their dehumanization. The communist movement is fittingly called the movement for equality, or re-humanization, since it insists that social, economic, and political rights cannot be differentially assigned on the basis of gender or social and national origin. In practice, the communist movement has been at the forefront of struggles for equality and is, in practice, a movement for the liberation of subordinate groups from oppression. Indeed, the Nazism of Hitler and Fascism of Mussolini were deliberately constructed as antitheses to the egalitarian credo of communism. Nazis, Fascists, and Japanese militarists loathed communists for their appeal to equality, an appeal which clashed violently with the empire-builders' doctrine of the hierarchy of races, civilizations, nations, gender, and class.

Under Japanese rule, Koreans were unequal and treated as subhumans and non-persons, as dumb beasts to be exploited for the benefit of Japan and, most especially, of the Japanese lords of humanity at the top of the Japanese colonial hierarchy. And so, Koreans quite naturally aspired to reclaim their humanity and dignity. Seeking liberation from their dehumanization they became participants in a great movement for equality, *viz.*, *de facto* communists, even if they weren't nominally so. Nonetheless, many were. Communist ideology, wrote Sarah Paine, "resonated globally among colonized and downtrodden peoples."[14] This single fact must be understood if the modern history of Korea is to be apprehended. Koreans opposed a hierarchy of humanity in which they were relegated to the bottom. They sought equality, and therefore were drawn to the communist movement because it championed the freedom from dehumanization to which they aspired, and it implacably opposed the hierarchical division of humanity. The yearning of Koreans for independence based on the equality of nations and of all people resonated with the communist program of emancipation, of tearing down hierarchies that divided humanity between those who could exploit and those who were relegated to existences as dehumanized objects of exploitation.

For all these reasons, the Korean people repudiated Roosevelt's trusteeship proposal, viewing it as the replacement of one system of domination (Japanese colonialism) by another (shared domination by multiple foreign powers.) Yearning for equality after four decades of subordination to Japanese rule, Koreans bristled at the idea that they were to be subjected to more foreign rule.[15] For his part, Stalin considered Roosevelt's trusteeship plans naïve, and fittingly, as a leader of a world movement for equality, reminded Roosevelt that "Koreans would want independence."[16]

US State Department planners also questioned Roosevelt's idea of trusteeship—not, however, because it was a system of domination. Their concern was that trusteeship as a system of domination wasn't strong enough; in its multilateralism it failed to grant the United States monopoly control over Korea, instead sharing control of the peninsula with other powers. Clearly, in either Roosevelt's multilateral trusteeship or the State Department's unilateral control, the United States had no intention of allowing Koreans their long sought-after independence. Rejecting Roosevelt's trusteeship idea, the State Department and Pentagon formulated plans for a post-war US military occupation to assure Washington would have the predominant voice in Korean affairs.[17]

However, there remained the Soviet Union to contend with. After much negotiation, Washington and Moscow arrived at an agreement. US and Soviet armies would occupy separate zones in Korea for a period of no more than five years. At the end of the quinquennium, an independent Korean government would be formed on a unified basis.[18] The Soviets adhered to their part of the accord, ending their occupation at the close of 1948. The US occupation continues.

Henry Heller, in his book *The Cold War and the New Imperialism*, described the scene in Korea immediately following the Japanese surrender on August 15, 1945:

> The sudden end of the war in August 1945 set off a popular revolution. In towns and villages across Korea the underground resistance surfaced in the form of a gigantic mass movement of people's committees. ... Seizing local government from the Japanese and their Korean collaborators, they demanded the restoration of Korean independence. ... In Seoul, the Korean capital, the national leadership of the popular movement proclaimed the establishment of the People's Republic of Korea.[19]

The people's committees usually consisted of community leaders and notable figures, some elected, some not, who organized civic administration, land reform, and the expulsion of the Japanese and their Korean collaborators from government.

Since the Japanese, along with their Korean turncoats, had controlled civil administration, the Japanese surrender meant (1) that someone had to take over the operation of government; (2) that Koreans, hungry for independence, would quickly fill the void; (3) that quislings were likely to be targeted for reprisals; (4) that the new native Korean administrators were likely to take government in the direction of egalitarianism; (5) that since the fourth point accorded with the Soviet worldview, the people's committees would be welcome in the Soviet zone; and (6) since the same point clashed with the US worldview, the US occupation would try to crush the people's committees.

The Soviets had entered Korea on August 8, fighting Japanese forces until August 15, the date Tokyo surrendered. They had pushed south of the 38th parallel, but once the Japanese had capitulated, the Red Army quickly withdrew to its pre-arranged occupation zone. US forces wouldn't arrive in Korea until September 8, a full month after the Soviets arrived, and three weeks after the Japanese surrendered. Hence, Soviet blood had been spilled in liberating the peninsula; US blood had not. For three weeks, from Victory over Japan Day forward, no undefeated occupation force was in Korea south of the 38th parallel. During this period Koreans in the south were able take control of civic administration, by their own efforts. They were also able to do the same in the north, where the Soviets allowed the people's committees to flourish.[20] By September 6, the Koreans had organized the people's committees into a peninsula-wide network, and proclaimed a Korean People's Republic.

In 1948, Lee Kang Kuk, head of foreign affairs in the provisional government north of the 38th parallel (the predecessor to the DPRK) told journalist Anna Louise Strong that:

> After the surrender of Japan, we organized People's Committees and set up local provisional governments all over Korea. We made no division between north and south for the Americans had not yet come. ... On September 6, 1945, three weeks after the surrender of Japan, we held our first congress in Seoul, of about one thousand representatives from all parts of the country. They had been chosen quickly and without full formality, but they were a fair representation of all the political tendencies in Korea, except the pro-Japanese. We took the name 'Korean People's Republic' and set up a People's Committee' of seventy-five members to hold provisional power and prepare for general elections.[21]

When the Red Army swept into Korea, the Soviet commander told Koreans that they had "happiness in [their] own hands" and that they must "make themselves the creators of their own" destiny.[22] The message of the US commander in the Pacific, General Douglas MacArthur, announcing the arrival of US forces on the peninsula, was very different.

> Proclamation No. 1 by General of the Army Douglas MacArthur
> Yokohama, September 7, 1945
> To the People of Korea:
> As Commander-in-Chief, United States Army Forces, Pacific, I do hereby proclaim as follows:
> - I hereby establish military control over Korea south of 38 degrees north latitude and the inhabitants thereof.
> - All powers of Government over the territory of Korea south of 38 degrees north latitude and the people thereof will be for the present exercised under my authority.
> - All persons will obey promptly all my orders and orders issued under my authority. Acts of resistance to the occupying forces or any acts which may disturb public peace and safety will be punished severely.
> - For all purposes during the military control, English will be the official language.[23]

With the stroke of a pen, MacArthur expunged the People's Republic of Korea. Korea's liberation from foreign rule had lasted exactly one day.

Lee Kang Kuk recalled that the Korean People's Republic sent delegates to greet the US forces. "They refused to deal with us, choosing rather to recognize the Japanese rule. The Americans disregarded and finally suppressed our People's Committees all over their zone. [The Soviets] recognized these committees as our local provisional government. Thus began the great split between north and south."[24] Lee's point is significant. The division of Korea into north and south began when the Soviets recognized the nascent indigenous governance structure in the north, which became the DPRK, and the United States refused to recognize the people's committees, imposing, instead, a military occupation on the south that continues to this day.

The commander of the US occupation forces, General John R. Hodge, who would become the military governor of the US zone, had a choice: allow the Koreans, through their newly created republic, to take over the reins of government, or retain the Japanese and their Korean collaborators in their positions in the colonial administration. He chose the latter. "We could [have] come as liberators," Anna Louise Strong lamented, but chose instead to come as conquerors.[25]

It was the same throughout East Asia. The journalist Israel Epstein observed that:

> British and Dutch troops landing to 'liberate' Java did not disarm conquered enemy units but ordered them to cooperate in subduing the local population, which had formed a government to rule itself. ... French forces in Indo-China, again with British support, employed Japanese soldiers against the independent Vietnam government. The British in Malaya allowed the Japanese garrison to keep a considerable part of their arms for 'self-defense' and began to hunt down the wartime anti-Japanese guerrillas there. In Burma friction developed between local antifascist forces and the victorious Allies. In the Philippines, General MacArthur disarmed and deported the Japanese. But he became the protector of Filipino landlords, commercial magnates and politicians who had been Japan's quislings during the occupation.[26]

The United States came as a conqueror because Washington wanted to incorporate Korea into the US empire and the aspirations of Koreans, yearning for freedom, were against the US project. "Koreans longed for independence after suffering four decades of Japanese rule," wrote US historian Melvyn P. Leffler, but the administration of US president Harry S. Truman "feared that... radical nationalists or communists would take control."[27] The US government, therefore, decided to deny Koreans the right to govern themselves. Instead, they brought conservatives and pro-Japanese collaborators to power, to establish a US-superintended hierarchy, with the Americans at the top, Korean elites and quislings immediately below them, and the bulk of Koreans at the bottom, precisely where they had been under Japanese rule. Koreans despised the new US-imposed imperial order, as much as they had despised the Japanese equivalent, and would vigorously oppose it as fervently as they had opposed the hated Japanese. In the war that would develop between a new colonial master and liberation forces, Koreans who had collaborated with the Japanese would play an important part, reprising their role as kapos in a Korean imperial prison, now under the supervision of a new warden.

Japan couldn't have maintained three and half decades of colonial rule without a fair degree of collaboration. The Japanese sought out Koreans willing to betray their compatriots, and found them. The collaborators were the landed class, the feudal elite who led parasitic lives feeding off the labor of the peasantry. Most Koreans were poor farmers—sharecroppers who paid rent to the landlords by handing over 50 to 80 percent of their crop.[28] "Korean landlords maintained relations with tenants that were not fundamentally different from those of the nineteenth century,"[29] observed Bruce Cumings. It was these very same parasites who ingratiated themselves with the Japanese.

The Japanese also found Koreans to fill the ranks of the national police and army. These were traitors, who helped their Japanese overlords quell opposition to colonial rule. Later, the same quislings would help the US occupation authorities suppress opposition to US rule. The collaborators included Chong Il-gwon, who was a captain in Japan's Manchurian garrison, the Kwantung Army. Chung transitioned easily from the Japanese army to the South Korean military, by way of the English Language School for officers, founded by the US Military Government in December 1945. He would later become the South Korean army's chief of staff, and after that, prime minister,[30] a direct path from collaboration with the enemy to head of the government of a collaborator state.

Paek Son-yop and Paek In-yop were turncoat officers in Japan's Kwantung Army. The former was involved in anti-insurgency warfare, hunting down patriots like Kim Il-sung. He would become the first four-star general in the South Korean army. His brother would command South Korea's 17th Independent Regiment. Park Chung-hee, or Lt. Takagi Masao, as he was known to his Japanese comrades, earned his spurs at an officers' school in Japan, before enlisting in the Kwantung Army, Japan's occupation army in Manchuria. A biography recounted how Park—a Japanese "hireling",[31] in the words of Bruce Cumings—had received a gold watch from Emperor Hirohito for his services to the empire—services which likely included hunting down Korean patriots who fought to slough off Japanese rule.[32] Kim Chae-gyu also served in the Japanese military as an officer. Both Park and Kim graduated from the US military government-established Korean Military Academy. Park—who was entangled with the Japanese right wing, including America's favorite war criminal, Kishi Nobusuke, maternal grandfather of Japanese prime minister Abe Shinzo[33]—became president of South Korea. Kim was his national intelligence director, head of the Korean Central Intelligence Agency, the KCIA, an organization very much of the same cloth and anti-Left political orientation as the *Geheime Staatspolizei*, the Gestapo.

Kim Sok-won, also known by his Japanese name, Kaneyama Shakugen, we have met already. As a colonel in the Japanese Imperial Army, Kim led the hunt for Kim Il-sung in the frozen mountains of Manchuria. The emperor of Japan had decorated him with the Order of Merit for 'bravery' in campaigns in the war against China. On June 2, 1948, Kim paraded 2,500 hundred Korean veterans of the Japanese army through the streets of Seoul, in the US occupation zone, an act which speaks volumes about the character of the political regime the United States was implanting in Korea. It is unthinkable that a pro-Japanese collaborator could openly parade a band of traitors through the streets north of the 38th parallel, brazenly celebrating their treachery. One reason why this tableau would never have been realized in the north is because turncoats fled the north, where they were unwelcome, to take up residence in the south, where they could bask in the warm embrace of the US military government. The US occupation government was much more accommodating of collaborators; indeed, they counted on them to run day-to-day affairs in the US occupation zone, as the Nazis had counted on kapos to administer the day-to-day affairs of their concentration camps. Later, Kim would lead a division of the newly-formed, US-commanded, South Korean army. During the Korean War, every division of the US-directed military was led by traitors who had served as officers in the Japanese army.[34] This was fitting, since, as veterans of armed forces dedicated to enforcing foreign rule over a recalcitrant population, they had years of experience in a role their new US master was looking for—as anti-insurgency specialists, skilled in the suppression of *maquis* resistance to foreign rule. Plus, the United States afforded them protection. If the turncoats were already inclined to collaborate with their foreign masters, their inclination was reinforced by the reality that without the aegis of the US occupation force, they would likely be strung up from light poles and other suitable gibbets by Korean patriots. Hence, a cadre of officers of the former Japanese Imperial Army would become the foundation of the South Korean army. The army would serve as "the preserve," Bruce Cumings wrote, "of those Koreans who, one would have thought, chose the wrong side during their nation's moment of maximum trial."[35] This illuminates the nature of the fratricidal intra-Korean war that would be fought in 1950 between, on the one side, an army whose officer corps was almost exclusively drawn from the pool of Korean turncoats who had served in the Japanese army, and on the other, an army whose officer corps was almost exclusively drawn from veterans of the guerrilla resistance to the Japanese—an army of traitors vs. an army of patriots.

William Langdon, a US State Department adviser to Hodge, wrote that "The old native regime internally was feudal and corrupt but the record shows that it was ... disposed toward foreign interests ... protecting foreign lives and property and enterprises and respecting treaties and franchise. I am sure that we may count on at least as much from a native government evolved above."[36] And so the landed elite, and traitors who had taken up positions as officers in the Japanese military, became the favored sons of the US occupation authorities. US authorities clearly knew they were siding with the most reviled sections of Korean society. Only a week after Uncle Sam's swaggering arrival on the Korean peninsula, US military intelligence reported that Koreans who "achieved high rank under the Japanese are considered pro-Japanese and are hated almost as much as their masters."[37] The United States—the self-appointed champion of freedom and democracy—arrogantly strode into Korea, looked about for a local ally, and immediately found one in a numerically insignificant group of parasites and pro-Japanese lickspittles.[38]

Washington's intervention on behalf of the tiny landlord class immediately fanned the flames of Korean resentment. By September 15, US military intelligence was describing southern Korea "as a powder keg ready to explode at the application of a spark." Denied independence, with their efforts to sweep out the Japanese countermanded by the new US military dictatorship, Koreans seethed with anger. "All groups," the report revealed, had "the common idea of seizing Japanese property, ejecting the Japanese from Korea, and achieving immediate independence."[39] And now the achievement of their idea had been thwarted. Hodge wrote that there "is growing resentment against all Americans in the area including passive resistance. ... Every day of drifting under this situation makes our position in Korea more untenable and decreases our waning popularity. ... The word pro-American is being added to pro-Jap, national traitor, and collaborator."[40] All the same, in Hodge's view, Koreans couldn't be allowed to run their own affairs. Southern Korea, he observed, was "extremely fertile ground for the establishment of Communism."[41] The masses, he confided, were looking to Russia as a model for their future.[42]

CHAPTER 5

The Patriot State

"In the night of our ignorance, North Korea confirms all stereotypes."—Bruce Cumings[1]

Of the two superpowers, the United States and Russia, the latter was clearly favored by Koreans and the former clearly spurned. Koreans certainly weren't going to look to the United States to determine their future, for the future Washington offered was one of perpetual Korean subordination to foreign rule within the US empire. Washington had assented to Japan's colonization of Korea, in return for Japan accepting the United States' colonization of the Philippines. Wilson had reneged on the promise (he never really made) to colonial peoples to usher in a new age of self-determination. And the United States, which hadn't spilled a single drop of blood in the liberation of Korea, had marched onto the peninsula, declared a military dictatorship, and rejected Korea's four decades-long struggle for independence. What's more, Washington had intervened on behalf of the most reviled groups in the country, and brought the Japanese and their Korean collaborators back into administrative positions, reversing efforts Korean patriots had made to purge them. Washington, then, had a long and ignominious record of opposition to Korean independence.

On the other hand, Koreans looked to the Soviet Union as a model because the communists genuinely supported national liberation, were against the landlords, and promoted women's rights.

Hodge's analysis that Koreans were inspired by communism was corroborated by Edwin Pauley, a friend and adviser to US president Harry S. Truman. After touring Korea, Pauley warned the US president that, "Communism in Korea could get off to a better start than practically anywhere else in the world."[2]

"In 1945 Koreans would have worked out a new destiny," wrote the historian Frank Baldwin in 1975. "That destiny almost certainly would have been a leftist, perhaps a communist, government."[3] Bruce Cumings echoed Baldwin's (and Hodge's and Pauley's) view: a "leftist regime would have taken over quickly, and it would have been a revolutionary nationalist government."[4]

Koreans in the US zone were also looking to the USSR because it was clear that in the Soviet zone, Koreans were allowed to build an independent Korea, emancipated from the exploitation of the indigenous landlord class, and liberated from the treachery of pro-Japanese collaborators. The Soviets, wrote Bruce Cumings, "stayed in the background and let Koreans run the government, they put anti-Japanese resistance leaders out front, and they supported radical reforms of the land system, labor conditions, and women's rights."[5] To Kim Il-sung, who had returned to Korea on September 19, the Soviet people were "our liberator and helper."[6]

In contrast to the US zone, where the Korean People's Republic was abolished, in the Soviet zone people's committees spread rapidly, developed into a network, and quickly evolved into a provisional government, which immediately undertook significant democratic reforms. Land was redistributed from the landlords to those who tilled it. Large enterprises, mainly Japanese owned, were nationalized. An eight-hour workday, an end to child labor, and a program of social insurance, were soon implemented. A law allowing Koreans to be educated in their own language, contrary to Japanese practice, which had discouraged it, was decreed. And Koreans, through their people's committees, abolished the differential assignment of rights and privileges on the basis of gender.[7]

The provisional government was established on February 8, 1946, with Kim Il-sung as its president.[8] On the eve of their return to Korea, the top Korean leaders of the Manchurian resistance had agreed that, owing to his reputation and charisma, Kim Il-sung would be promoted as the principal political leader of a liberated Korea.[9] Kim had considerable charm[10] and his organizational and leadership abilities, demonstrated through his leadership in the Chinese Communist Party and Communist Party-led armies,[11] were *nonpareil*. His reputation and magnetism would allow him to command popular support, while his leadership and organizational skills made him the perfect candidate to oversee the administration of a new government.[12]

Kim's ascension to power, then, was not a Soviet-orchestrated plan to impose a dictator on a resistant population, as anti-DPRK propaganda, disseminated by US intelligence services and ignorant Western journalists, would have it. The revolutionary situation was endogenous to Korea, and Kim's elevation to the presidency of the provisional government was an expression of Koreans' aspirations for independence. The autonomous development of the provisional government from the spontaneously developed people's committees arose from Korean ambitions to overcome four decades of hardship and humiliation under Japanese rule, while Kim Il-sung's ability to command the popular support of Koreans in the Soviet zone was attributable to his personal qualities, his undeniable patriotic credentials, and his outstanding commitment to the historical aspirations of Koreans.[13] He was not imposed on Koreans by Moscow, and his revolution was not exogenous, imported from the USSR. He had the support of his compatriots, and the reforms his government implemented were demanded by Koreans themselves.

In some ways, the cult of Kim Il-sung that would grow up around the guerrilla leader obscured the role that Koreans *en masse* played north of the 38th parallel in collectively bringing about their liberation. True, the Soviets furnished Koreans space to work out new modalities of independent rule, free from the stifling hand of the United States. Without the Red Army's presence from 1945 to 1948, Korea's independence movement in the north would have been quashed by the US empire, as it was in the south; hence Kim Il-sung's designation of the Soviets as our "liberator and helper."

In North Korea, Kim is revered as a semi-deity, a god-like figure who, it might be supposed, single-handedly delivered his people to freedom. There is a parallel with Fidel Castro, another revolutionary nationalist, also of considerable personal magnetism, who is often portrayed as playing a larger-than-life role in his country's liberation, overshadowing the significant contributions of countless others. When Castro died, historian Louis A. Perez Jr. wrote what might be called a historian's elegy of a great figure. His remarks on the passing of Castro, however, apply equally to Kim. Replace Castro with Kim, and Perez's requiem becomes:

> [Kim Il-sung] was in many ways defined through his confrontation with the [Japanese]. His uncompromising defense of [Korean] claims to self-determination as a matter of a historically-determined mandate and a legacy to fulfil more than adequately validated his moral claim to leadership. To confront [Japan, and later the United States] in defense of national sovereignty was to make good on the internal logic of [Korean] history.
>
> What resonated in [1946] and in the years that followed was the very phenomenon of the [Korean] revolution, of a people summoned to heroic purpose, to affirm the right of self-determination and national sovereignty. [Kim Il-sung] was the most visible representative of that people.
>
> However large a role [Kim] played in shaping the course of [Korean] history, it bears emphasizing that the success of his appeal and the source of his authority were very much a function of the degree to which he represented the authenticity of [Korean] historical aspirations. [Kim Il-sung] was an actor, of course, but he was also acted upon. He shaped the history of his times in discharge of the history in which he was formed. The meaning of his life must be situated within that history, as it was lived and learned, as the circumstances that acted to forge self-knowledge and knowledge of the world at large, and served to inform the purpose of his presence.
>
> To subsume outcomes of [decades] of [North Korean] programs and policies to the will of one man is facile. It is bad history. Worse still, it is to dismiss the efforts of countless hundreds of thousands of other men and women who—with ill-will or good intentions—played important roles in the decisions, deliberations and discharge of the purpose that has moved the history of [Korea].[14]

How, then, did the countless men and women of the Korean north move the history of Korea? Apart from forming people's committees through which they consented to their own representatives, Koreans—peasants in the majority—demanded land reform. Six of every 10 members of the provisional government were peasants. Fittingly, on its very first day, the provisional government announced that redistributing land from parasitic landlords to the peasants who toiled it would be its first order of business.[15] As president of the provisional government, Kim Il-sung reported:

> Already in March this year [1946], the agrarian reform was carried out in the rural areas of north Korea, bringing about a radical change in production relations. The agrarian reform dealt a decisive blow to the landlord class, the most reactionary class in Korea, wiping out its economic base. The peasantry was freed from feudal exploitation and oppression and became the master of land, which had been their centuries-old aspiration. The peasants have not only come to work the land as their own land which was distributed free by the people's committee, but also have got rid of the system of exorbitant forced delivery of farm produce plus all kinds of exacting taxes and levies extorted from them in the years of Japanese imperialism and have become free to dispose of their farm produce after delivering only 25 percent of the harvests as tax in kind.[16]

"The Land Reform Law was sweeping," wrote Anna Louise Strong. "It confiscated all Japanese lands, whether public or private, all landlords' lands, if the landlord owned more than twelve acres, or if, owning less, he systematically rented the land and did not work it himself, and all land of churches and monasteries that exceeded twelve acres." The lands, recovered on behalf of the people, "were given to village committees to distribute on the basis of the number of people in each farm family, and also with reference to the number of adult workers. Landlords also might get land to till but not more than twelve acres, and this must be in another county where they would have no traditional influence. Of the 70,000 landlords" in the Soviet occupation zone "3,500 took advantage of this permission."[17]

The remainder of the north's landlords fled to the US occupation zone, where the governing authorities had a more tolerant—indeed, favorable—attitude to parasites. Korean landlords in the US occupation zone continued to oversee the production of rice for export to Japan, a continuation of the colonial regime.[18] While completed by 1946 in the north, land reform wouldn't be carried out in the south until 1950, and it was North Korean forces, advancing south of the 38th parallel, clearing away the landlord regime and their US patrons, that allowed Koreans of the south to implement the land reform their compatriots to the north had already completed. Hence, the advancing force of the DPRK military played the same role the Red Army had played from 1945 to 1948: it created the space Koreans needed to carry out democratic reforms.

In the north, the work day was set at eight hours for non-hazardous jobs and seven hours for hazardous ones. Workers were guaranteed annual two-week vacations with pay. Workers in hazardous jobs got a full month. This contrasted sharply with labor conditions under the Japanese, marked by work days of 15 hours or more and no paid vacations. Child labor was outlawed, as was discrimination against women in pay.[19] Lee Mai-Hwa, a female gold miner, told Anna Louise Strong that during the colonial era she worked 13 hours or more per day, loading ore onto carts underground. In 1949, she was a pneumatic drill operator, working only seven hours per day.[20] Kim Il-sung explained: the "Provisional People's Committee of North Korea promulgated the Labour Law freeing factory and office workers from harsh, colonial-type exploitation and introducing the eight-hour working day and a social insurance system. And a law was passed to guarantee the women social rights equal to those of the men for the first time in the history of our country."[21]

On the heels of the labor reforms, the provisional government nationalized all industry belonging to Japanese and quislings.[22] The government, Kim said, had also "proclaimed the law on the nationalization of industrial, transport and communications facilities, and banks which had been owned by the Japanese imperialists, pro-Japanese elements, and traitors to the nation. With this we have brought under national ownership, ownership of the entire people, the backbone of the economy which constitutes the material basis for building a fully independent and democratic state."[23] The new law, Kim pointed out, had "wiped out the foundation of Japanese imperialist colonial rule and deprived the traitors to the nation who had collaborated with Japanese imperialism of their economic footholds." The institution of paying rent to private landlords was eliminated. "Thus, all the forces that had oppressed and exploited the Korean people hand in glove with Japanese imperialism," he explained, "were deprived of their economic footholds and politically liquidated."[24]

Concurrently, Kim's government introduced an economic plan to convert the economy, which had been tailored to meet the needs of Japanese, to meet the needs of Koreans.[25]

In 1965, Joan Robinson, the Cambridge economist, visited the DPRK and declared that North Korea was an economic miracle. "There is a complete system of social security for workers and employees," she wrote. "Pensions are at the level of 50 percent of wages. ...The medical service is free." North Korea, she concluded, is a "nation without poverty."[26]

Reflecting the reforms Kim's provisional government introduced in 1946, there existed, Robinson observed, in all enterprises "an eight-hour day, with an hour's break for lunch; there is a six-hour day for heavy work and for occupations dangerous to health. Workers receive holidays with pay for fifteen days a year (a month for heavy and dangerous work)."[27]

"Women are 51 percent of the population and 49 percent of the labor force," Robinson continued, "which means that few except the elderly are not employed." Women could fully participate in the work force because paid maternity leave, day cares, nursery schools, and prepared meals, freed them from the childcare and domestic burdens they alone had once shouldered. Regarding income inequality, Robinson noted that the "spread of income is very narrow, both between town and country and within industry."[28]

The Soviet zone was a living laboratory whose experiments showed the United States what would happen in their own zone if Koreans of the south were allowed to organize their own affairs. Decisions about public administration would be democratized, driven into the people's committees, rather than held in the hands of a landlord class answerable to foreign patrons; landlords would be expropriated, and their land distributed to those who worked it; and industry would be nationalized. Since these outcomes would fail to comport with the US vision of a world organized as a hierarchy, with the titans of US finance, industry, and commerce at the top, Korea's landed elite in the middle, and 98 percent of Koreans at the bottom, the latter group would have to be prevented from ever laying its hands on the levers of power. In order to accomplish this negative goal, the movement for Korean independence in the south would have to be crushed. After it was crushed, it would have to be forever repressed. This would be accomplished by building an anti-communist state, staffed by anti-communist zealots and former Japanese army officers whom Washington would hand pick to operate a police state, as viciously anti-Left as the Nazi's anti-communist police state. Eventually, the citadel of the Korean independence movement in the north would have to be weakened, degraded, and ultimately destroyed (to borrow the words that a future US president, Barack Obama, would use in connection with ISIS.) But for the moment, the task at hand was to repress the homegrown movement for equality in the south. It was to this immediate task that US military governor General John Reed Hodge turned his attention in November of 1945.

CHAPTER 6

The War Against Communists of the South

"We have got to kill them."
—Senior South Korean intelligence officer, referring to communists of the south.[1]

At the end of 1945, Hodge and his advisers created a four-point plan to destroy the movement for independence in southern Korea. First, they would build an army staffed by former officers of the Japanese army to isolate the south from the independence movement in the north. Second, the Korean National Police, the instrument of violence the Japanese had used to suppress opposition to Japanese rule, would be rebuilt. Where the KNP's original mandate had been to crush opposition to the Japanese occupation, the organization's new mandate would be to quell opposition to the successor occupation of the United States. Third, the occupation government's alliance with right-wing, anti-egalitarian, pro-collaborationist forces would be strengthened. And fourth, opponents of the new regime would be rounded up and jailed.[2] This amounted to a declaration of war on the Korean People's Republic.[3] By 1948, Hodge's war on the independence movement in the south had driven the movement's supporters into graves, into jail, underground, or to the north. "Germany was built up by Hitler to fight Communism," Hodge had observed.[4] The US military governor was building a parallel state in Korea to achieve the same anti-Left goals that had animated the Nazi project in Germany. Hodge and his successors, a string of South Korean strongmen, belonged to the same class as Hitler, Mussolini, Franco, Pinochet, and Suharto—dictators whose chief political goal was the extermination of communists.

Hodge created the Korean Military Academy as the first step toward building a South Korean army. The army's political function would be to isolate the south from the north so that the KNP would have space and time to eliminate the independence movement in the south. The first graduating class comprised 40 traitors, Korean officers who had served in the Japanese Imperial Army, along with 20 patriots, Koreans who had served in the army of the exile Korean Provisional Government, fighting the Japanese from China. The patriots refused to work with the traitors, and the new south Korean army accordingly became predominantly staffed by turncoats.[5] According to Bruce Cumings, "Virtually the entire officer corps of the Republic of Korea army" that Hodge would eventually build "was drawn from Koreans with experience in the Japanese Imperial Army."[6]

The KNP became Hodge's principal apparatus for crushing the independence movement in the south.[7] Hodge recruited the Koreans whom the Japanese had hired to staff their colonial force to staff the new KNP, establishing a continuity between Japanese and US rule.[8] US military officials described the KNP as "thoroughly Japanized and efficiently utilized as an instrument of tyranny" during the colonial period,[9] making it especially attractive to Hodge as the main instrument of repression to be used by the anti-communist police state he was building.

Under the Japanese, 40 percent of KNP personnel were Korean traitors. The police carried out a number of colonial functions, from ordinary policing to tax collection, dragooning Koreans for road construction, administering land purchases, enforcing landlord-friendly tenancy agreements, and teaching school.[10]

Anna Louise Strong wrote that, "Within a year [of US troops landing in Korea] great uprisings took place in eighty cities and in hundreds of farming villages against the 'police state' that the

American armed forces kept in power."[11] For his part, Henry Heller wrote that "Following the suppression of the Korean People's Republic by the United States, widespread strikes, mass demonstrations, rebellions, and, finally, large-scale guerrilla movements continued at the grassroots."[12]

In Bruce Cumings' words, the US occupation "immediately ran into monumental opposition from the mass of South Koreans. Most of the first year of the occupation, 1945-46, was given over to suppression of many people's committees that had emerged in the provinces. This provoked a massive rebellion that spread over four provinces in the fall of 1946; after it was suppressed, radical activists developed a significant guerrilla movement in 1948 and 1949."[13] Three years into the US occupation, most villages in the Korean interior south of the 48th parallel were under the control of liberation forces.[14]

By December 1947, Hodge's KNP force had rounded up and jailed 21,458 leftists. Lee Kang Kuk, head of foreign affairs in the north's provisional government, told Anna Louise Strong that the figure exceeded the number of political prisoners under Japanese rule.[15] By 1949, the number swelled to 30,000.[16] The magnitude of opposition to the US occupation regime was so great, that the KNP's jails could not hold all the dissidents the KNP arrested. To handle the excess, concentration camps, euphemistically denominated as 'guidance camps,' were established to immure the 70,000 leftists who exceeded the capacity of the overcrowded prisons, already teeming with 30,000 communists.[17] Hitler, it should be noted, also relied on concentration camps, or *konzentrationslager*, to do what Hodge's forces were doing in Korea. Roger Baldwin, the head of the American Civil Liberties Union, visited Korea in May 1947, reporting that "The country is literally in the grip of a police regime and a private terror." One prison he toured contained 1,000 inmates who had been jailed for organizing unions and strikes.[18] In Bruce Cumings assessment, Hodge had "created one of the worst police states in Asia."[19] The anti-Left ethos of the state, and its police state methods, as we'll presently see, never disappeared. South Korea very much remains an anti-communist police state today.

In a 1948 report the CIA described the overt political structure in the US zone "as under the control of 'extreme Rightists,'" who were "ruthlessly brutal in suppressing disorder" mainly "through the agency of the National Police." Although membership in leftist organizations was legal, the police ran roughshod over communists, harassing them, jailing them, and not infrequently gunning them down. Moreover, noted the CIA, the "alliance of the police with the Right has been reflected in the cooperation of the police with Rightist youth groups for the purpose of completely suppressing Leftist activity. This alignment has had the effect of forcing the Left to operate as an underground organization since it could not effectively compete in a parliamentary sense even if it should so desire."[20]

In contrast, there was little suppression of political opposition in the north, mainly because there was not much political opposition to suppress. Most Koreans, no matter where they lived on the peninsula, wanted the same things: government by Koreans; land reform; the deportation of the Japanese and expulsion of collaborators from the government; and economic development to meet domestic, not foreign, needs. Kim Il-sung's government immediately delivered on all of these demands. The opposition would come from landlords and collaborators. But the collaborators had fled to the US zone, and the landlords either accepted the land reform law, and worked the land they were allotted, or migrated to the south. Anna Louise Strong explained the lack of political opposition in the north this way: because the United States "ruled at first through the Japanese and then through the Japanese-appointed Korean officials and police ... all of the pro-Japanese Koreans—former police and officials, landlords and stockholders in Japanese companies—fled south" to the US zone.[21] The flight of pro-Japanese collaborators and parasitical landlords to the south simplified politics in the Soviet zone, by cleansing it of enemies who would have otherwise needed to be suppressed. At the same time, militants who had been jailed by the Japanese for opposing colonialism were freed from jail, and brought back into politics in the north.[22]

By 1950, between 100,000 and 200,000 southern patriots had been killed by US occupation forces and their Korean subalterns.[23] At the head of the South Korean police state was a fanatical anti-communist who had spent four decades in the United States, accumulating degrees from Ivy League universities and hobnobbing with US government officials while Kim Il-sung battled the Japanese army and Korean turncoats in the frozen mountains of Manchuria. His name was Syngman Rhee.

Unlike Park Chung-hee, the military dictator who would succeed him as president, Rhee cannot be characterized as a traitor *tout court*. Park helped the Empire of the Rising Sun keep his native Korea in chains. Rhee, unlike Park, was not a traitor, in the sense of collaborating with the Japanese. Collaborating with the new US occupation, however, was another matter.

Rhee immigrated to the United States in 1904, before Japan made Korea into a protectorate. He was absent from Korea for the entire Japanese colonial period, returning only in October 1945, aboard a US military aircraft, spirited into the country to head a new pro-US anti-communist police state.

Rhee opposed the Japanese colonization of Korea and fought against it, lobbying US politicians, including two presidents, Theodore Roosevelt and Woodrow Wilson, to intercede on Korea's behalf. This strategy, thought Kim Il-sung, was tantamount to appealing for help to an armed robber waiting outside your door while another armed robber plunders your house from within. The only effective solution to the problem of occupation, Kim concluded, was to take up arms to drive the robber out, and prevent the other robbers from entering, a strategy Kim would take up, while Rhee pounded the streets of Washington, seeking help from one imperialist power (the United States) against another (Japan).

Kim Il-sung's communism made him attractive to many Koreans but *persona non grata* to the US government. Syngman Rhee's anti-communism made him attractive to the US government but *persona non grata* to many Koreans. But Rhee had something that other Korean anti-communists lacked: a record free from pro-Japanese collaborationist taint. Exiled in the United States during the course of the Japanese colonial period, Rhee never had the opportunity to collaborate (and may not have taken it if he had.) Plus, he had been the president (though disgraced) of the Provisional Republic of Korea government in exile. Washington hoped that Rhee's anti-Japanese credentials would make him acceptable to South Korean public opinion.

As head of a puppet state, Rhee would have other attractions for US officials. His long-time residency in the United States practically made him an American, and certainly inclined him toward the US point of view. He had travelled in the same circles as the US politico-economic elite, meeting US politicians in Washington as a lobbyist and establishing contacts with the US ruling class at the elite universities he attended (BA from George Washington University, MA from Harvard and PhD from Princeton). Indeed, as the US geopolitical strategist Zbigniew Brzezinski pointed out, the transmission of US ruling class ideology and values to talented foreigners who pass through elite US universities *en route* to jobs in government back home is one of the foundations of US global power.[24] The Office of Strategic Services (forerunner of the CIA), with which Rhee worked during the Pacific War,[25] valued Rhee above all other exiled Korean leaders for having more of an "American point of view." Accordingly, it was Rhee, instilled with US ruling class values, whom the OSS selected to install in Korea in October of 1945,[26] a Trojan horse in which to smuggle into Korea the thinking of the US ruling elite.

CHAPTER 7

Suppressing a Worldwide Movement for Liberty, Equality and the Unity of Humankind

"The 'national security institutions' were staffed by Wall Street lawyers with a keen interest in American economic supremacy."[1]

While Hodge was building his Gestapo state in the south to suppress the Korean movement for equality, planners at the US State Department in Washington were worrying about the advance of communism on a world scale. According to Melvyn Leffler, "Elaborate studies undertaken by the State Department and the Council on Foreign Relations in New York demonstrated that" corporate America couldn't thrive in a world in which its access to foreign markets, raw materials, and investment opportunities was restricted.[2] The United States' opposition to Nazi Germany and militarist Japan was related, not to the Axis powers' treatment of the peoples they conquered—about whom US leaders cared not one iota—but to Germany's and Japan's efforts to construct zones of economic exclusion in Europe and East Asia respectively. It was Axis domination of Eurasia and the concomitant exclusion of US capital from European and Asian markets which thrust Uncle Sam into the wars in Europe and the Pacific.

Similarly, socialism and revolutionary nationalism abroad threatened US capitalism at home. Socialists and revolutionary nationalists in power brought their countries' markets, labor, and raw materials under indigenous control, closing off corporate America from important profit-making opportunities, forcing US capital to live with limited money-making opportunities at home. Hadn't Kim Il-sung nationalized Japanese-established industry in Korea, bringing it under a regimen of economic planning guided by Korean needs, thereby denying potential profit-making opportunities to wealthy US investors and business people? Walter Lippmann, the most renowned US journalist of the time, opined that US capitalism could not "survive in a world that is elsewhere under" the control of socialists and revolutionary nationalists; it needed access to profit-making opportunities on a world scale.[3]

The United States had always been "a nation without borders," as historian Steven Hahn called it.[4] Driven by economic interests, it had expanded inexorably, growing from 13 former British colonies on the Atlantic coast of North America to a vast continental empire based on the conquest of the land of North America's indigenous peoples, which would inspire Hitler's drive for *lebensraum* and Mussolini's wars for *spaze vitale*. The Spanish-American War added territory, some of which—Puerto Rico and Guam, for example—remain, even today, as *de facto* US colonies. The expansion was driven initially by a slave-owning elite's hunger for land and later by an industrial elite's hunger for markets and investment opportunities. "The basis for America's expanding geopolitical ambitions," wrote Zbigniew Brzezinski, citing the Spanish-American War and the Monroe Doctrine, "subsequently justified by America's 'alleged manifest destiny,'" was "provided by the rapid industrialization of the country's economy,"[5] which demanded access to foreign markets and raw materials. The problem was that the people of other countries didn't always want to give US industrialists and investors access to their labor, markets, and raw materials—at least, not on terms which allowed US investors and business executives to accumulate handsome profits while local populations were left in poverty or driven into pauperism. And sometimes the industrialists and investors of other countries wanted to keep foreign markets and raw materials out of the hands of their US competitors.

Post-war Western Europe struggled economically, and US officials feared that the region's economic travails did nothing to shore up the credibility of the capitalist economic order, which was already viewed with suspicion by Europeans who had lived through the failure of capitalism during the Great Depression. With no sign that capitalism was about to pull Western Europe out of its post-war morass, US planners feared a turn toward communism. The US ambassador to Italy warned Washington that "all the indications we receive ... show that the Communists are consistently gaining ground."[6] In the Western occupation zone of Germany, food riots led the US military governor, General Lucius Clay, to sound the alarm over what he described as a growing communist movement. French conservatives warned Washington that local communists—who had enjoyed enormous prestige owing to the lead role they had played in the resistance to German occupation—might take power. In Greece, communists had also led the resistance to German occupation, and had significant popular support. If the United States failed to eclipse the growth of Communist parties, vast areas of the globe could be walled off from exploitation by US firms and investors.[7] At the same time, if Communist forces were to consolidate their control of Manchuria and northern China, US officials believed that the region's resources would be forfeited to indigenous anti-colonial and anti-feudal forces, who would use the region's bounty of natural resources to address local development needs at the expense of corporate America's profit imperatives.[8]

Truman raised the alarm about the world's growing turn to communism and the implications of this trend for US business in a major foreign policy address delivered at Baylor University in March of 1947. The US president noted that the destruction of national economies during the war and the requirements of reconstruction had compelled governments to favor central planning and internal development at the expense of open markets and free enterprise. The implications for the United States, Truman warned, were grave. Unless Washington acted, corporate America would be forced to operate within attenuated economic frontiers.[9] Socialism and revolutionary nationalism abroad were imperiling the US system of free enterprise[10]—that is, were endangering the profit-making opportunities of the wealthy owners of major US enterprises. Truman didn't present the problem in quite these terms, portending instead, that the American way of life was at stake, but it was the shareholders and financiers whose wealth depended on open access to the world's markets, raw materials, and labor who were at risk.

Truman foresaw the possibility that weaknesses inherent in capitalism could touch off a systemic collapse. "If the countries of middle-western and Mediterranean Europe sink under the burden of despair and become Communist, Scandinavia will fall in the same camp. The strategically and economically vital North African and middle-western areas will follow. The transfer of Western Europe, the second greatest industrial area in the world, and of the essential regions which must inevitably follow such a lead, would radically change the American position. If it should prove that a weakened United Kingdom could not resist so powerful a current, the shift could be cataclysmic."[11] In other words, forces guided by the Enlightenment values of equality and inclusion would become hegemonic. Economies would be reconstructed on the basis of publicly-owned enterprises, organized by a plan, and guided by the goal of satisfying human needs, rather than being based on privately-owned enterprises, organized by markets for the sole reason of channeling profits, rents, and interest to a numerically tiny class of capitalists.

US planners feared that communist governments would come to power in the industrial core of Western Europe and Japan on a wave of popular support. Governments would take control of local economies through state-owned enterprises and implement programs of industrial planning in order to deliver the economic and social security that the core industrial populations had been denied during the great crisis of capitalism that swept the world from 1929.

Meanwhile, anti-colonial movements in the periphery planned to implement a similar program. They aimed to build planned economies, using tools of nationalization, state ownership, incubation of industry behind protective tariff walls, land reform, subsides to domestic firms, controls on foreign investment, and other measures to lift their countries from their subordinate positions in the international division of labor. For half a millennium, colonial powers had accumulated vast wealth by plundering the periphery, creating a "great divergence," which saw the core countries shoot ahead economically, militarily, technologically, and culturally, while the plundered periphery lagged behind.

The communist movement, with its emphasis on social and economic security in the industrial core, and national liberation in the periphery, was decried in Washington as the bearer of a hostile ideology, which, it was feared, might bring the resources of Eurasia under popular control. The conditions of post-war Germany and Japan, marked by economic collapse, demoralization, and widespread disaffection with the capitalist economic order, were viewed by US planners as fertile soil in which attachment to planned economies and social security could take root and flourish.[12]

Truman and his advisers "felt real apprehension," observed Leffler. "The growth of autarky and state planning, the strength of the Communist parties," the disillusionment of people in Japan and Germany, "and the vitality of revolutionary nationalist movements," portended a shift to growing equality and democratization on a world scale.[13] US officials saw themselves as engaged in an enormous geopolitical struggle whose outcome would determine whether globe-girding US capitalism survived or perished.[14] Unless the communist trend was reversed, US corporations and investors would have to turn inward, as people abroad organized their economies to suit their own interests, rather than those of Wall Street. The United States' political economy—atop which sat its principal beneficiaries, a numerically small inter-marrying class of wealthy bankers and industrialists—was under a threat of a greater magnitude than any it had ever faced, borne by a movement of workers and colonial *untermenschen,* whose origins lay in the Bolshevik revolution.[15]

Resurrecting Japan was seen by US strategists as the key to breaking the back of the growing democratization movement in Asia. Japan couldn't be allowed to embrace a communist future. If it did, the socialist bloc would acquire incomparable assets. An army of skilled laborers and a great industrial armamentarium would fall into the hands of a movement which aspired to build a world of plenty, in which the exploitation of man by man was proscribed. The balance of world power would shift away from the United States and its corporate elite toward a worldwide movement of workers and liberated colonial people.[16]

But how was Japan to be resurrected? US policymakers worried that pressure to revivify the Japanese economy would compel Japanese politicians to look to Manchuria, north China, Taiwan, and Korea, its traditional sources of raw materials and agricultural goods.[17] But these areas were now partially under the control of the communist forces of Mao Tse Tung and Kim Il-sung and might soon come under the complete control of leaders who would use central planning, state-owned enterprises, and cooperatives to develop their economies, and would insist on selling their raw materials only on terms that met domestic needs, if they sold them at all. Might Japan be absorbed into a communist East?

By 1947, it was clear to US strategists that Japan's failure to recover economically had become a boon to the Japanese Communist Party, whose popularity was being borne aloft on a rising tide of disenchantment with the capitalist economic order and its attendant plagues of recurring economic crises and industrial wars of extermination.[18] Communism, observed Sarah Paine, "resonated among Japan's poor, threatening" plutocratic rule.[19] If Japan was denied access to its former colonies, its economy would remain in crisis, and the tide of Japanese who looked to communism as a solution would become overwhelming.[20] Owing to its industrial assets and skilled workforce, Japan was the most valuable country in Asia, in the view of US strategists. These assets might escape the control of the United States.[21] A communist Japan would become a model for the world. Communism in Russia and China had been disadvantaged by a low starting point. But a powerful industrial economy, oriented toward the development of human potential rather than profit, and guided by goals of economic and social security, would be a formidable foe in the ideological struggle for the hearts and minds of humanity.

Furthermore, a highly developed Japan, integrated into the world communist movement, would facilitate the industrial development of China, the Soviet Union, and other socialist bloc countries. The Bolsheviks had always expected that industrially-advanced Germany would come to the aid of Red Russia after it had its own socialist revolution. Lenin and his colleagues expected a revolutionary Germany to help build socialism in under-developed Russia. Now, US officials feared that Japan could play the role the Bolsheviks had once imagined Germany would play.

The key to re-animating Japan's economy, and, therefore, to eclipsing the emergence of a communist Japan, US planners believed, was to strengthen Japan's links to its former colonial possessions, including Taiwan and Korea. At the same time, new links would be established with surrogate peripheral economies to replace the ties severed by revolutions in China and North Korea. The markets and raw materials of Southeast Asia would replace those lost to communist advance in Northeast Asia.[22] US planners envisaged a network of interconnections, plugging Japan into the resources, labor, and markets of South Korea, Taiwan, Southeast Asia, and the Persian Gulf.[23]

This plan, however, was not without its challenges. Revolutionary nationalists in Indonesia and Vietnam, having ejected the Japanese at the end of the war, were now threatening to overturn the colonial rule Western Europe had sought to re-establish over its former colonial domains. If the liberation forces succeeded, it was unlikely that either country would allow itself to return to its previous role as purveyor of cheap labor, raw materials, and investment opportunities for wealthy Japanese.[24]

The efforts of the Indochinese to free themselves from French colonial rule presented another difficulty. Already weakened by the war, the French were embroiled in an expensive campaign to retain their empire in Southeast Asia, expending blood and treasure, and consequently exacerbating the economic crisis at home. French capitalism depended on the plunder of the country's colonial possessions. But the expense of maintaining these possessions in the face of revolutionary movements of the oppressed was threatening to bankrupt the economy. This redounded to the benefit of the French Communist Party, which increasingly more French citizens saw as offering the only cogent exit from the crisis.

From Washington's point of view, it was imperative that the flame of Vietnamese independence be extinguished. Apart from the dangers a Viet Minh victory posed for the capitalist interests of hexagonal France, if Ho Chi Minh's army succeeded, the people of Malaya might take heart, and try to shake off the oppressions of the British. Malaya was a rich source of tin and rubber, and the dollar earnings the British Empire reaped from its plunder of the Malayan people underwrote London's financial solvency. Britain's economy had failed to rebound after the war. Economically prostrated, London was no longer able to suppress revolutionary nationalist movements in its vast overseas colonial empire.[25] It was unlikely to survive a further blow. Hence, the United States would have to intervene in Vietnam, to arrest further decay in the French economic position, which was fueling the growth of French communism, and to discourage independence movements in the British Empire, which threatened to precipitate an economic catastrophe in metropolitan Britain, creating fertile soil in which communism could take root and blossom. The consequences for Washington of communist and revolutionary nationalist advance, then, were grim: more economic territory turned to the development of local populations; continued capitalist failure in Western Europe and Japan; the growing chances of Communist revolution in the industrial core; and all of this threatening the project of creating a globe-girding US-led capitalist economic order.

Into this world of impending doom for the US empire stepped US Secretary of State George Marshall. To provide a fillip to Japan's economy, in order to arrest the growing attractions of communism, the Korean peninsula—or as much of it as possible—had to be reintegrated into the Japanese sphere. In late January 1947 Marshall sent a note to under-secretary Dean Acheson: "Please have plan drafted of policy to organize a definite government of [South] Korea and connect up its economy with that of Japan."[26] The implication of Marshall's plan for rescuing capitalism in Japan was that the US occupation zone in Korea would be transformed into a US-aligned state, betokening the country's indefinite political division.

Koreans hadn't asked for a partition. Most vehemently opposed it, and a Calvary of millions—the grim outcome of a war which began three years later to reverse the partition—stands as a testament to their opposition. The few Koreans who weren't opposed were distinguished by their minority status; they were mainly anti-communists who had collaborated with the Japanese and were no less eager to lick the boots of the Americans. The decision to organize a definite government of South Korea was taken to benefit Japan's titans of industry, finance and commerce in service to the construction of a US empire, and in opposition to the worldwide movement for liberty, equality and human solidarity.

CHAPTER 8

The Political Partition of Korea

During WWII, the agreement Washington and Moscow had arrived at on Korea was that the post-war zonal division of the peninsula would be temporary, lasting no more than five years. Within five years, a pan-Korean government would be elected, and US and Soviet troops would withdraw from the peninsula, leaving Koreans to govern themselves. Between 1945 and 1947 the Soviets and Americans met to discuss the formation of a provisional government which would administer Korean affairs preparatory to country-wide elections. "Nothing came of these talks but increasing bitterness," reported Anna Louise Strong. The United States insisted on including conservative pro-Japanese collaborators in the provisional government. The Soviets demurred. The Soviets insisted on including communist workers and farmers. The Americans objected.[1]

By 1947, the United States had abandoned any intention it ever had of honoring its agreement with the Soviet Union on Korea's future. An ongoing US presence on the Korean peninsula offered too many attractions to Washington to leave Korea to Koreans. Apart from putting Washington in a position to orient the Korean economy to Japan, a continued US military presence on the peninsula would facilitate the goal of containing and possibly rolling back leftist movements in nearby China, Russia, and North Korea. Hence, rather than working towards a democratically elected pan-Korean government and mutual Soviet-US withdrawal, Washington obstructed the plan.

Abandoning further talks on national elections with their presumed Soviet partners, the Americans persuaded the newly inaugurated and US-dominated United Nations to form a committee to initiate and observe elections in Korea. The committee was stacked with US allies: Canada, Australia, the Philippines (a former US colony which had recently been granted nominal independence), and the Kuomintang (the communists' hated enemy in China). Since the Americans had walked away from talks held to work out a mutually agreeable plan for the elections, and since the UN committee members could be counted on to follow US directions, Koreans of the north, and the Soviets, refused to endorse the US-initiated, UN-approved plan.[2] All the same, the elections would go ahead—in the US occupation zone alone. And the election's remit wouldn't be limited to the south but would cover the entire country! Whoever won the election, would form a government to administer all of Korea.

This not only rankled Moscow, it rankled Koreans, as well, and Koreans more strongly, since they would have to live with the consequences of Washington's divisive machinations. In an effort to pre-empt the US plan, Koreans organized a National Unity Conference at Pyongyang, which met three weeks before the scheduled date of the US-orchestrated poll. The conference included delegates from both the north and south, who declared themselves implacably opposed to the impending elections, denouncing them as a maneuver by the United States to politically partition Korea by creating a separate government south of the 38th parallel.[3] In lieu of fissiparous elections, which virtually no one in Korea wanted, the conference proposed the immediate withdrawal of the two occupation armies, a national political conference to organize a provisional government to draw up a constitution, and elections to follow with the goal of forming a national government.[4] US officials ignored the Koreans' proposal, pushing ahead instead with their own plan to hold a centrifugal election limited to the US occupation zone for a national government.

Much to Washington's surprise, even most Korean conservatives, whom US officials counted on to back their scheme, expressed opposition to what appeared as an obvious device to partition the country politically in order to establish a US puppet regime in the south.[5] The election was widely viewed by Koreans as signaling their country's permanent division. For this reason, and owing to the pro-landlord, anti-communist ethos of the Rhee government, parties of the left and center,[6] and even some of the right, boycotted the election. In other words, the election was repudiated by the USSR, shunned by the provisional government in the north, and opposed by most Koreans of the south. All the same, the Americans obstinately pushed ahead, unrestrained by even the slightest qualms about trampling upon the aspirations of Koreans. Koreans, after all, weren't the object of the exercise; the building of a global US empire was. Leaving nothing to chance, the UN allowed the Korean National Police, dominated by pro-Japanese collaborators and assisted by the Korean equivalent of Nazi storm troopers—right-wing thugs recruited to crack communist heads—to organize the voting.[7] Voters were threatened with the loss of their land and ration cards if they failed to show up at voting stations.[8] Through these illegitimate means, Washington midwifed the birth of a pro-US, anti-communist police state with Syngman Rhee as the state's nominal leader. Within three weeks of the election, the traitor Kim Sok-won, who had been decorated by Emperor Hirohito for bravery in Japanese military campaigns to colonize China, was leading a parade of twenty-five hundred Korean veterans of the Japanese army through the streets of Seoul. The quisling state had been born.

"The United States now has a puppet state in South Korea," wrote Israel Epstein. "Elections held under a 'protecting umbrella' of US troops have put a discredited rightist, Dr. Syngman Rhee, in power."[9] The Rhee government formally superseded the US military government, which was replaced by the Korean Military Advisory Group and the Economic Cooperation Administration, the US deep state in South Korea, comprising 500 US personnel. The US military government faded from public view,[10] but continued to govern from behind the scenes, much as the Japanese had pulled Chinese strings in Manchukuo. The formal, public agreement Washington struck with Seoul, to create the illusion of South Korean sovereignty, was that the Korean Military Advisory Group would retain operational control of the Korean police and military only so long as US combat troops remained on the peninsula.[11] However, secret protocols granted the Pentagon command of South Korean police and troops *sine die*.[12] Even after most US combat troops were withdrawn in the summer of 1949, US advisers continued to be embedded with South Korean army units, US military aircraft continued to transport Korean troops and materiel, and US intelligence officers continued to work with the ROK army and KNP.[13]

With the political partition of Korea now a (US-engineered) *fait accompli*, there was little choice for Koreans in the north but to declare a separate republic, a democratic republic, to operate on behalf of the social strata to which 98 percent of Koreans (i.e., the *demos*) belonged. The dream of Korean self-determination, seemingly promised by Wilson, urged by Lenin, for which thousands of Korean patriots had been martyred, had been blocked on a pan-Korean scale and restricted to the north. The declaration of the Democratic People's Republic of Korea on September 9, 1948, was therefore only a partial victory. "Two months after the end of the Second World War," wrote Kim Il-sung, "the 30 million Korean people were still intoxicated with the joy of liberation. None of these people, however, imagined that the liberation of the country would end in a territorial division and national split, resulting in a great national disaster."[14] A great national task remained, announced Kim: to "drive the U.S. imperialist aggressors out of south Korea, accomplish the national liberation revolution and realize the reunification of the country."[15]

A day after its birth, the newly formed DPRK, acting as a representative of all Koreans and considering itself on strong grounds to be the sole legitimate government in Korea, asked the Soviet Union and the United States to withdraw their military forces from Korean territory. The Soviets complied, exiting the peninsula by December 25. Washington ignored the request, even though the Soviet withdrawal meant there was no longer a justification for US forces to remain on Korean soil under the terms of the occupation agreement worked out between the two wartime allies.

Meanwhile, in the south, the US-led war against Korean patriots continued. By early 1949, there were between 3,500 and 6,000 guerrillas fighting the ROK government, according to a CIA estimate.[16] A declassified February 1949 CIA report noted that South Korea faced a "strong and efficient" communist underground and recognized that US troop withdrawal would be met by "countrywide internal disorders"—in other words, uprisings to topple the government few Koreans wanted—accompanied by "large scale border penetrations." The CIA warned that in "the face of combined invasion and uprising" the South Korean government would collapse.[17] In September of 1949, the head of the US advisory government working behind the scenes, General W.L. Roberts, ordered all ROK army units diverted from the 38th parallel to an anti-insurgency campaign in the interior to wipe out the Korean *maquis*. Roberts requisitioned additional infantry officers from the Pentagon, to lead the campaign to "*exterminate* guerrilla bands"[18] (emphasis added).

Rhee set up the National Guidance League to coerce patriots in the south to disavow their commitment to national and social revolution and forced 300,000 of them to join. When war broke out in June 1950, the South Korean military and police, under US command, rounded up league members. Many, presumably executed, were never heard from again.[19]

Within four months of the ROK's proclamation, Rhee introduced the notorious National Security Law, still on the books, which has been used to lock up—sometimes for decades—Korean patriots who have worked for, even only aspired to, the independence of their country. The key to the law lies in South Korea's definition of the DPRK, not as a state, but as an illegal anti-state organization. With unbridled shamelessness originating in the US-engineered elections to politically divide the country, the ROK defines itself as Korea's only legitimate government, with jurisdiction over the territory controlled by Pyongyang, which the North Korean state is deemed to be occupying illegally. The law provides for punishment up to and including death or life imprisonment for anyone who joins an anti-state organization, praises or sympathizes with it, furnishes it with money or other material assistance, or communicates with its members. Indeed, the law goes so far as to prohibit the expression of praise of, or sympathy with, the DPRK , a prohibition which extends to publicly articulating the main arguments of this book. Since the advent of the ROK in 1948, its governments have used the law to arrest Koreans for anything from extolling North Korea in casual conversation to running as an opposition candidate in presidential elections.[20] By December 1949, the National Security Law had been used to arrest 188,621 people committed to Korean independence and other Leftist causes,[21] including members of the National Assembly.[22] Hence, in the space of less than four years, a resident of Seoul could have travelled the road from jubilation at the fall of the Japanese empire and an expectation that her country would now be free from foreign domination, to running afoul of the National Security Law and languishing in prison for demanding what the fall of the Japanese empire had presumably signified: self-determination.

CHAPTER 9

The Campaign of 1950-1953

What you see here, caught in your night defenses
These steel and glass cocoons for killing people
With tons of bombs, are just the consequences
For all, and not the causes of the evil.—Bertolt Brecht [1]

Our understanding of the Korean War is based on a flawed premise, namely, that there existed on June 25, 1950 the date traditionally marking the beginning of the conflict, a legitimate international boundary separating two countries that, if crossed, would constitute an act of international aggression. The premise is flawed because neither state recognized the other as legitimate; each state claimed the same territory; and the two states did not recognize the *de facto* border that separated them as a *de jure* international frontier.

From the perspective of the Republic of Korea, the movement of its military forces north of the 38th parallel did not constitute an act of aggression across an international boundary, since all Korean territory, including that north of the 38th parallel, was territory under its jurisdiction. The Democratic People's Republic of Korea had a parallel view. The advance of its forces south of the 38th parallel was perfectly legitimate, since Korean territory south of this line fell under the DPRK's purview. In other words, no matter what their differences, both sides agreed on this: the sole legitimate government of Korea could move its military forces into territory over which it had a sovereign claim. The legitimate government of Korea could not invade its own territory.

Since the United States accepted South Korea's claim to be the sole legitimate state in Korea, and the Soviet Union accepted North Korea's parallel claim to be the only state in Korea representing all Koreans, it was clear that the two superpowers also rejected the 38th parallel as a legitimate international frontier. For such a frontier to exist, two separate nations would have to exist on either side, and no party—not Pyongyang, not Seoul, not Moscow, not Washington—recognized the existence of two separate legitimate states on the peninsula. Hence, the condition for an international frontier to exist, was absent.

The United States acknowledged that the 38th parallel had no legal status as an international border when, on September 30, 1950, lacking a UN mandate to cross the dividing line, MacArthur's forces did so anyway, pushing north into territory controlled by the DPRK, and the US ambassador to the UN justified the action by dismissing the 38th parallel as "an imaginary line."[2] Yet when DPRK forces earlier crossed the 38th parallel on June 25, Washington obtained a UN mandate to intervene in Korea on the ground that the KPA had committed an act of international aggression across an international border.

The creation of an imaginary line along the 38th parallel was simply an expedience used by Washington to *temporarily* divide the peninsula into separate US and Soviet occupation zones, in order to accept the Japanese surrender in Korea. Dean Rusk and Charles Bonesteel had no legal authority to draw an international boundary, when, on August 10, 1945, the day after an atomic bomb was dropped on Nagasaki, they etched a line along a map to separate Soviet and US forces in Korea. The conflict, then, was not a matter of one state initiating a war of aggression against another by launching a general invasion across an international frontier, since no international frontier existed. But if the war cannot be cogently characterized in these terms, how should it be characterized?

One view is that it was a civil war, a quarrel between Koreans over how to organize the social, political, and economic life of the peninsula, on whose soil existed a single nation. At the heart of the debate was the question of equality. Are people, as individuals, and peoples, as nations, equal, and should they enter into associations on the basis of mutual benefit, or are some people or nations destined to lead others, and to have rights, responsibilities and privileges senior to others? Should the exploitation of man by man, be prohibited or welcomed? Should the country be aligned with, and integrated into, the US empire, or independent? And who should form the governing elite—collaborators with the Japanese empire, or those who waged war against it? These questions were at the core of the conflict.

"In the American Civil War," observed a British cabinet minister in the early 1950s, "the Americans would never have tolerated for a single moment the setting up of an imaginary line between the forces of North and South, and there can be no doubt as to what would have been their reaction if the British had intervened in force on behalf of the South. This parallel is a close one because for [the United States] the conflict was not merely between two groups of [US citizens], but was between two conflicting economic systems as is the case in Korea."[3]

William R. Polk, a former US State Department adviser, marks the beginning of the war, not as June 25, 1950, but as August 15, 1948, the day the quisling state was proclaimed. In Polk's view, the unilateral creation by the United States of a separate state in the south was a declaration of war. If the state was "allowed to stand," argues Polk, "that action as Kim Il-sung clearly understood, would have prevented unification. He regarded it as an act of war."[4] Polk's argument has merit. But was the proclamation of the Republic of Korea an act of war only because it prevented unification, or was it an act of war for other reasons, as well?

At the most inclusive level, the founding of the Republic of Korea on August 15 was an act of war against the Korean people. The proclamation of the republic imposed on Koreans a political structure they had clearly rejected. Koreans north of the imaginary line objected to the elections that brought the quisling state to life, and Koreans of the south rejected it as well by resisting the election on which the proclamation was based. Thus, the founding of the ROK was an imposition of the will of the United States on the Korean people—a bellicose and profoundly anti-democratic act.

On another level, August 15 was a declaration of war on Koreans of the south, for it marked the birth of a state whose anti-communist orientation clashed with the pro-communist aspirations of its citizens. Koreans of the south, as much as their compatriots of the north, wanted self-determination, not incorporation into another empire. They also wanted an economy that was directed toward meeting their own needs, not Japan's. In addition, they wanted land reform. Since the Republic of Korea was pro-landlord and anti-communist, the state would be incessantly at war with its citizens. That the political partition of the peninsula would inevitably lead to war was apprehended at the time the partition was effected. Following the elections, at least one US-based journalist predicted that the creation of a US "puppet state in South Korea ... probably marks the birth of a new civil war in which American forces are likely to be heavily involved."[5]

Another view dates the commencement of the civil war to December 1945, the beginning of the war that US military governor General John Reed Hodge would declare on the indigenously founded Korean People's Republic, using Korean quislings who had served in the Japanese army and colonial police as his front line troops. Hugh Deane's history of the conflict, *The Korean War: 1945-1953*, follows along these lines.

An alternative view is that the civil war began in 1932, when Kim Il-sung formed his first guerrilla unit to fight the Japanese, and collaborators like Park Chung-hee chose another route, joining the Japanese army and the Korean National Police to enforce Japanese rule over their compatriots. This is a perspective offered by Bruce Cumings, who has argued that the Korean War "was a civil war" that was "fought primarily by Koreans from conflicting social systems" that began "in 1932" when Kim Il-sung and other Koreans began "guerrilla, secret society, and bandit resistance" to the Japanese in Manchuria, and that the war "has never ended."[6] In Cumings's view, the war is a conflict between "North Koreans" and

"Korean quislings" who are the North Koreans' "blood enemies." The phase of the war that lasted from 1950 to 1953 was a campaign in a continuing civil war that was fought as a way for North Koreans to "settle the hash of the top command of the South Korean army, nearly all of whom served the Japanese."[7]

But while a civil conflict lay at the heart of the war fought on the Korean peninsula from 1950 to 1953, the war was also an international conflict. Apart from Koreans, the participants included combatants from: the United States, Great Britain, Canada, Turkey, Australia, the Philippines, New Zealand, Ethiopia, Greece, Thailand, France, Colombia, Belgium, South Africa, the Netherlands, Luxembourg, and China.

Most of the combatants fell under the US-led UN command. The principal foreign combatant forces were the United States and its auxiliaries—which is to say the US empire, fighting under a UN flag, and the People's Republic of China, newly emerged from a long but successful anti-colonial and anti-feudal struggle, which had secured for China freedom from foreign control and domination, including by the United States. On an international level, the war was a conflict between forces of empire and forces of self-determination, between imperialists and anti-imperialists. The conflict of 1950 to 1953 was, then, an imperialist war fought on a Korean battlefield overlaid upon a civil war between patriots who rejected empire and traitors who collaborated with it.

Whether we date the commencement of the civil war from 1932, 1945, or 1948, it continues to be fought today, if only at a low level of intensity. Formally, the imperialist war continues, as well. The end of open hostilities from 1950 to 1953 was secured by an armistice, or cease-fire, and not a peace treaty, though the DPRK has repeatedly offered to sign one, and the United States has just as frequently rejected the DPRK's offers. As for the ROK, it refused even to sign the armistice agreement ending open hostilities. Technically, then, the United States and South Korea remain at war with the DPRK, despite entreaties by the latter to end the conflict.

What are the aims of the contending sides in this ongoing civil war? For the DPRK, the goal is to wrest control of Korean territory from the empire which now dominates the southern half of it, and whose domination is enforced through the empire's military forces stationed on the peninsula and by its Korean representative, the ROK. In effect, the DPRK's struggle is with the United States (the globally hegemonic empire) and its Korean proxy (the ROK), just as in the 1930s, the struggle of the DPRK's predecessor, the Manchurian guerrilla army, was with the regionally hegemonic empire of the time (Japan) and its Korean proxies (the quislings, like future ROK president, Park Chung-hee, who fought for the Japanese.) In 1971, Kim Il-sung defined the DPRK goal in the civil conflict as driving "the U.S. imperialist aggressors out of south Korea," in order to "accomplish the national liberation revolution and realize the reunification of the country."[8] The ROK's contending objective is to wrest control of the northern half of Korean territory from the anti-imperialists who now dominate it, and to fold the entire Korean peninsula into the US empire.

"The basic military history of the 1950-53 phase" of the imperialist war has been succinctly summarized by Bruce Cumings. He divides the conflict "neatly into three parts: the war for the South in the summer of 1950, the war for the North in the fall and winter of 1950, and China's intervention, which soon brought about a stabilization of the fighting along what is now the demilitarized zone, or DMZ, even though a form of trench warfare went on for another two years."[9]

But the campaign might be more insightfully dated from late 1948, with the founding of two separate states, each claiming jurisdiction over the entire peninsula. The Korean War could never have broken out had the United States not drawn a dividing line along the 38th parallel and the Soviet Union not accepted it.[10] Without a divided Korea, there would have been no division to fight over. But what turned the division into a potent cause of war was its transformation from a temporary zonal division, scheduled to disappear within five years, to a continuing political division, inaugurated by the ROK's proclamation.

What would have happened had neither the United States nor the USSR entered Korea in 1945, and had instead allowed Koreans to direct their own liberation? That's clear from what did happen up to the point Hodge's forces arrived in Korea. Koreans purged the Japanese and their collaborators from civil administration, brought civil administration under their own auspices, began land reform, and met to organize a central government and proclaim a republic. The US historian Frank Baldwin figured that in "1945 Koreans would have worked out a new destiny if the US and Soviet Union had not intervened. That destiny almost certainly would have been a leftist, perhaps a communist, government."[11] What would have happened if the United States and the Soviet Union had accepted the Japanese surrender and then quickly left Korea? Bruce Cumings figures "a leftist regime would have taken over quickly, and it would have been a revolutionary nationalist government."[12]

But neither of these potential outcomes materialized. Instead, the Republic of Korea was established, headed by a fanatical anti-communist and US proxy who believed his state had sovereignty over the entirety of the Korean peninsula, and that it was his duty to bring all of its declared domains under his control. Rhee frequently promised to undertake a "northern expedition" to "recover lost territory," and in the summer of 1949 his army started to provoke fighting along the 38th parallel with the forces of the DPRK.[13]

On the other side of the parallel, Kim Il-sung headed a state that had a legitimate claim to represent all Koreans. He had the moral authority of having been the maximal Korean leader in the anti-colonial struggle in Manchuria. He commanded significant support among Koreans in the north, on the strength of his considerable charisma and organizational abilities (in contrast to Syngman Rhee, who had been handpicked by US masters, and then brought to power in a boycotted election held after the US occupation government led a three years-long campaign to exterminate the opposition.) Plus, it was clear to most observers that in fair national elections, Kim Il-sung would have been elected president.

Kim believed it was his patriotic duty to recover the southern territories held by Rhee's illegitimate US puppet government in order to unify the country. His forces also provoked fighting along the old zonal division line. Indeed, through 1949 there were numerous skirmishes between ROK and DPRK forces along the separation line. But most skirmishes, according to Bruce Cumings, were started by the ROK army.[14] The movement of DPRK forces south of the 38th parallel on June 25, 1950 came after nine months of clashes between the two armies, involving thousands of troops and hundreds of fatalities.[15]

Washington regarded Rhee as a hot-head, and worried that his skirmishing with Kim's forces would escalate into all-out war. And so, the Pentagon declined to supply him with tanks and warplanes.[16] US planners recognized that Rhee lacked popular support and would likely take a drubbing if he launched his promised drive to the north.

A declassified February 1949 CIA report had recognized "an inherent Korean sentiment against foreign interference," that is, against the US presence on the peninsula. It also noted that Rhee's government faced a "strong and efficient" Korean patriot underground.[17] Hadn't Hodge, and after him Rhee, spent the last four years rounding up leftists, immuring them in concentration camps, and fighting guerrillas in the countryside? Despite their efforts, culminating in 100,000 to 200,000 Korean patriots killed,[18] 30,000 in prison and 70,000 in concentration camps,[19] the resistance continued. And that's because Rhee's government was the manifestation of the foreign interference the CIA observed an inherent Korean sentiment against. So long as the affront to Korean sovereignty existed that was the anti-communist US puppet state, there would be a patriot underground. And that meant the ROK would always be vulnerable to a fifth column liberation movement.

On June 25, North Korean forces crossed the imaginary line Rusk and Bonesteel had drawn to divide US and Soviet forces. According to the DPRK, ROK forces crossed the line first, and were met by an immediate DPRK counter-offensive.[20] The UN issued a report on June 26 blaming the outbreak of the fighting entirely on North Korea. But the report was based on US and South Korean sources—hardly unbiased. In this way, US officials were able "to define the war as they saw fit, making their official story of what happened definitive and lasting,"[21] as Bruce Cumings put it. However, it's

Marking the beginning of the "independence" of the Republic of Korea, Syngman Rhee, President of the Republic of Korea, embraces his guest General Douglas MacArthur, who commanded the UN troops in Korea during the war. (Photo: Alamy Stock).

not clear which side crossed the 38th parallel first, and while the reigning view, reflecting US ideological hegemony, is that it was the DPRK which initiated a general invasion, the matter of who initiated the fighting remains *sub judice* in the court of scholarly research.[22] But does it matter? Hostilities had broken out between the two sides months earlier. And does a general invasion across an imaginary line neither side recognized have any significance?

The ROK collapse was immediate. Syngman Rhee and his inner circle immediately fled, soon followed by the ROK army. Those of the South Korean military who didn't flee defected to the North Korean side.[23] DPRK forces liberated Seoul within three days. By late August, Kim Il-sung's patriots had liberated nine-tenths of the peninsula from Rhee's grip. ROK and US forces held on only in Pusan, on the southeast tip of the peninsula.

The United States sought and obtained a UN mandate to intervene *manu militari* in Korea. The authorization of the US-dominated world body was secured in the absence of the USSR, which was boycotting the Security Council for its refusal to recognize the People's Republic of China as the legitimate holder of China's seat on the council. (China was represented by the Kuomintang based in Taiwan.) The authorization merely formalized an intervention that had already begun, for US forces were already present on the peninsula and engaged in combat by the time the UN gave its blessing. In the words of Frank Baldwin, the "US government led the UN into the Korean War; the Truman administration then claimed that it was supporting the United Nations by providing forces to fight in Korea!"[24]

The US-led force fought under the banner of the UN flag and relied on token troop contributions from UN members to create the impression that it represented an international coalition. In reality, it was a US force under US command dressed in UN camouflage. The UN Commander, Douglas MacArthur, was a US general who reported directly to the US Joint Chiefs of Staff, not to the United Nations.[25]

In his first radio address after North Korean forces surged into the south, Kim Il-sung called for the restoration of the people's committees. Kim's goal was to revivify the people's committees which had existed prior to the establishment of the DPRK, not to impose the North Korean political structure on the south. As the US puppet regime collapsed, thousands of Korean patriots, of both the north and south, began to resurrect the people's committees disbanded by Hodge. In Seoul, the city's people's committee was re-established, led mainly by southerners. Within weeks it had confiscated the property of the Japanese, traitors, and wealthy industrialists.[26]

The advance of DPRK forces into the south also gave patriots space to organize land reform. South Korea's landed class, the darlings of the Rhee government, had blocked all attempts at democratizing patterns of land distribution. Farmers now set about confiscating land from parasitic landlords and allocating it those who toiled on it. Redistribution was carried out hastily and under conditions of war, but, according to Bruce Cumings, "it cleared away class structures and power that later made possible Rhee's" mimetic land redistribution program.[27]

Rhee's land reform program was not only made possible by the foundations laid during the brief period of liberation, but was also an effort to win the loyalty of farmers of the south. As Walter Scheidel argues in his book *The Greater Leveler,* "South Korea undertook land redistribution in order to mollify its peasants and discourage them from allying with communist North Korea."[28] Hence, the ROK's land reform program owes its existence to the DPRK in two ways: first, in the space the advancing KPA established for peasants to liberate themselves from feudalism, and second, in establishing a model for land reform in the north which Seoul felt compelled to match in order to earn the allegiance of its rural citizens.

As patriot forces set about reclaiming Korea from the despised Rhee regime, Rhee's government, which was evocative of the Nazi regime in its fierce anti-communism, did what a fiercely anti-communist police state could be expected to do: carry out a massacre of the left.

Early in the war the ROK army and Korean National Police, officered by Japanese collaborators and under US command, carried out a program of extermination. Communists held in South Korean prisons and concentration camps were executed, as were people suspected of communist sympathies. The aim was to prevent the Left from aiding advancing DPRK forces. Lee Soon-chang, a member of an ROK militia, "escorted men and women, detained by pro-government villagers on suspicion of being Communist collaborators, to a hill where the police executed them in groups of five and pushed their bodies into an abandoned mine shaft,"[29] according to Choe Sang-hun, the *New York Times'* Korea correspondent.

There were "tens of thousands of victims of hurried mass executions carried out ... by South Korean authorities, bent on ridding the nation of communists in the early days of the Korean War,"[30] reported the Associated Press. According to Korean historian Hun

Joon Kim, "at least 300,000 people were detained and executed or simply disappeared by the South Korean government in the first few months after conventional war began."[31]

Bruce Cumings has written about Alan Dower, and Australian journalist, who "witnessed a retinue of hooded women, many with babies, roped together and dragged along by ROK police." Dower "followed them until they were kneeling before 'a deep freshly dug pit,' ringed by machine guns."[32] US soldiers witnessed the ROK army routinely execute North Korean POWs, and occasionally turned over captured DPRK troops to the KNP to be executed on the spot.[33] One US GI watched as KNP officers forced scores of civilians, including children, pregnant women and the elderly, to dig their own graves, before being shot.[34]

A Truth and Reconciliation commission was established by the ROK government in 2005 to resolve issues related to animosities that carry over from the war. It found that "wartime South Korean authorities ... summarily executed ... leftist prison inmates or machine-gunned villagers during their mountain operations to exterminate guerrillas, dumping their bodies in the sea or mass graves."[35] According to the Associated Press, family members of the victims "hold not only President Syngman Rhee's right-wing regime responsible for their loved one's deaths," but also the United States, arguing that "the mass killings" would not "have been possible without tacit support from the" United States, which "supplied weapons and ammunition used in the executions and took photographs at some sites."[36] Significantly, the United States had operational control of ROK force as the extermination campaign—reminiscent of the Nazi's Commissar Order, an order issued by the German High Command during the invasion of the USSR to exterminate communists—was underway.

There are strong parallels between Rhee's regime and the fanatically anti-communist Nazi regime, with its concentration camps in which Communists, Socialists and labor activists were the primary victims;[37] its abhorrence of the Soviet Union; and its extermination of communist partisans. The only difference is that the Nazis were empire-builders who had a good deal of popular support, while Rhee, the acolyte of US empire-builders, had practically none. In this regard, Rhee's state was more like the SS, not a state itself, but merely a component of an empire, and the principal instrument of violent political repression on the Korean peninsula. In Bruce Cumings' words, "South Korea always had a strong state vis-à-vis its own people,"[38] beginning with Rhee and continuing to the present.

The first phase of the war, the war for the south in the summer of 1950, came to an end on September 15 when MacArthur landed his forces at Inchon, the port of Seoul, halfway up the peninsula. Had the United States not landed an invasion force, the DPRK would have quickly won the war, the lives of millions would have been spared, and Koreans would have experienced the sweet taste of freedom for the first time in four decades.[39] But this happy occasion did not come to pass. Instead, the second phase of the war, the war for the north in the autumn and winter of 1950, began.[40]

MacArthur's amphibious invasion at Inchon cut off KPA forces from the north. To escape, patriot soldiers were forced to melt into the countryside and retreat. The UN resolution authorizing US intervention had demanded that DPRK forces pull back to the 38th parallel. Therefore, once the KPA had withdrawn from the south, the matter should have been resolved, and MacArthur should have held the line there and gone no further. But on September 11, four days before landing at Inchon, MacArthur had obtained Truman's authorization to launch an offensive north of the 38th parallel.[41] US forces captured Seoul on September 25, and five days later pushed into the north, across the imaginary line Rusk and Bonesteel had drawn five years earlier.

MacArthur's northward drive to the Yalu River (one of two riparian boundaries separating Korea and China) brought the Chinese into the war. On October 25, Mao deployed to Korea an army of 300,000 Chinese "volunteers" to arrest the US advance. Mao designated the army a volunteer force, calling it the Chinese People's Volunteer Army, to avoid a formal clash with the United States.[42] Thus began what some have called the Sino-American War. The Chinese virtually eliminated the remnants of the South Korean army and quickly drove US forces back across the 38th parallel by December.[43] By December 5, combined PVA and KPA forces had liberated Pyongyang.

Stunned by the collapse of MacArthur's forces at the hands of a lightly armed army of peasants, Truman declared a national emergency, and MacArthur called for a nuclear strike, importuning the president to authorize the use of 50 nuclear bombs to reverse the setback.[44] Truman declined. But for the next two years the United States set about producing, by conventional means, the equivalent destruction of many nuclear attacks. MacArthur called on US bombers to create a wasteland, ordering the use of incendiaries to burn to the ground every city, every village, and every factory between the 38th parallel and the Chinese border.[45] US "planes dropped 635,000 tons of bombs on Korea—that is, essentially on North Korea—including 32,557 tons of napalm, compared to 503,000 tons of bombs dropped in the entire Pacific theatre of World War II. The number of Korean dead, injured, or missing by war's end approached three million, ten percent of the overall population,"[46] wrote historian Charles Armstrong.

The extent of the physical destruction visited upon Korea north of the 38th parallel by US carpet bombing is horrifying. It's not clear that every building over one story was destroyed, as some have claimed, but it is clear that the USAF created a desert. Joan Robinson claimed, though with a touch of hyperbole, that by the end of the war "there was not one stone standing upon another" in Pyongyang,[47] although the level of destruction was close to Robinson's account. By the end of the war, only two modern buildings remained standing in Pyongyang.[48] US carpet bombing "destroyed some 8,700 factories, 5,000 schools, 1,000 hospitals and 600,000 homes," according to the DPRK.[49] Dean Rusk, when he was the assistant secretary of state for Far Eastern affairs, said that everything "that moved in North Korea, every brick standing on top of another," we bombed.[50]

With the US Air Force spreading its dark wings over North Korea, the DPRK created a subterranean life as a necessity of survival. Factories, schools, hospitals, government offices, and people were moved underground. Farmers worked at night and retreated to underground lairs in the morning.[51] Bruce Cumings called North Koreans a "mole people" who "learned to love the shelter of caves, mountains, tunnels and redoubts."[52]

By the autumn of 1952, MacArthur's ambition to create a wasteland north of the 38th parallel had been realized. No city, town, or building of significance remained to be incinerated.[53] So, US forces targeted irrigation dams on the Yalu River. Five reservoirs were destroyed by US bombers, inundating thousands of acres of farmland, flooding towns, and destroying a vital source of sustenance for millions of North Koreans.[54]

The number of fatalities produced by the war can only be estimated. Estimates range from 3 to 4.5 million, with Koreans accounting for 2.3 to 3 million deaths. Chinese fatalities in the war ranged from an estimated 600,000 to one million. US fatalities were a comparatively insignificant 36,574, one to two percent of the total. Given that the population of Korea in 1950 was approximately 20 million, the war destroyed 10 to 15 percent of the population.[55] Charles Armstrong estimates that the fraction of Koreans killed is in the range of "the proportion of Soviet citizens killed in World War II."[56] About 2.3 million Japanese perished in the Pacific War,[57] or roughly three percent of the population, much lower than the Korean fatality rate in the 1950-1953 holocaust. Curtis LeMay, who directed the terror bombing, estimated that "Over a period of three years or so, we killed off—what—20 percent of the population."[58] It's not clear whether LeMay's figure was based on a methodical estimate. It was offered more than 30 years after the war ended, and may have been only a very rough guess. In any event, whether 10 percent or 20 percent, it's clear that the United States exterminated a significant proportion of the Korean population.

US officials have exhibited no restraint ever since, in threatening to carry out additional demographic holocausts against Koreans of the north. Wesley Clark, for example, a US general who commanded NATO forces in Europe and led NATO's air war on Yugoslavia in 1999, warned DPRK leaders that the United States had the capability to completely destroy North Korea; it "would literally cease to exist," he said.[59] In 1995, Colin Powell, who had served as chairman of the US Joint Chiefs of Staff and would later serve as US secretary of state, warned the DPRK that the United States had the means to turn North Korea into "a charcoal briquette."[60] In 2017, US Senator John McCain, chair of the Senate Armed Services Committee, warned the DPRK that the price of acting "in an aggressive fashion ... will be extinction."[61] For his part, US president Donald Trump "warned that if North Korea threatened the United States or its allies, Washington would have 'no choice but to totally destroy North Korea.'"[62]

The United States bears the main responsibility for the millions of lives destroyed in the war. At every point, US leaders made decisions that guaranteed that the mountain of corpses would pile ever higher. In the first instance, Washington made war inevitable by politically partitioning the country. Then, when the 1950 conflict broke out, it immediately intervened, rather than allowing a quick resolution with a minimal loss of life, as would have happened, with a DPRK victory, which was imminent. When the KPA withdrew north of the 38th parallel, Washington could have chosen to break off hostilities, as the UN resolution authorizing the use of force indicated it should. Instead, MacArthur pushed forward, intent on rolling back the independence movement in Korea and establishing an anti-communist US puppet state over the entire Korean peninsula. When Chinese forces pushed the United States back over the 38th parallel, Washington could have agreed to end the war. Instead, it fought on for two more years, before finally accepting a restoration of the *status quo ante*. But in those two years US bombers burned North Korea to the ground. US carpet bombing, observed Bruce Cumings, created "a subterranean world that became the basis for reconstructing the country and a memento for building a fierce hatred through the ranks of the population. The leaders who survived draw a straight line from 1932, when their struggle began, through this terrible war, down to the present."[63]

Syngman Rhee, President of the Republic of Korea, delivers a speech in English at the US Congress on July 28, 1954. Sitting behind to the left is Vice President Richard Nixon, who had gained his anti-communist credentials with Joseph McCarthy. (Photo of Youtube video, Robin Philpot)

CHAPTER 10

The Anti-Communist Police State

"The country is literally in the grip of a police regime and a private terror."
—American Civil Liberties Union chief Roger Baldwin[1]

After 1953, the movement for liberty and equality in the north deferred plans to exercise sovereignty over all of Korea and concentrated on defending itself against the hostility of Washington, which remained committed to the objective of rolling back communism in Korea. For the movement in the south as well, the primary task was to survive. From the very first moments that Koreans had fought for freedom from foreign domination and exploitation at home, they had met the fierce resistance of traitors backed by empires—Japan, until 1945, and the United States thereafter. Collaborators with the Japanese empire quickly became collaborators with the US empire. In 1960 there remained approximately 600 KNP officers, the main instrument of anti-communist suppression, who had served the Japanese. Nearly all were in senior positions.[2] Because the aims of the ROK were antithetical to the goals of national and social revolution which, as indicated above, inspired most Koreans, the South Korean state had to become—and was from its birth to the present—a very strong police state, with all the trappings of one: military dictatorship, extreme ideological control, a security police force recalling the Gestapo, concentration camps for leftists and their extermination during periods of crisis, designation of all socialist countries as enemy states, and a draconian anti-Left National Security Law which locked up Koreans for even sympathizing with the DPRK.

Joan Robinson had remarked that in the mid-1960s the ideological control of Koreans of the south was so extreme that no "Southern eye can be allowed a peep into the North."[3] Until 1973, Kim Il-sung's photograph was banned from publication in the ROK. South Korean censors combed through foreign publications, redacting photos of Kim with splotches of black ink.[4] Kim, whose contribution to the project of liberating Korea was second to none, was demonized by ROK authorities and traduced. South Korean security agencies disseminated the myth that the DPRK leader was not, in fact, Kim Il-sung, but an imposter beholden to the USSR who had stolen the famed guerilla leader's identity. Immersed in anti-DPRK slanders, Koreans had no real conception of who Kim Il-sung really was. In 1989, Suh Dae-sook, South Korea's leading scholar of Korean communism, was granted leave to finally tell the true story of Kim Il-sung. A large audience of South Korean youth erupted in applause when Suh explained that Kim was a hero of the guerilla struggle for Korean independence, this revelation being completely new to them.[5] So militantly anti-leftist is South Korea that "a brand of crayon called Picasso was once banned because of the artist's Communist associations,"[6] explained Choe Sang-hun, the *New York Times'* Korea correspondent. In 1951, Picasso, a member of the French Communist Party, painted a famous work, *Massacre in Korea*, which depicted the slaughter of Korean civilians by anti-communist forces during the Korean War. The ROK authorities didn't take kindly to their atrocities becoming the subject of a famous artwork—and by a communist no less!

The ROK police state has cracked down, with varying degrees of intensity over the years, on virtually every public expression of leftism, including anti-capitalism, anti-colonialism, and anti-imperialism—in other words, all genuine expressions of unalloyed liberalism. What the historian Arno J. Mayer said about Hitler, namely, that he abhorred communism because it "was the final culmination and distillation of the Enlightenment"[7] can equally be

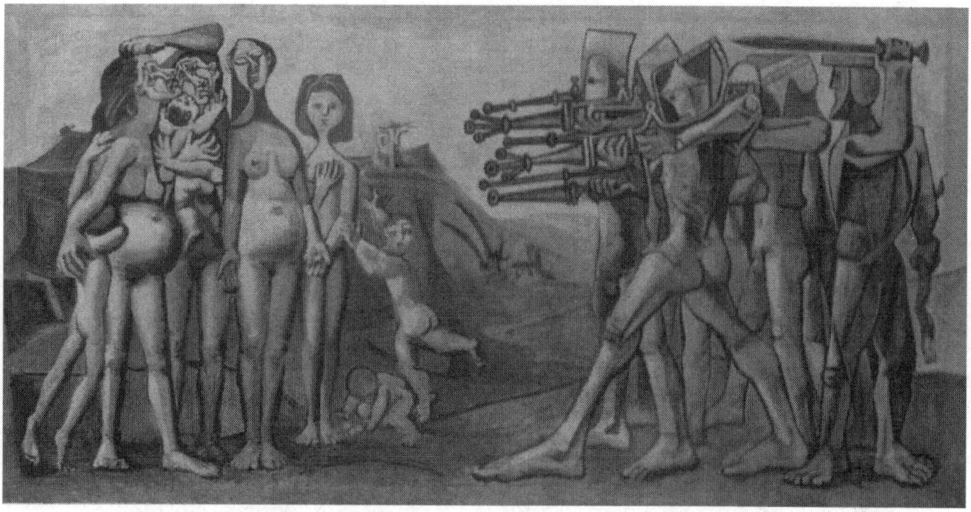

Pablo Picasso completed Massacre in Korea on January 18, 1951. He was depicting the 1950 Sinchon Massacre in northern Korea carried out with the blessing of US military authorities in the fall of 1950. It is exhibited at the Musée Picasso in Paris.

said about the animus of the South Korean state and its US sponsors toward Korean communism.

Some degree of intolerance of leftist dissent is emblematic of all states in capitalist societies, and the ROK is assuredly a capitalist state; that's the way it was designed by its creator, the United States, even if most Koreans wanted a socialist state. But in Washington, where billionaire investors carry the day, the political views of Koreans are of no consequence. As a US secretary of state, Henry Kissinger, once famously remarked in connection with Chile: "I don't see why we need to stand by and watch a country go communist due to the irresponsibility of its own people."[8] Kissinger was echoing Woodrow Wilson, whose rhetorical commitment to self-determination was matched only by his actual commitment to overthrowing foreign leaders he didn't like, even if they happened to be elected by their own people. Wilson would stop intervening in other people's countries, he said, if only they learned to "elect good men."[9] For the United States, good men meant anti-communists like

Syngman Rhee rather than communist national liberation leaders like Kim Il-sung.

Even in self-declared liberal democratic societies, which are erroneously believed to tolerate dissent to a higher degree than other societies, the security services have had a long history of surveillance against those who challenge the rich and powerful. The history of the political police in such societies is one of conservatism where the targets of surveillance are militant leftists who challenge the *status quo*. Those who pursue the class war from the bottom are regarded as subverting the established political and economic order and therefore are deemed legitimate subjects for surveillance and disruption.[10]

The ROK anti-communist police state differs from that of other capitalist countries in degree only, the difference due to its daily confrontation with the DPRK, which embodies genuine Enlightenment values, and which, in its rejection of foreign domination, acts as an inspiration to many Koreans of the south. It's virtually impossible to be committed to anti-imperialism and convinced there's a better alternative to capitalism without espousing values that significantly overlap those of the DPRK. Consequently, it's virtually impossible for South Koreans who embrace any kind of commitment to authentic Enlightenment values not to be accused of being a DPRK fellow traveler, and therefore of transgressing the National Security Law.

Consider the platform of the Unified Progressive Party (UPP), a leftist party founded in 2011, which was dissolved in 2015 by the ROK's Constitutional Court on the ground that its goal was "North Korea-style socialism." The party sought an end to the US military presence in Korea (as does Pyongyang) and advocated an end to Korea's subordinate relationship to the United States (another DPRK demand.) The party talked of "rectifying" Korea's "shameful history tainted by imperialist invasions, the national divide, military dictatorship, the tyranny and plunder of transnational monopoly capital" and large family-owned conglomerates, like Samsung and Hyundai[11]—also DPRK positions.

UPP members were widely denounced by conservatives as *jongbuk*, a derogatory term denoting followers of the DPRK accused of spreading subversive ideas challenging the merits of capitalism and the ROK's subordinate relationship to the United States.[12]

The centerpiece of South Korea's anti-communist police state is the notorious National Security Law, created by Syngman Rhee in 1948 to criminalize communism, or more precisely, the DPRK, the embodiment of Korean communism, and to criminalize its many supporters, which included the bulk of Koreans, before decades of ROK brainwashing produced an epistemology of ignorance. Criticized by Amnesty International,[13] Human Rights Watch,[14] and the United Nations,[15] the National Security Law has been variously used to lock up South Koreans for any expressions of leftism.[16] South Koreans have run afoul of the law for making comments that were construed as supportive of the DPRK, setting up websites with pro-DPRK content, calling for the establishment of a socialist state, discussing alternatives to capitalism in public forums, re-tweeting messages from the DPRK's Twitter feed, possessing books published in the DPRK, listening to radio broadcasts from Pyongyang, and visiting the DPRK without Seoul's permission. Promoting conciliation between the two states has also been punished under the law.

In the 1970s, the poet Kim Chi-ha was jailed because his poems advocated "class division." In 1976, South Koreans who signed a declaration commemorating an uprising against Japanese rule were imprisoned, under the provisions of the law. In 1987, a publisher was arrested for distributing travel essays written by Korean-Americans who were sympathetic to the DPRK. The law has been used to jail university students for forming study groups to examine DPRK ideology. In 1989, the ROK police state arrested an average of 3.3 citizens per day for infractions of the anti-communist regulations. In the first half of 1998, more than 400 were arrested under National Security Law provisions for demonstrating against unemployment. In 2001, sociology professor Kang Jeong-koo was jailed for visiting the birthplace of Kim Il-sung while on a visit to the DPRK.[17]

One man was convicted of having in his possession "printed matter aiding the enemy." The offending material included E.H. Carr's *The Russian Revolution*, Maurice Dobb's *Capitalism*

Yesterday and Today, Eric Fromm's *Socialist Humanism*, and Paul Sweezy's *Theory of Capitalist Development*.[18] In 2007, Kim Myung-soo was confined to a jail cell so small "he could spread his arms and touch the facing walls." His crime: aiding the enemy by operating a website that sold Edgar Snow's *Red Star over China*, a biography of Karl Marx, and other titles deemed to be pro-DPRK.[19] In 2008, ROK military personnel were banned from reading *Bad Samaritans: The Secret History of Capitalism* by Chang Ha-Joon (Chang is no Marxist, just critical of capitalism), Noam Chomsky's *Year 501: The Conquest Continues*, and Hyeon Gi-yeong's novel *A Spoon of the Earth*, all of which were labeled subversive books under an order that banned pro-DPRK, anti-capitalist, and anti-US publications.[20]

If Seoul suppresses books, it no less vigorously wipes out online content it doesn't want South Koreans to see. According to the *New York Times*, "When a computer user in South Korea clicks on an item on the" DPRK "Twitter account, a government warning against 'illegal content' pops up."[21] In 2011, ROK authorities blocked over 53,000 Internet posts for infractions which included having a kind word to say about the state founded by Kim Il-sung.[22] In the same year, the ROK deleted over 67,000 web posts that were deemed favorable to the DPRK or which criticized the US or ROK government. Over 14,000 posts were deleted in 2009.[23]

In August 2011, Prosecutor General Han Sang-dae "declared 'a war against fellow-travelling pro-North Korean left-wing elements,' and said, 'We must punish and remove them.'"[24] The government kept Han's promise, disbanding the left-wing UPP, stripping its legislators of their parliamentary seats, and jailing a handful of its members, including the lawmaker Lee Seok-ki. Lee was convicted under the National Security Law for, among other things, singing the *Song of the Red Flag*. The song is a socialist anthem, but so anodyne that even members of the British Labor Party occasionally sing it at party meetings. Another of Lee's transgressions was his calling Korea "Chosun," the country's last official name before colonization by Japan, and the DPRK's autonym for the country; in contrast, the ROK denotes Korea as Hanguk. The ROK police state regards Chosun as a pro-DPRK shibboleth.[25]

Conservatives and liberals have vociferously criticized *jongbuk*, accusing them of spreading subversive ideas and worming their way into positions of influence. Lee rejoined that *jongmi*, blindly following the United States, is a problem of far greater magnitude.[26] Lee was also accused of calling, at a closed meeting, for the sabotage of South Korean infrastructure in the event of war with the DPRK. He was convicted of inciting an insurrection and sentenced to a nine-year jail term, just one of hundreds of thousands of Koreans who have, since 1905, been locked up for promoting Korean independence and socialism.

While Lee's case was before the courts, the ROK government referred the UPP to the Constitutional Court, asking for the party's dissolution, owing to its program mirroring the aims and values of the DPRK. The government called the UPP's commitment to "overcoming foreign domination and dissolving" the ROK's "dependence on the alliance with the US," as well as its defining South Korea as "not a society where the workers are master, but the reverse, where a privileged few act as masters," as being "identical to the argument coming from Pyongyang,"[27] which indeed it was. The court accepted the government's brief, ruling that the UPP sought to undermine South Korea's liberal democracy (hardly a fitting description of a pro-imperialist police state) and its goal was to establish DPRK-style socialism. Far from seeking to undermine an authentic liberal democracy, the UPP was actually seeking to create one. A liberal democracy, by any unbiased definition, unaffected by an epistemology of ignorance, would look exactly like the system Lee advocated: one committed to *freedom* (from foreign domination and exploitation in the workplace), *equality* (of nations and individuals) and the *unity of humankind* (rather than peninsular division to suit the geopolitical goals of a foreign hegemon), i.e., *liberté, égalité, fraternité*—the liberal democratic goals of the revolution inaugurated in 1789, carried forward by the revolution of 1917, and advanced during the great twentieth century wave of decolonization

President Kim Dae Jung used the law to arrest people who demonstrated against unemployment and the government's response to an economic crisis. He also used it to arrest the filmmaker Suh

Joon Sik, who screened *Red Hunt*, a film about anti-communist suppression on Jeju Island in 1948, at the Korean Human Rights Festival in 1997. But Kim refused to prosecute Hyundai Business Group for clandestinely giving nearly $200 million to North Korea, a blatant violation of the law's prohibition against knowingly providing monetary benefits to the DPRK.[28]

Conservatives believe that the law and its enforcement are necessary to prevent political unrest, an acknowledgement that Koreans of the south remain committed to the emancipatory goals of the DPRK's political program, and that absent the threat of punishment for overtly espousing these values, South Koreans would mobilize to demand change. Conservatives insist that the National Security Law must remain until North Korea abandons its ideology.[29] In other words, so long as an ideology of liberation continues to be articulated by Pyongyang, the principal legal instrument of the South Korean police state must remain on the books to suppress the emancipatory movement of the south.

One South Korean newspaper editorial expressed the trepidation of conservatives this way: "What then would happen if we had completely abolished the National Security Law? There would be no legal way to block a South Korean citizen from joining the North's Workers Party ... Even if one established a [DPRK] ideology research institute ... and instruct[ed] the ideology to students, nobody would be able to block it ... Few citizens believe that our society is fully capable of digesting such confusions."[30]

The National Security Law has not only been invoked to round up Koreans committed to prosecuting the class war from below, it has also been used to incarcerate Koreans who struggle for national self-determination. Kim Sun Myung served almost 44 years in an ROK prison for political crimes. He was 70 years old when he was finally set free. Kim served over four decades in jail because he was committed to Korea's struggle for liberation. Despite being threatened with beatings and torture, he never recanted his communist beliefs, obstinately refusing to renounce his advocacy of Korea's struggle for freedom, despite witnessing the fatal prison tortures of a number of comrades who defied demands to disavow their communism.[31]

Kim's political journey began when Hodge landed at Inchon and refused to recognize the indigenously formed republic. Although an ROK citizen, Kim immediately joined the KPA when DPRK forces crossed the 38th parallel in June 1950, eager to participate in the Pyongyang-led project to unify the country and achieve its long sought-after independence.[32]

Kim's active participation in the project came to an abrupt end on October 15, 1951, when he was taken prisoner. As a South Korean citizen who had joined the North Korean army, Kim faced capital punishment, but was sentenced to life imprisonment. Kim's prison experience was austere. Placed in solitary confinement, without books or anyone to talk to, his verbal skills atrophied. Prison officials refused to treat his cataracts, leaving him blind. Kim's immediate family members were harassed and threatened by ROK authorities; they never visited him, fearing their visits would place them at risk of further government harassment.[33]

In the 1970s, the anti-communist police state undertook a campaign to use corporal punishment and starvation to induce political prisoners to denounce the DPRK. Prison guards promised Kim meals, only if he renounced his beliefs. He chose hunger.[34]

Political prisoners who were thrown into the hell of ROK political prisons, and emerged, say that three factors stiffened the resolve of Kim and his ilk. First, their utter conviction that their cause was just. Second, the inspiration provided by Korean national heroes who had survived torture at the hands of the Japanese. And third, the dignity their resistance offered them, in a prison life otherwise lacking in dignity, where prisoners were forced to bathe in their own urine.[35]

Kim Suk Hyun, another Korean inspired by the DPRK, was released at age 79 after serving 32 years in jail for refusing to denounce North Korea.[36]

On the day of his release, Kim Sun Myung was transported through bustling Seoul. Reporters were eager to find out how Kim would react to the vast changes that had transformed the capital city Kim had last seen four and a half decades earlier. Kim wasn't awed.[37] "It's changed so much that I don't recognize any of it," he said, "But this kind of thing doesn't impress me, because there are still a lot of poor people. These tall buildings are the labor of poor people. Did you ever see any rich people digging on a construction site?" Unbowed, Kim declared that the fight goes on.[38]

On the day Kim was released, two dozen DPRK sympathizers continued to languish in prison, each having served more than two decades in ROK dungeons.[39] The unbowed conviction of Koreans like Kim Sun Myung, and the conservatives' fear of what might happen if their compatriots are allowed to openly embrace the values embodied by the DPRK—indeed the very existence of the National Security Law—speaks volumes about the continuing attachment of Koreans of the south to the emancipatory goals that have always animated Korea's fight for freedom.

In 1961, the same year the ROK government enacted an anti-communist law, declaring all socialist states enemies, the Korean Central Intelligence Agency, or KCIA, was founded. The KCIA operated, according to William R. Polk, "like the Gestapo. It routinely arrested, imprisoned and tortured Koreans suspected of opposition."[40]

The KCIA was ubiquitous, infiltrating its agents into newspaper offices, radio stations, TV networks, political parties and discussion groups, trade unions, and classrooms, both in South Korea and abroad.[41] KCIA surveillance was panoptic—its agents were everywhere, and watched everyone, all the time. So pervasive was KCIA spying, that South Koreans believed it was best to say nothing about politics to anyone, even loved ones.[42] Had the ROK been communist, rather than capitalist, it would have been branded a "totalitarian" state of the very worst kind.

Recalling trade unions organized by the Nazi Party and Italian Fascists, the KCIA imposed a state-directed trade union structure on South Korean labor, creating workplace unions by sector. In August 1961, the KCIA appointed a committee to found a national labor federation comprised of twelve industrial unions. Labor leaders were required to pledge loyalty to the South Korean state. Once again, the label "totalitarian," in the West, usually reserved as a term of vilification to be attached to communist countries, is a fitting description of a state in which the political police organized trade unions. Two years later, the state prohibited unions from engaging in political activity.[43]

George Ogle, an American United Methodist Church missionary, led a ministry for South Korean factory workers, whose hours were punishing and working conditions often hazardous. He helped found the Urban Industrial Mission, whose goal was to acquaint workers with their rights and offer advice on contract negotiations. When eight workers were arrested under the National Security Law, convicted of treason, and sentenced to death, Ogle sprang to their defense. This ultimately led to his deportation, but not before he was whisked to the KCIA headquarters for interrogation. Ogle was questioned for seventeen hours straight by Yi Tong-taek, chief of the KCIA's sixth section. How could he possibly defend men about to be executed for treason as socialists, Yi demanded. Wasn't he aware that one of the defendants "had listened to the North Korean radio and copied down Kim [Il Sung]'s speech?" The KCIA chief screamed,"These men are our enemies. We have got to kill them. This is war. In war even Christians pull the trigger and kill their enemies. If we don't kill them, they will kill us. We will kill them."[44]

The Agency for National Security and Planning, the successor to the KCIA, had in excess of 70,000 employees in 1998, not counting informal agents and spies, and a yearly budget of about $1 billion, making it the capitalist version of what the East German secret police, the *Stasi*, was reputed to be, to say nothing of its being a first cousin of the Gestapo. On top of its omnipresence in the mass media, political groups, universities, and trade unions, it also controlled organizations that publish well-placed English-language academic journals.[45]

The movement against foreign domination of Korea and for what the historian Hakim Adi calls a "people-centered" economy[46] was strong enough that despite the regular unimpeded operation of the oppressive instruments of the National Security Law and the secret police, the anti-communist state continued to be threatened by the unremitting democratic demands of South Koreans. These demands included the exit of US forces from Korea and an economy that was responsive to the needs of ordinary people. Whenever pressure for these democratic goals exceeded a red line, the army would oust the civilian government and install a flag officer as president, all with the implicit approval of the US government, whose military commander on the peninsula had operational control of the ROK army. Washington's interest in the suppression of the democratic demands of Koreans was obvious: it desired a continued US military presence on the peninsula to contain and possibly roll back communism, not only in Korea, but in contiguous China and Russia, as well. Korea was a valuable, geopolitically strategic perch from which the American eagle could overlook communist prey. And the Wall Street bankers and lawyers who played a central role in US policy formulation certainly didn't want all of Korea converting to a people-centered economy. It was bad enough that the Koreans of the north had taken the socialist path.

Syngman Rhee had been brought to power by Washington in a flawed election that no one, except the US government and the few Rhee supporters, wanted. Rhee's popular support was always limited and therefore winning a fair election was always going to be a challenge, and underhanded measures would be needed to pull off an election win. And so, in the weeks leading up to the March 1960 election, Rhee supporters routinely beat opposition supporters. On voting day, March 15, ballot boxes disappeared from areas in which the opposition was expected to win. At the same time, ballots were stuffed with fraudulent votes. All of this happened in full view of US and UN election observers, who, Bruce Cumings observed, "apparently were present to legitimate, not monitor, the validity of election." Rhee claimed an improbable victory—almost 90 percent of the vote—sparking protests across the south. In the southwest, police killed several demonstrators. The army was called out to suppress the protests—with the approval of the army's US commander, General Carter Magruder.[47]

Midway through August, Kim Il-sung made a proposal to unify the country. The proposal excited the imaginations of South Koreans, but alarmed US collaborators. Kim's proposal, which he would table repeatedly throughout the years, was for a confederation. It would comprise one nation, one state, and one flag, but would have two sub-national governments, corresponding to the ROK and DPRK, each of which would maintain its own economic system. A national government—which would consist of representatives from both north and south, would look after foreign affairs, national defense, and intra-confederal relations. But there was a *proviso* that guaranteed that the US officials who dominated South Korea from behind the scenes would be hostile to the plan: Kim insisted that no foreign troops remain on Korean soil.

Students of the south were galvanized by the idea and set to work organizing a movement to link up with students of the north, in order to work for unification along the lines Kim proposed. This agitated the right wing and the security services,[48] and greatly displeased US planners, for whom maintenance of South Korea as the largest power projection platform in the Pacific (in the words of the US military),[49] was essential to the US imperial project.

In 1991 Kim Il-sung resurrected his proposal. Korea, he said "should be reunified by founding a confederacy based on one nation, one state, two systems and two governments. We consider that this conforms with the desire of the Korean nation to develop independently as one reunified nation and meets the requirement of the present era of independence and peace. We recognise that it is also the most feasible way of reunifying the country peacefully when different ideas and systems actually exist in the north and the south."[50] Once again, the proposal was rejected by ROK leaders. Subordinate to Washington, South Korean officials were duty-bound to reject a plan that demanded the exit of the US military from Korea. Besides, by 1991, the USSR and the Warsaw Pact had dissolved, and Communist East Germany had been absorbed into

West Germany. US and ROK officials believed it was only a matter of time before the same scenario of a communist collapse followed by integration into a capitalist neighbor would play out on the Korean peninsula.

On April 19, 1960, a teeming multitude of angry students, numbering more than 100,000, descended on the presidential palace, demanding an audience with Rhee. Terrified palace guards discharged their weapons directly into the throng, precipitating mayhem on the streets of Seoul. Over 100 students were killed and nearly 1,000 were injured.[51]

Nearly a week later, hundreds of university professors held a peaceful demonstration demanding that Rhee step down. Matters became violent later that evening when 50,000 demonstrators attacked the home of the vice-president. The next day, a crowd of 50,000 people was back out on the streets of Seoul. With Rhee's presidency now obviously untenable, the US ambassador and US military commander—the true power behind the puppet state of South Korea—paid a visit to the embattled president. Three days later he was gone, returning to the metropole from which he had come.[52]

Rhee was succeeded by the opposition Democratic Party's Chang Myon. Chang was from a landlord family, spoke English fluently, and had been ambassador to the United States. As prime minister he consulted with the US ambassador and CIA station chief on most matters, significant and otherwise.[53]

Rhee's succession by Chang Myon began what Bruce Cumings has called, "the ordeal that sent shivers up the spine of Seoul's ruling groups"—a move to the left.[54]

On May 16, 1961, Park Chung-hee and a group of Army and Marine officers under his command seized control of strategic points in Seoul. The Army Chief of Staff, General Chang To-yong, appealed to his superior, the US commander, General Carter Magruder, to mobilize troops to put down the coup. Magruder refused. The next day a conspiracy of senior officers shut down the National Assembly, banned political activity, and pledged anticommunism and fealty to Washington[55]— precisely what the Americans who ran the show insisted on, and precisely the inverse of what Koreans, who didn't, demanded. For the next 32 years, military leaders would occupy the presidency.

Like Rhee, Park was a vehement anti-communist. He was also a quisling, ready to sell out his compatriots to not one, but two empires. He carried with him the vile taint of Japanese collaboration, and added the vile taint of US collaboration. From 1961 until 1979, when Park's presidency would end in his assassination at the hands of the head of the KCIA, the leaders of Korea's two contending states were thesis and antithesis. The leader in the south had hired out his services to the Japanese to enforce their colonial rule over his compatriots. The leader in the north had led a guerrilla struggle to free his compatriots from the yoke of Japanese colonialism. The leader in the south nurtured a capital-centered economy, in which Koreans "had the right to work the longest hours in the industrial world at wages barely able to sustain one's family."[56] The leader in the north preferred a people-centered economy and had introduced an eight-hour work day and social security within months of coming to power. The leader in the south was greatly hemmed in by the influence exercised behind the scenes by the US military commander, US ambassador and CIA station chief. Tens of thousands of US troops occupied the domain over which the southern leader's state ruled. And his military reported, not to him, but to a US general. In the north, there were no foreign troops, and the leader preached a doctrine of self-reliance, which eschewed dependency on foreign powers. In the south, the top political leader was a traitor to the Korean project of national liberation; in the north, the top political leader was a patriot who had devoted his life to Korea's liberation. In the south, the state was part of an empire. In the north, the state rejected empire. The state of the south was founded by a foreign hegemon. The state of the north was founded by guerrilla leaders who had fought against foreign hegemony.

To kick off his regime, Park trod a path blazed by other anti-communist dictators, as his US patrons watched and silently applauded. He dissolved the legislature and suspended the constitution. He rounded up communists and other political dissidents, tossed them into prison, and had them tortured. Among his victims were Kim Dae-jung and Kim Yong-sam, men who would later become presidents.[57]

Next, he oversaw the writing of a new constitution to replace the one he had expunged. The new foundational law granted him presidential powers indefinitely. He could appoint and dismiss the prime minister and cabinet at will, and suspend or abolish civil liberties by decree. He also granted himself the authority to exercise whatever additional powers he thought he might need.[58] In effect, Park could have accurately declared, "*L'état, c'est moi.*" Except behind Park's power lurked the far greater authority of Hirohito's successors, the serial emperors whose abode lay in Washington. In 1973, Park prohibited all work stoppages. The year after he banned all criticism of his government.[59]

By 1979 Park's capital-centered economy was sputtering. Growth had dipped below zero. The economy continued to contract, shrinking six percent in 1980.[60] Growing unemployment and economic hardship touched off a wave of unrest. Massive demonstrations unsettled the country as workers and students took to the streets demanding relief from growing hardship.[61]

How to arrest the growing distemper? The options were repression or accommodation. On October 26, 1979, Park travelled to a KCIA safe house for discussions with Kim Chae-gyu, the KCIA supremo, on how to bring the distemper to an end. The discussion went horribly wrong, ending with Kim fatally gunning down the president.[62]

Park's presidency was quickly followed by a December 12, 1979 military *coup d'état*, carried out by General Chun Doo Hwan, commander of the ROK army's Ninth Division. Chun, at the time, was under the command of US General John A. Wickham, Jr., head of the US-ROK Combined Forces Command.[63] A veteran of military intelligence, Chun, in power, expanded the intelligence function as a force of internal repression. The paramilitary riot police force was expanded, until it numbered around 150,000 by the mid-1980s.[64] Wickham approved a role for the ROK military in politics. The army would vet political candidates. At the same time, it would supervise all political activity, preventing challenges to the state.[65]

In the spring of 1980, students took to the streets of Gwangju to protest Chun's dictatorship. Wickham approved the deployment of two ROK special forces brigades to quell the disturbance and enforce martial law. On May 18, elite paratroopers landed in the city and began to indiscriminately murder demonstrators, including women and children.[66] Outraged, the citizens of Gwangju fought back. Hundreds of thousands of local people drove the soldiers out of the city. It's estimated that as many as 1,500 people died in the fighting. In the aftermath, a citizens' council was established. Resembling the Paris Commune, the revolutionary people's government that ruled Paris in the spring of 1871, the council governed Gwangju for the next five days.[67]

As the citizens of Gwangju were driving the US-commanded South Korean army out of the city, the US National Security Council was meeting at the White House to plan a response. US President Jimmy Carter, along with Zbigniew Brzezinski, his national security adviser, and Assistant Secretary of State Richard Holbrooke, decided to approve a military intervention.[68] Wickham ordered the ROK army's Twentieth Division to deploy to Gwangju to crush the rebellion, a mission it successfully carried out a few days later. But Washington took no chances. To guarantee the success of the mission, the arrival of troops in Gwangju was delayed by three days to allow a US naval armada led by the aircraft carrier Midway to reach Korean waters, should reinforcements be required.[69]

Less than a year later, Chun had himself inaugurated president. Recalling the Nazi's use of concentration camps in the early 1930s as instruments of terror against the Left, Chun established a network of concentration camps in mountain areas to terrorize the Left and bring it to heel. The police rounded up and incarcerated 37,000 known or suspected leftists, including journalists, students, teachers, labor organizers, and civil servants.[70]

One survivor recalled:

> Right before supper we were beaten out of our minds and at supper-time we were given three spoonfulls of barley rice. Even though we offered thanksgiving for this, we were beaten again. For one laugh—80 lashings. In the morning there is a marching period which is called

> a screaming time but we were so hungry we couldn't shout [so] then they beat us with clubs until we screamed. One friend of mine, a Mr. Chai, could not scream because of a throat infection and therefore, he was beaten to death. Another person, a Mr. Lee, was also beaten to death. Two out of the eleven in our group were killed.[71]

Military leaders would continue to fill the post of president until 1993. Over the entire span of that period, the United States had operational control of the ROK military, the institutional body from which South Korean presidents sprang. Hence, political authority in South Korea ran in a straight line from the White House to the US viceroys in Korea (the US commander of the joint US-ROK military structure, the US ambassador and the CIA station chief), and, last and least, to the Blue House, the official residence of the ROK president.

CHAPTER II

Washington's Power Projection Platform in the Pacific

There was a marked shift in politics in South Korea by 1993, but also profound changes in the larger world, which were causally related. The Berlin Wall had fallen, the German Democratic Republic had dissolved, and Germany had reunified under a capitalist economic system, betokening, it seemed, a model for Korean reunification, in which the DPRK would surrender and willingly accept absorption into the ROK. More significantly, the USSR had thrown in the towel, and the Warsaw Pact had dissolved. The Cold War was over and capitalism had won. Or so it appeared.

These tectonic shifts ignited a crisis in the Left around the world. Communist parties dissolved, or abandoned communism for social democracy. Social democrats abandoned social democracy and embraced austerity. The threat of the Left to the established order melted away, allowing governments that had been on the frontline of the war against movements for self-determination and people-centered economies to scale back the politically repressive functions of the state. If there's no Left to repress, the full armamentarium of repressive instruments need no longer be deployed. And since military rule, dictatorship, and concentration camps provoked embarrassing comparisons to Nazism, these institutions could be happily placed in storage, pending future eruptions of leftism.

Hence, by 1993, the context of global developments allowed political space to open up in South Korea. The military was no longer needed to repress the Left, now in a period of retrenchment. Military rule—from the point of view of the empire-builders in Washington and their collaborators in Seoul—could be shelved and replaced by civilian rule. Of course, the National Security Law would remain to keep the Left reined in, and the secret police would continue to function, carrying out their mandate of penetrating and undermining leftist groups, while shaping the ideological space by covertly funding academic journals, conferences and mass media. But secret police and anti-communist laws would operate in the background. The integument of the South Korean state would become liberal democratic, but the underlying tissue would remain viciously intolerant of the Left.

At the same time, it would no longer be necessary for Washington to maintain operational control of the ROK military at all times. In 1994, South Koreans were granted command of their military, but during peacetime alone. At a time of war, command would revert to a US general.

There is an important question of sovereignty here. A country whose military is under foreign command can hardly be said to be sovereign. Indeed, no less than a former commander of US forces in Korea, General Richard Stilwell, described US operational control as the "most remarkable concession of sovereignty in the entire world."[1] Many South Koreans were embittered by their country's flagrant abnegation of sovereignty to the United States, and the transfer of peacetime operational control of their military was a concession to them—though one of limited significance.

A military exists to wage war. War-making can be defensive, what it's supposed to be, or aggressive, what it shouldn't be, but almost invariably *is* where the United States is concerned. Andrew Bacevich, a US historian and retired career US Army officer, points out that the function of the US military is not self-defense, but "power projection"—the use, or threat, of violence to impose Washington's will on other countries. Self-defense is what Homeland Security does.[2] Washington's granting the ROK control of the South Korean military in peacetime, i.e., when it's not fulfilling its primary power projection function, is tantamount to the United States yielding control of an asset when it's not in use but insisting on full command when it's needed. In other words, Washington's ceding peacetime operational control of its East Asian army in reserve—a military which has been historically used as a US auxiliary power projection force in Korea, Vietnam, Afghanistan and Iraq—was nothing more than a sop to mollify South Koreans.

Promises were made to grant South Korea full control of its military by 2015, including during times of war, but as the date neared, it was pushed off by South Korea's military chiefs to the future—sometime in the mid-2020s.[3] But as Tim Beal has pointed out, it is inconceivable that the Pentagon would ever allow its forces to fall under the command of a South Korean general. If US forces remain on the peninsula in large numbers, operating conjointly with the ROK military, the combined forces will always be under US command, whether openly or covertly. The United States leads military coalitions, even if leadership is provided from behind, as in the NATO war on Libya or the Saudi war on Yemen, or in placing military advisers with local combat forces. The only conceivable circumstance in which wartime control of ROK forces would devolve to an ROK general, is that in which the United States decided to sit out a war, either because its forces were not necessary to achieve victory, the war did not comport with US objectives, or Washington had abandoned the ROK as a political project. This might explain why transfer of operation control is regularly postponed—because no one of consequence realistically expects it's ever going to happen, or wants it to.

Moon pressed ROK commanders to assume wartime operation control, or op-con. The commanders balked. Moon persisted. Eventually Washington stepped in to rein in the South Korean president. As the *Wall Street Journal* explained, many South Koreans "see the lack of military control as an embarrassment that exposes the country to criticisms from Pyongyang that South Korea is a puppet state of the U.S." Accordingly, Moon pushed the United States to allow South Korea "to take control of its own military forces should war break out on the Korean peninsula." But Washington wasn't "inclined to relinquish control," the newspaper reported, adding that US officials had concluded that, "Seoul isn't ready." Said one US official, "I don't think anyone [in Washington] is eager to see op-con transfer."[4] Washington's denial of Moon's op-con demand—indeed, even the fact that the South Korean president has to petition the United States for control of the South Korean military—proves a point Pyongyang makes almost daily and which embarrasses South Koreans: the ROK *is* a puppet state.

The ROK military is certainly capable of defending itself against the DPRK without US assistance. Compared to the DPRK, Seoul can draw on twice the population and many times the GDP to meet its military needs; hence, compared to its northern neighbor, the ROK is capable of fielding a much larger military and sustaining a much larger military budget and therefore of purchasing much more lethal weaponry. South Korea's planned 2018 military budget was $38.4 billion, up from $35.9 billion in 2017.[5] The DPRK, in contrast, spends from $3.4 to $9.5 billion on its military, 75-90 percent less, and about as much as the City of New York spends on its police force.[6] The ROK has 600,000 active-duty service members, backed by 3.5 million reservists. It's not clear how large the KPA is, but a "number of scholars both inside [South Korea] and in other countries have concluded that the [KPA] is composed of around 700,000 soldiers",[7] according to the South Korean newspaper, *The Hankyoreh*. Despite a rough parity in the number of active service personnel between the two militaries, ROK forces have far more sophisticated and deadly weaponry. For example, the ROK air force is equipped with F-15 and F-16 jetfighters, while the KPA has obsolescent MiG fighter jets which are often *hors de combat* for lack of aviation fuel or parts.[8]

The ROK's military superiority over its DPRK rival was acknowledged in 2017 by the country's president. Moon Jae-in reassured South Koreans that ROK forces had "the power to destroy" the DPRK "beyond recovery."[9] Our "economy has been stronger" than the DPRK's, he said, "since the 1970s and our military expenditures have topped theirs for decades."[10] With comparative advantages like these, only sheer incompetence could put the ROK at a disadvantage in a head-to-head contest with the KPA.

Military weakness, then, is not the reason the United States maintains operational control of South Korea's armed forces. The ROK military remains under the command of a US general because it is, and always has been, an extension of the Pentagon, and an instrument of US power projection, which continues to have utility in connection with US foreign policy goals. It was established by the United States, its officers are trained by the United States, its units are equipped by the United States, its component parts are integrated into the military of the United States, and its general staff is under the command of the United States. To be sure, ROK service personnel defend their country, but the ROK itself is an extension of the Pentagon. Therefore, the defense of the ROK is equivalent to the defense of an instrument of US foreign policy. Should South Korean soldiers perish in battle, they will die as cannon fodder sacrificed to the defense of the largest US power projection platform in the Pacific,[11] and not in defense of the welfare, dignity, and self-determination of Koreans.

In 1949, after the Pentagon had withdrawn its combat troops from the peninsula (before rushing them back a year later), the journalist Marguerite Higgins remarked on how the advisers the United States had left behind became "a living demonstration of how an intelligent and intensive investment of 500 combat-hardened American men and officers can train 100,000 guys to do the shooting for you."[12] The 100,000 guys would eventually become 600,000 men and women, with a reserve force of 3.5 million, but the principle is the same. As we've seen, the United States puts this principle to work around the globe, using special operations forces to train local militaries to do the shooting for them in over eighty countries.

In the late 1960s and early 1970s, hundreds of thousands of ROK troops were deployed to Vietnam, where they were integrated into the US military command as mercenary soldiers in a war to crush a communist-led national liberation movement. In effect, South Korean combatants were employed in Vietnam to do what they had already attempted to do under US command in Korea a decade earlier—thwart an anti-colonial struggle for independence. Indeed, the ROK military has only ever been used in campaigns to put down movements to eject US occupation forces.

In exchange for helping the United States wage a war of empire against an East Asian anti-colonial independence movement, the ROK received injections of cash and economic perks that contributed significantly to South Korea's subsequent economic take-off. Most accounts of the ROK's stellar growth conceal this dirty secret.

Washington injected about one billion dollars into the ROK from 1965 through 1970 (equal to nearly $8 billion in 2018) to cover the cost of ROK troop deployments to Vietnam. These payments accounted for an estimated 7 to 8 percent of South Korea's GDP from 1966 to 1969 and almost one-fifth of its total foreign earnings.[13] In addition, Washington accoutered the ROK military with billions of dollars of equipment and opened up Vietnam to South Korean businesses as a market and sphere of investment.[14] Vietnam became a cornucopia of profits for Korean firms, as US officials showered Korean corporations with contracts to support the US war effort. Under US direction, Vietnam soaked up more than 90 percent of the ROK's steel exports and half of its transportation equipment exports.[15]

The South Korean army took on the role of the Pentagon's East Asian army in reserve. Rather than acting as a means of ROK self-defense, it was deployed as an auxiliary force in the US fight against revolutionary nationalism in Vietnam.[16] In the mid-1960s, Washington said it needed 50,000 US troops in Korea to defend the ROK, but arranged to ship hundreds of thousands of South Korean troops from the peninsula to Indochina. It didn't add up.

More recently, the ROK has deployed its armed forces to serve under US command in wars of empire in Afghanistan and Iraq. From 2003 to 2008, Seoul sent 20,000 troops to Iraq to help Washington engineer, by force, a transition from a socialist economy under an Arab nationalist government to a capital-centered, foreign-investment-friendly economy, under a government beholden to Washington. From 2001 to 2014, 5,000 ROK military personnel participated in the US-led war on Afghanistan.

The KPA, in contrast, has never fought beyond Korea's borders and has never engaged in an aggressive war. Since the latter point challenges a popular misconception that North Korea initiated a war of aggression against a sovereign state on the Korean peninsula in 1950, it is fitting to recapitulate points made earlier on this matter. First, the question of which state initiated the attack ignores the reality that both states had been engaged in a series of reciprocal attacks for months in advance of June 25, 1950, and that most of the attacks were initiated by the ROK. Second, the question of which side opened a general offensive has never been settled and remains a matter of historical uncertainty. The UN determination that it was the North Korean side that was the first to strike was based exclusively on US and ROK reports, hardly unbiased. The DPRK has always hotly contested this claim. Third, an invasion across the 38th parallel by either side was a matter of no moment, since no one recognized the parallel as an international border. A North Korean push to the south could not have been an invasion any more than a South Korean push to the north would have been. Koreans cannot invade Korea. The notion, then, that the KPA initiated a war of aggression in 1950 is without foundation. The only war the KPA has ever fought has been within its own country to establish sovereignty over territory it arguably has the sole legitimate claim to. In contrast, ROK forces have waged four wars (Korea, Vietnam, Afghanistan, and Iraq), all under US command, and all in defense of US occupations and against forces of national liberation.

Emblematic of the epistemology of ignorance is the accustomed portrayal of the DPRK as belligerent and the ROK as fairly peace-loving, when exactly the reverse is true. So it is that *The Diplomat*, a publication which covers the Asia-Pacific region, could describe the Republic of Korea as a state that "has rarely deployed troops outside its borders" (only three times!) while at the same time referring to the DPRK, a state that has *never* deployed troops outside its borders, as "a belligerent North Korea."[17] Perhaps the North Korean belligerence the publication refers to pertains to Pyongyang's rhetoric toward Washington and Seoul, which, to be sure, is often belligerent, but no less bellicose than Moon's assertion that the ROK has "the power to destroy" the DPRK "beyond recovery," to say nothing of the highly aggressive threats of total extermination US officials have frequently directed at the DPRK. States which regularly deploy troops beyond their borders and participate in wars for empire, as is true of the United States and the ROK, are not, by any reasonable definition, peace-loving. Conversely, a state which has never deployed troops beyond its borders, and has never participated in a war of empire, can be described fairly as a state that rejects wars of aggression. Indeed, the very idea that the DPRK could engage in a war for empire is inconceivable; it is entirely antithetical to its core values.

There are "not two but three Koreas," observed William R. Polk: the DPRK, the ROK, and US military bases.[18] Actually, there is only one Korea, and that Polk can point to three (or even two) is emblematic of the power Washington has to create artificial political constructions and an ideology to explain them. There is, in reality, one Korea. But grafted onto the one indivisible country is an illegitimate state, the ROK, ("basically set up" by Washington, as Bruce Cumings observes[19]) and roughly two dozen US military bases on which nearly 30,000 US service personnel are stationed as an occupation force.

The US military presence in Korea began with the establishment, in 1945, of the US military government, which spent its three-year tenure engaged in a war to suppress the Korean People's Republic, at the time, the organically created state of the one true Korea, from whose people's committees the DPRK sprang. Once Soviet forces exited the peninsula at the end of 1948, the reason for US troops to remain in Korea, under the original US-Soviet agreement on Korea's occupation, dissolved. All the same, Washington maintained its garrison on the peninsula until the summer of 1949. "Americans usually perceive an important gap between the withdrawal of US combat forces in July 1949 and the war that came a year later," observes Bruce Cumings. But, in reality, the US military never left. US "advisers were all over the war zones in" South Korea, "constantly shadowing" their ROK charges "and urging them on to greater efforts" in the war to suppress the guerrilla uprising against the US-ROK occupation.[20]

The number of US soldiers on the Korean peninsula swelled to nearly 330,000 during the conflict of 1950-1953, but a residual force of 50,000-70,000 US troops continued to occupy South Korea in the immediate aftermath of the war. US military advisers trained the ROK military, evaluated its performance, and sent its officers to war colleges in the United States.[21] Over the years, the size of the US occupation force has diminished to its current level just shy of 30,000.

Until 2017, the Pentagon's main base in Korea was at Yongsan, a facility that had also been the main Korean base of the Japanese Imperial Army during the Japanese colonial period. The base of one imperial army in Korea became the base of its successor. The Yongsan base was a conspicuous foreign implantation in the middle of the ROK's capital city and a constant reminder of a more than century-long imperial military presence in Korea. Perhaps for this reason the Pentagon moved US forces to a less conspicuous location in 2017. Another reason, more significant, was that the base was within range of KPA artillery.

The Pentagon built a new main base, Camp Humphreys, at Pyeongtaek, beyond the reach of North Korea's heavy cannons. Like the base at Yongsan, Camp Humphrey's has been built on the site of a former Japanese military installation. The base covers an area equivalent to more than four Central Parks. *The Diplomat* calls it "the largest overseas American military base in the world."[22]

The US installation has "apartment buildings, sports fields, playgrounds and a water park, and an 18-hole golf course with the generals' houses overlooking the greens. There is a 'warrior zone' with Xboxes and Playstations, pool tables and dart boards, and a tavern for those old enough to drink," according to *The Washington Post*—which is to say, all the amenities an occupation army could desire. The base is also outfitted with "two elementary schools, a middle school and a high school," as well as a "68-bed military hospital."

There is housing to accommodate as many as "1,111 families and a total of about 45,500 people."[23]

Despite the gross imbalance in conventional military force that divides the ROK from the DPRK—an imbalance strongly in Seoul's favor—South Korean officials have never asked Washington to withdraw US troops. The military imbalance is even greater if nuclear weapons are taken into account. The ROK is, along with some 30 other countries, sheltered under the US nuclear umbrella, and Washington has announced on several occasions that it will reduce North Korea to ashes if ever the DPRK attempts to assert its sovereignty over the entire peninsula. That threat alone, issued by the world's most formidable nuclear power, ought to be reason enough to believe that the chances of a DPRK attack on the ROK are vanishingly small. The ROK can readily defend itself, a point made by two ROK presidents, (even if to an unreceptive military brass and an equally unreceptive Washington.) In contrast, the DPRK is the weaker military force on the peninsula and no state provides it a sheltering nuclear umbrella.

The reality that Seoul fails to demand US troop withdrawal hinders the possibility of reunification. "In the question of the country's reunification," Kim Il-sung declared in 1971, the US army must be "withdrawn from south Korea."[24] In Kim's view, reunification and independence are inseparable. In contrast, Seoul insists that any reunification be accompanied by Korean integration into the US military command structure[25]—in which case there would two Koreas: one of the colonizers, and one of the colonized. The ROK has no intention of building one united, *independent*, Korea. That aim is embraced by the DPRK alone. For the ROK, the subordination of Korea to the US-dictated global order is a goal whose primacy exceeds the recovery of the one Korea.

CHAPTER 12

US Supremacy's All-Conquering March

"The United States today is, by its own reckoning, the overwhelmingly dominant power of the globe in nearly all spheres, with the determination to impose its will by one means or another."—Graham E. Fuller, former vice-chair of the US National Intelligence Council[1]

As he was leaving office in 2017 after eight years as US president, Barack Obama wrote a letter to his successor, Donald Trump. "American leadership in this world really is indispensable," Obama told Trump. "It's up to us, through action and example, to sustain the international order that's expanded steadily since the end of the Cold War, and upon which our own wealth and safety depend."[2]

There was nothing new in what Obama had to tell the incoming president. These themes had pervaded the utterances of US administrations, senators, scholars and editorial writers for decades. The themes were that US leadership is necessary; that it maintains an international order; and that the US-created international order is the basis of US prosperity. Senator John McCain, a principal figure in the Republican Party, echoed Obama. "We are the chief architect and defender of an international order governed by rules derived from our political and economic values," McCain averred. "We have grown vastly wealthier and more powerful under those rules."[3] The dual statements, one by a Democrat, the other a Republican, represented the consensus position of the US foreign policy establishment. The United States has created an international order; that order has made the United States vastly wealthier and more powerful; and the US government intends to enforce the global economic order it created. Unspoken, but true nonetheless, is the reality that the global economic order the United States has created caters, not to US citizens *en masse*, but to a numerically tiny class of billionaire investors and shareholders who wield an influence in Washington that vastly exceeds their numbers. To construe McCain's use of the plural pronoun "we" as denoting all Americans is to make what Jean-Paul Sartre called the error of confusing the elite with the genus.[4] Anyone who doubts that billionaire investors and shareholders wield inordinate influence in Washington should consider the backgrounds and careers of appointees to the top positions in the US state—the secretaries of defense, treasury, state, and commerce; the national security advisers; ambassadors to the UN; World Bank presidents; and so on. If not immensely wealthy themselves, they are connected to the wealthy in important ways as political lieutenants and acolytes. When Obama and McCain say "our" and "we" they mean the top one percent of US citizens, the stratum of US society that matters in the political and economic life of the country—the United States' very *raison d'*être.

One ought to consider too who US public policy favors. As political scientists Martin Gilens and Benjamin I. Page concluded in their 2014 analysis of over 1,700 US policy issues, "economic elites and organized groups representing business interests have substantial impacts on government policy, while average citizens and mass-based interest groups have little or no independent influence."[5] In other words, the *demos,* ordinary people, have virtually no influence on US public policy, while wealthy business people and their lobbies, who constitute only a tiny fraction of the US population, have substantial impacts. The United States, then, is a plutocracy ruled by the wealthy, not a democracy ruled by the people. And the foreign policy of a plutocracy is one which addresses the concerns, interests, and aspirations of Wall Street, not Main Street.

The architects of the post-World War II, US-led international order were Wall Street bankers and lawyers, most of whom were members of the Wall Street foreign policy think tank, the Council on Foreign Relations (CFR). McCain was a member of the CFR, as has been virtually every person who plays, or has played, a significant role in the US departments of state, defense, treasury, national security, US intelligence, the Pentagon, or as ambassador to the UN.[6]

The Wall Street politicos—to coin a term denoting people with strong Wall Street connections who take on leading roles in public policy—sought to build a post-war world in which US investors and shareholders would be able to exploit labor and resources over as much of the face of the globe as US power could make possible. Anathema to their vision of a post-war world were Germany's and Japan's closed economies, which, for roughly a decade beginning in the mid-1930s, had locked US businesspeople out of lucrative profit-making opportunities in Europe and East Asia. Equally repellent was the people-centered economy being built in the Soviet Union, which clashed strongly with the capital-centered economy on which Wall Street's very prosperity depended. The last thing Wall Street politicos wanted was the advance of communism, which appeared poised to take off in war-torn Europe and East Asia. The international order the Wall Street politicos would seek to establish would be one of an open world economy; it would be capitalist, and all parts of the globe would be open to exploitation by US investors and shareholders.

The "containment of Communism and Soviet power," noted historian Melvyn P. Leffler, "was essential to preserve an open world economy."[7] Hence, gradually, "between 1947 and 1950, the United States took on the role of hegemon in the international system."[8] Washington would assume a "leadership role around the world,"[9] as Germany had assumed a "leadership role" in Europe, Japan had done in East Asia, Italy had tried to do in the Mediterranean, and Britain and France had done in Africa and parts of Asia; except that, with other imperialist powers defeated, or greatly weakened, the United States would capitalize on the opportunity to exercise primacy on a world scale, to construct what Brzezinski had called a global power—that is, an unsurpassed empire of unprecedented scope and reach.

Washington saw itself as having a continuing role in "shaping an emerging global economic order" that continued "to reflect [US] interests and values." But there were impediments. "Despite its success, our rules-based system," noted Obama, "is now competing against alternative, less-open models." These include models based on "state-owned enterprises,"[10] which are prevalent in China, Russia, Venezuela, the DPRK, Cuba, Iran, and Syria. Indeed, every country in the Pentagon's cross-hairs since the dissolution of the USSR, from Milosevic's Yugoslavia, to Saddam's Iraq, Gaddafi's Libya, Assad's Syria, and the Islamic Republic of Iran, have embraced "alternative, less-open models" of economic organization based on "state-owned enterprises." In his last address to the United Nations General Assembly, Obama referred to the economy of the DPRK as a "wasteland" and a "dead end." It too, with its central planning and state control, was an alternative, less open model. In other words, the countries which have come to be the targets of US hostility are the very same ones which have built economies that are non-compliant with the US-led global economic order. The US president promised to address these "challenges."[11]

When McCain said "we" are the chief architect and defender of an international order governed by rules derived from "our" political and economic values, what he really meant was that Wall Street is the system's chief architect. When he said that "we" have grown vastly wealthier and more powerful under rules which reflect "our" political and economic values, what he really meant was that *Wall Street* had grown vastly wealthier and more powerful—and that the rules reflected Wall Street's political and economic values.

Even a cursory survey of US society quickly reveals that vast wealth and power can hardly be claimed by Main Street, but is conspicuously evident on Wall Street. Therefore, the use of words such as "we" and "our" to attribute ownership of the global economic order to all Americans, misleadingly conflates the interests of Wall Street with those of all US citizens, the overwhelming majority of whom are not in any way a part of Wall Street and, on the contrary, stand in relation to Wall Street as Korean tenant famers stood in relation to absentee landlords—as the exploited, not beneficiaries. The purpose of conflating Wall Street and Main Street is to disguise the reality that the United States is class-divided, and that the global international order which US citizens are expected to salute and pay homage to as the guarantor of their prosperity is, in reality, the guarantor of the prosperity of a numerically miniscule economic *uber*-class, the one percent, whose vast wealth is as dependent on the exploitation of its American compatriots as it is on the exploitation of foreign populations.

"Ideology," Joan Robinson is reputed to have once remarked, "is like your breath. You never smell your own." The ideology inhered in the statements of US officials, like one's own breath, may be difficult to detect. Ideology is a formal concept which denotes a set of ideas used to justify a socially-constructed order. It performs the following functions:

- presents the interests of a dominant group as universal.
- conceals the exploitation of subordinate groups.
- presents a socially-constructed order as originating in nature or God (and therefore as immutable) rather than being the creation of human beings (and therefore as changeable).

Washington presents the imposition of its will on the rest of the world, not as imperialism—the process of empire maintenance and building—or as the international dictatorship of the United States, or as despotism, but as "US leadership." References to US leadership abound in the statements of US politicians, military leaders, and commentators. "We lead the world," declared US ambassador to the UN, Samantha Power.[12] "The question is never whether America should lead, but how we lead," asserted Obama's National Security Strategy.[13] Barbara Stephenson, president of the American Foreign Service Association, described the United States as having a "global leadership role."[14] After Trump was elected, Newt Gingrich said that the new president, a reality TV star, would have a new show to star in: "'Leading the World.'"[15] The political scientist and journalist David J. Rothkopf defines the White House and, more specifically, the National Security Council, as "the nerve center" from which the world is led.[16] In his second inaugural address, Bill Clinton described the United States as "the world's greatest democracy" imbued with a mission to spread its "bright flame ... throughout all the world" and to "lead a whole world of democracies," because "America stands alone as the world's indispensable nation."[17]

Other statements of US leadership refer explicitly to an international order. US Defense Secretary James Mattis issued a statement "to the Pentagon work force that cast the United States as a bulwark of the international order."[18] Sohrab Ahmari, who had spent years as an editor of the *Wall Street Journal*, defined US leadership as "essential to global order" and opined that the United States' "combination of military supremacy and decent values makes our leadership essential."[19] John McCain referred to the United States as having "an obligation" to the lead the world and a "duty to remain 'the last best hope of earth.'"[20]

US military strategy defines US interests to include "an open international economic system" advanced by "US leadership." US national security interests are equated with the "security of the global economic system"; and the "presence of US military forces in key locations around the world" is characterized as underpinning this system.[21] US military leaders see US leadership as global and enforced by US military supremacy. "If you have a global economy, I think you need a global navy to look after that economy," remarked the head of the U.S. Pacific Fleet, Admiral Scott Swift.[22] This resonates with Alexander Haig's admission that tens of thousands of US troops occupy Europe to ensure that European markets remain open to US exports and investment. James Stavridis, who, as a US naval flag officer, had command of all NATO forces in Europe, said that the United States regards the world's oceans as "a vast American lake" and that the role of its navy is to dominate "a defined sea space anywhere on the globe."[23] (Mussolini regarded the Mediterranean as a vast Italian lake, but then his imperial ambitions were a good deal more modest than Washington's.) In

2017, the chairman of the US Joint Chiefs of Staff, General Joseph Dunford, declared that his country is "a nation that both thinks and acts globally."[24] He might have added that the United States both thinks and acts in terms of global markets, and its military functions to keep those markets open and free from challenges by alternative, less open models that rely on state-owned enterprises.

US leadership, moreover, is framed as an institution that other countries of the world consent to, and even ask for. Hence, US leaders present themselves as benevolently acceding to the world's demand to be led. We "welcome our responsibility to lead," declared Obama, as if the mantle had been thrust on Washington.[25]

Washington also presents itself as leading on behalf of universal welfare and universal values. For example, the US National Security Strategy of 2015 declares that American leadership is exercised "in the cause of universal values."[26] Washington tells us that "US leadership is a global force for good" and that there "is no substitute for American leadership ... in the cause of universal values."[27] Obama, who left a trail of chaos and destruction across the Muslim world in his wake, could say, with apparent detachment from reality, that "I believe we [the US government] have been a force for good."[28] Delusion? Yes, but only if we assume that Obama was referring to a *universal* good. Since it is almost axiomatic that the United States has not acted as a force for universal good, unless Obama was detached from reality, the force for good to which he referred could only be specific to the interests of the Wall Street politicos who shaped the global economic order in whose interests Obama acted. Obama's presidency was a force for good for a numerically small section of the US population that matters in US political life—billionaire investors and the immediate circle of professionals who attend to their profit-making needs, all of whom continue to enjoy rising wealth at the expense of everyone else.

Obama's presidency was marked by true statements delivered with strategic omissions that made them into masterpieces of equivocation. If, through the brilliance of his equivocations, the bulk of the US population believed that the United States acts for the benefit of all, well, then, that was well and good, for the United States could hardly act as a force for the good of its wealthiest citizens without the consent and cooperation of the bottom 99 percent. And the *menu peuple* would hardly voluntarily cooperate if they believed that the movement of their government was along an arc defined by the interests of billionaire investors. The function of US presidents, as the principal face through which the Wall Street-dominated US government presents itself, is to manage the ideological environment. They must present Wall Street's interests as Main Street's interests and the United States' interests as the world's interests; US leadership must be presented as benevolent and universally beneficial, rather than exploitative and aimed at aggrandizing a hyper-wealthy Wall Street-centered minority. And US leadership must be presented, not as constructed and imposed by the United States, but as something everyone desires, except those deemed evil. In an instance of circular reasoning, the turpitude of the latter is defined by their rejection of US leadership. Forces which reject US leadership are evil. How do we know? Because they reject US leadership.

Over and over, US officials repeat a mantra—US leadership is "indispensable"—but they don't say who it is indispensable to. The truth of the matter is that US leadership is indispensable to US billionaires as a class; it is a desideratum of their vast wealth and power. But the continual references to indispensability, made with the strategic omission of who US leadership is indispensable to, become invocations of "desirability." We're to believe that US leadership is universally desirable and good.

What qualities does the United States uniquely possess to make its leadership on a global scale desirable? The answer, apparently, is its "unique contributions and capabilities," according to the 2015 National Security Strategy. But the strategy document fails to spell out what these contributions and capabilities are, leaving us to guess. One argument might be that the United States has constructed an international order that benefits all, and that the United States is the only country wealthy and powerful enough to enforce the universally beneficial international order; consequently, its leadership is desirable. Only an epistemology of ignorance can rescue this view from its utter disregard of reality.

US ideology has historical resonances. Claims to benevolent leadership have been used by other empires to beautify their projects of domination. Japanese empire-builders made clear their "intent to ... lift Korea out of endemic poverty, eliminate governmental dysfunction, and bring prosperity to Korea in the process through expanded trade." Japan "would open Korea to the global economy, a win-win solution for both countries."[29] We saw how that worked out. The journalist Hugh Byas condemned Japan in 1942 for sharing the same belief as Nazi Germany—the belief that Japan had "unique qualities that [made] it superior to its neighbors and [gave] it a special mission to perform."[30] Who can deny that the same imperial arrogance of superiority, accompanied by a special mission to lead, has not touched US leaders?

European empires, along with the Empire of Japan, invoked the concept of racial superiority to justify their exploitation of subject peoples. Relationships of domination were presented as relationships of benevolence. The superior race was taking inferior people in hand, and guiding them for their own benefit until they were able to govern themselves. Consider that Washington today refuses to yield op-con to South Korea because it deems Seoul not yet ready to handle its own self-defense. Today, concepts of white (or Japanese) supremacy are no longer formally tolerable, and qualities said (against the evidence) to be unique to, or more fully developed in, the United States (industriousness, inventiveness, equality of opportunity) assume the role previously played by racial superiority.

The French imperial theorist, Jules Harmand, justified European domination by reference to its "superiority" which provided it with the moral legitimacy to lead in order to bestow its blessings on lesser people. The frequently offered justifications of US leadership come remarkably close to Harmand's justification of European empire. For example, US ideology constructs an international hierarchy, not of races, but of nations. It declares that the United States is the superior nation, or, if we like, the superior civilization. Its superiority is to be understood as based not merely on mechanical, economic, and military superiority, but on moral superiority, which US presidents and other ideologues define as commitment to "human rights and democracy" (conspicuously absent in US support for every dictator, king, emir, or sultan who facilitates Wall Street's wealth accumulation). The United States' right to direct the rest of humanity is presented as springing from its ostensible commitment to universal values which make it a shining beacon on a hill—the last best hope on earth, as John McCain emetically put it.

Additionally, US ideology presents US leadership as enforcing order on the world, and of bringing security to other countries, on whose soil US military personnel are implanted, for reasons we're to believe are due to the host countries lacking the aptitude or means to defend themselves. Like European civilization, which flattered itself that it was conferring its blessings on inferior people, the United States establishes missions in the name of spreading democracy, human rights, economic aid, and military assistance on lesser countries implied to be incapable of self-governance, self-defense, or economic policy-making. With these mental and material instruments which "lesser" countries lack and now receive, the inferior countries of the globe, owing to the largesse bestowed upon them by a selfless America, now gain the idea and ambition for a better existence, and the means of achieving it.

Cutting through the dense, all-surrounding fog of US imperialist ideology, the grand strategy of the US state is revealed to be one in which Washington imposes an economic order on the world, at the center of which lurks Wall Street's interests, and which is hostile to alternative economic orders that do not prioritize the interests of US capital—namely, those in which the state has a role to play in the economy, through planning or enterprise-ownership or tilting the playing field in favor of local business interests or imposing conditions to protect labor or the environment to a degree corporate America deems to be onerous. If we take "America" to represent the numerically insignificant class of billionaires at the apex of US political and economic life, then US grand strategy is to "corporate Americanize" the world economy—that is, to order it in the interests of Wall Street.

If that is the United States' grand global strategy, what then is its Korea strategy? When John Bolton, then US undersecretary of state for arms control, was asked this question in 2003 by *New York Times*' reporter Christopher Marquis, Marquis said that Bolton "strode over to a bookshelf, pulled off a volume and slapped it on the table. It was called 'The End of North Korea.'" That, Bolton said, "'is our policy.'"[31] Richard N. Haas, who was director of policy planning at the US State Department before becoming president of the Council on Foreign Relations, described the goal of US Korea policy as "ending North Korea's existence as an independent entity and reunifying the Korean Peninsula."[32] In other words, Washington's goal vis-à-vis Korea is to eliminate the DPRK, and bring the peninsula under the proximal control of the ROK, and therefore, under the distal control of Washington.

The reason Washington seeks this outcome has more to do with China, and secondarily Russia, than the DPRK itself. China and Russia are strong enough that they cannot be easily coerced by Washington into accepting subordinate roles in the Wall Street-defined global economic order. And both countries, China perhaps more strongly than Russia, have adopted "alternative economic models" which feature a strong role for state-owned enterprises, that vile apparatus of state-directed development so loathed by the owners of private capital. Washington would like to make both countries more open to exploitation by private US economic interests than they already are—that is, the goal is to order US-Chinese and US-Russian economic relationships so that they preponderantly benefit private US enterprises. To that end, Washington aspires to successfully pressure Moscow and Beijing to abandon *dirigiste* economic policies which favor local businesses and publicly-owned enterprises.

Washington also has concerns about the rise of China as an economic power. China's growing economic dominance threatens to supplant US capital from the Asia-Pacific region. For this reason, the Obama administration began to shift US military forces more heavily toward East Asia and the Pacific to accomplish the goal of what was called "balancing China's rise," where "balancing" was used as a euphemism for "eclipsing." This was the so-called "pivot" to the Far East. In addition, an investor agreement was championed, the Trans-Pacific Partnership, to thwart the establishment in Asia and Oceania of a Chinese-centered economic area. The impetus for the agreement was to prevent "countries like China" writing "the rules of the global economy," announced Obama. "We should write those rules," he declared.[33] Indeed, that is the whole point of US imperialism—to write the rules of the global economic order to favor US free enterprise. By "we" Obama meant Wall Street. Wall Street should write the rules of trade, commerce, and investment, to suit Wall Street's interests.

A US military presence in Korea, a country which shares a border with China and Russia, helps Washington pursue its goal of containing these two potential challengers to Wall Street's hegemony. Washington would like to block Beijing and Moscow from drawing other countries into the Chinese and Russian economic orbits. It also aspires to dislodge countries already strongly economically linked to China and Russia in order to absorb them into the Wall Street-centric global order. To this end, Washington spent $5 billion on regime change to draw Ukraine out of Russia's economic orbit, and into that of the US-superintended Western European economy.[34] While this has no direct relevance to Korea, it does illustrate the lengths to which Washington will go to capture markets and investment opportunities for corporate America.

Employing Korea as a fixed aircraft carrier, located menacingly on the peripheries of China and Russia, helps Washington create a "security architecture" for Japan. By playing the lead role in guaranteeing Japan's security against threats from China and Russia, the United States partly relieves Japan of the burden of funding its own self-defense. This in turn makes Japan militarily dependent on the United States, unable to use arms to challenge the US-defined global economic order in favor of one that is more directly congruent with the aspirations of Japanese investors and businesses.

Of course, a US troop presence in Korea is greatly facilitated by a subservient Korean state. The security needs of the state in the face of the hostility of the DPRK provide a public justification for the presence of tens of thousands of US military personnel. In reality, the ROK is militarily stronger than the DPRK and capable of defending itself. What's more, the ROK is sheltered beneath a US nuclear umbrella. Washington has declared on several occasions that an attack by North Korea on the ROK will be met by overwhelming force. In short, South Korea does not face a significant security threat from its northern neighbor. Pyongyang has no desire to commit suicide by crossing the armistice line, nor is it unaware of its limited military capabilities vis-à-vis its southern rival.

Pyongyang long ago abandoned any hope of unifying Korea by military means, recognizing that the imbalance in military strength in the ROK's favor makes the project quixotic. As an alternative, on many occasions North Korean leaders have proposed a peaceful reunification. Under the plan first sketched out by Kim Il-sung, the South Korean economy would continue to be capitalist, but US troops would quit the country. A united Korea, under one flag and one government, would strongly foster intra-Korean security. And yet, just as often as Pyongyang has proposed this arrangement, Seoul has rejected it. A US military presence, from the point of view of the ROK government, is non-negotiable. US troops must remain on the peninsula for US geostrategic reasons, to stifle China and Russia.

A related goal of Washington's Korea strategy is to use the ROK military as an Asian army in reserve. From Washington's point of view, the 600,000 active-duty personnel of the ROK military, and its 3.5 million reservists, all under US wartime command, are of far greater significance than the comparatively tiny US military garrison in Korea, numbering less than 30,000. From the very beginning, South Korean soldiers trained for, operated on behalf of, and fought for, US goals, under the direction of US advisers and US commanders. The model that journalist Marguerite Higgins observed in the late 1940s, of a comparatively small number of US soldiers training a much larger force of South Koreans to do the shooting for them, is still in place. The significant South Korean military is a chess piece to be moved about on a grand chess board by planners in Washington seeking domination of Eurasia.

This is in keeping with European colonial tradition. European powers sought colonies, not only as markets, sources of raw material, and soil on which to settle surplus populations, but also as sources of manpower for wars. The British, for example, drew heavily on India to supply their fighting forces in the Great War. Mohandas Gandhi, known today as a great advocate of non-violence, engaged in recruiting 500,000 of his compatriots "for the British army and did it with such zeal as to write to the Viceroy's personal secretary: 'I have an idea that if I became your recruiting agent in chief I might rain men on you.'"[35] The French, similarly, relied heavily on colonial troops. Canada contributed 600,000 of its citizens to the war, which was declared on its behalf by Britain, with not a single Canadian consulted. David Olusoga's book, *The World's War,* makes the point that World War I was truly a world war, largely because the European powers at the center of it called on their vast colonial possessions for manpower[36]. Hence, Washington's goal in Korea of maintaining a puppet state capable of disgorging trained military personnel to fight in US wars continues a hoary imperial tradition.

Washington seeks the end of the DPRK, to use John Bolton's description of US aims, because Pyongyang is against the aforementioned US goals. The DPRK has a people- and Korean-centered economy, rejects US leadership and the idea that countries can be arranged in a hierarchy with the United States at the top, and demands the exit of US troops from the peninsula. North Koreans also repudiate the idea of a US puppet state of Korea. While they're willing to tolerate a capitalist economy in the south under their proposed plan for reunification, they insist that Korea be a truly sovereign, independent state. No state can be truly independent if it hosts foreign troops on its soil and places its military under foreign command. No country can be truly sovereign if it submits to US leadership. Leadership, as Washington means it, is the negation of sovereignty; it is the process of yielding decision-making authority to Washington and, indirectly, to Wall Street.

CHAPTER 13

Sabotaging an Alternative to the US-Led Global Economic Order

"America always targets countries that have had an anti-colonial and anti-feudal revolution."—Domenico Losurdo[1]

The DPRK's constitution shows that the North Korean state has an orientation that is diametrically opposed to the Wall Street-directed project of empire building. The DPRK defines itself as a socialist state representing the interests of all Koreans, independent and politically, economically, culturally and militarily sovereign, self-sufficient and self-reliant in defense, and guided by the supreme national task of reunifying the country.

The ROK also seeks, so it says, "unification based on the principles of freedom and democracy,"[2] namely, on its own terms, though without defining what "freedom" and "democracy" are to be taken to mean. However, given the state's history of military dictatorship, concentration camps, extermination of leftists, and anti-Left secret police, we can infer that freedom and democracy are not intended in a universal sense, but as applying exclusively to right-wing collaborators with the US occupation. The ROK speaks of "unification" *contra* the DPRK's "re-unification," consistent with the former's shamelessly defining the Republic of Korea as encompassing the Korean peninsula in its entirety.

The DPRK defines itself as "a revolutionary State" originating "in the struggle to achieve the liberation of the homeland." The state, then, is conceived as developing out of the national revolution for independence. It is guided by *Juche* (self-reliance and independence in matters of politics, economics, culture and the military) and *Songun* (the primacy of self-defense in the allocation of resources). *Juche* is a reflection of the reality that only Koreans can vouchsafe Korea's freedom, and *Songun* a *sine qua non* in the face of the existential threat North Korea has faced from the United States from the very moment of its birth. Absent North Korea's policies of *Juche* and *Songun,* the patriot state would have long ago succumbed to the tyranny of the United States. Without US tyranny, the DPRK's *Juche* and *Songun* policies would not exist.

The constitution defines working people as sovereign, with peasants, blue-collar workers, white-collar workers, and soldiers constituting the only groups invested with sovereignty, in contradistinction to those who once generated income by renting out access to land (landlords) or industrial economic assets (mainly Japanese industrialists). With sovereignty vested in laborers as a class, the party which consciously seeks to represent labor, the Workers' Party, is accorded the lead role of organizing the country's affairs and defending its revolution and independence from the forces that aspire to return the country to the *status quo ante* of servitude to an empire.[3]

The external relations of the DPRK emphasize principles that a country which has historically been dominated by larger powers and has carried out a national revolution would wish other countries to embrace: equality, mutual respect, non-interference in the affairs of other nations, and mutual benefit—contrary to the unequal benefit which characterized Korea's external relations in the past, with great powers imposing relationships of domination which served their interests at Korea's expense, a situation that carries on in the relationship of the United States to South Korea today.[4]

The DPRK also pledges to "promote unity with people all over the world who defend their independence, and resolutely support and encourage the struggles of all people who oppose all forms of aggression and interference and fight for their countries' independence and national and class emancipation."[5] Speaking at the United Nations General Assembly in 2017, DPRK foreign minister Ri Yong-ho expressed his country's "strong support" and "solidarity" with Cuba in its fight to defend its national sovereignty, with Venezuela in its fight to defend its "national sovereignty and the cause of socialism," and with "the Syrian government fighting to protect its national sovereignty and security."[6] All three countries are targets of Wall Street-driven US hostility, and Pyongyang's support for them as a manifestation of its opposition to empire-building is yet another reason Washington seeks to bring about the end of the DPRK.

North Korea constitutionally prescribes a socialist and independent national economy. Two forms of economic enterprise are permitted: State-owned enterprises and cooperatively-owned ones. State-owned enterprises belong to the people as a whole. All natural resources, railways, air transport service, post and telecommunication establishments, as well as major factories and enterprises, ports, and banks are owned solely by the state. Land, farm machinery, and ships, as well as small and medium-sized factories and enterprises may be owned jointly by workers as cooperatives.[7] By contrast, the South Korean constitution prescribes an "economic order" based on "freedom and creative initiative of enterprises"—an allusion to "free" enterprise and the power of a minority to command the labor of others—and prohibits the nationalization of private enterprises "except to meet urgent necessities of national defense or the national economy."[8]

Capitalism, Joan Robinson is reputed to have once remarked, has no goal but to keep the show going. In contrast, North Korea sets "the steady improvement of the material and cultural standards of the people" as the "supreme" goal of its economic system and seeks to leverage technological gains to "free the working people from difficult, tiresome labor."[9] In contrast, employers in the capitalist worlds seek to leverage technological gains to free workers from their jobs and to free themselves from the burden of having to pay wages and salaries. The DPRK works toward a communist society in which technological advancement is harnessed to reduce the burden of ceaseless toil on everyday working lives in order to afford people time to realize their potential as creative human beings.

North Korea's constitution limits the work day to eight hours and mandates a shorter work day for people engaged in "arduous tasks."[10] The eight-hour workday's elevation to a matter of constitutional principle establishes the *bona fides* of the country's claim to have consciously formulated a people-centered system—designed to meet the needs of people, rather than people existing to keep a system of capital accumulation going—that contrasts sharply with the capital-centered economy of the ROK.

"South Koreans work the second-longest hours among OECD countries,"[11] with "many salaried workers at manufacturing companies working for more than 60 hours per week." Many "do not take their paid vacations."[12] A person working a forty-hour workweek without vacation puts in 2,080 hours per year. In 2014, South Koreans worked an average of 2,124 hours, more than a full week in excess of a forty-hour workweek without vacation, implying that many South Koreans aren't taking vacation at all; or are taking vacation, but are working punishingly long hours; or both. And that figure was down from the year 2000, when South Koreans averaged 2,512 hours at work per year, 40 percent higher than the number of hours US workers put in on the job and 80 percent more than Germans worked.[13] South Koreans, then, work some of the longest hours in the industrial world—which means that conditions haven't substantially improved from when Japan occupied Korea, and Koreans were compelled to toil long hours in Japanese-owned mines and factories.

Have long hours made South Koreans marvels of productivity? Apparently not. Despite their lengthy hours on the job, Koreans of the south are less productive than workers in other OECD countries.[14] ROK citizens work long hours, ultimately, not to make their lives better, but to enlarge the inherited fortunes of the pampered sons and daughters of the founders of the country's handful of giant conglomerates which dominate South Korea's economy. And the privileged children of the country's corporate elite use their accumulated wealth—accumulated for them by long-toiling South Koreans—to dominate those spaces of the country's political life left open to indigenous South Korean influence by the otherwise smothering influence of the United States. As a consequence, corporate royalty exists on a legal and material plane high above that of the overworked South Korean *hoi polloi*.

The DPRK proscribes child labor, building a minimum working age of 16 years into its highest legal document.[15] In contrast, South Korea's constitution recognizes that child labor exists in the south, but simply pledges that "special protection shall be accorded working children."[16] The ROK's "Labor Standards Act sets the minimum age for employment at 15 years but provides that children between the ages of 13 and 15 may work if granted a work permit by the Ministry of Employment and Labor."[17]

North Korea's constitution prescribes the organization of the country's economic life in accordance with a rationally developed plan. Planning aims at developing the economy in order to provide a steadily rising standard of living, while at the same time providing for the defense of the country against the unremitting threat of external aggression. Threats against the country are significant, indeed, existential, and originate in the hostile activities of a world power, the United States, which is many orders of magnitude more powerful militarily than North Korea. Even the ROK alone, with twice the population of North Korea and a GDP that is 45 times larger—and therefore the capability to field a much larger and more formidably equipped military—is a threat of considerable magnitude to the DPRK. In light of this, the DPRK's embrace of economic planning—a measure of coordination that Germany turned to in WWI, as did other countries in times of national emergency and war—may be seen as both a matter of necessity and choice. In fact, absent an ideological commitment to socialism, the framers of the DPRK constitution may well have committed the country to an economy guided by a consciously formulated plan as the best way to meet its defense requirements. Central planning in North Korea may, then, be overdetermined—a product of multiple independent and mutually reinforcing causes.

Contrary to a naïve, but widely held misconception about socialist countries, North Koreans are neither told what jobs they must work at nor paid the same wage. Instead, the DPRK constitution guarantees that all "able-bodied citizens may choose occupations in accordance with their wishes and skills" and further requires that North Koreans be "paid in accordance with the quantity and quality of their work," a basic socialist principle.[18] Lenin gave the principle a biblical flourish, quoting Paul the Apostle: "He who does not work, neither shall he eat."[19] Moreover, the state requires all Koreans to work, and maintains a program of full-employment. North Koreans are "provided with stable jobs and working conditions" and "unemployment is unknown."[20]

The major aim of Washington's Korea policy is to maintain a puppet state on the peninsula for the purposes of furnishing the Pentagon with two advantages: (1) a geostrategically important space from which to menace China and Russia as potential threats to a global economy open to US businesses on Wall Street's terms, and (2) access to a large body of "colonial" soldiers, trained and equipped by US advisers, interoperable with the US military, and under US command, which can be used in furtherance of US military projects in East Asia (and beyond). These goals explain Washington's hostility to the DPRK. The DPRK is the major organized force in pursuit of a mission of Korean independence that is fundamentally at odds with the goals of the United States on the peninsula. That the DPRK is socialist is also a reason for US hostility, but inasmuch as North Korean socialism reduces Wall Street's sphere of exploitation only marginally, it is but a nugatory cause of Washington's inimical stance toward the country; the opportunity cost to corporate America of the DPRK's people-centered economy is miniscule, since the opportunities for profit-making in northern Korea are insignificant on a world scale. In the simplest terms, the major reason US policy toward the DPRK is "the end of North Korea" is because Washington wants the Korean peninsula as a military outpost in East Asia, and the DPRK wants its country back.

Before moving on, a final point should be addressed about Washington's aims. Some argue that US policy toward the DPRK is not the demise of the country, but only its permanent weakening. Weakening the DPRK, the argument goes, allows Washington to attribute North Korea's crippled state to the DPRK's alternative, state-owned, enterprise-dependent economic model (rather than to the measures the United States has taken to weaken it). Undermining the DPRK, and then attributing its consequent difficulties to its economic model, has the advantage of strengthening the grip on the public mind of the US-led program of anti-communist slander, producing the mass misconception that alternatives to the US-superintended global economy are a "dead-end" (as Obama called them). It also keeps the DPRK functioning (though barely), so that it can be used as an alleged menace to justify a continued US military presence on the peninsula, and to generate billions of dollars in sales for the US arms industry. Citing North Korea, US president Donald Trump encouraged Japan and the ROK to purchase "massive amounts of military equipment" from the United States.[21] The idea is that if the DPRK didn't exist, it would have to be invented, otherwise the United States would be bereft of a pretext to station troops on Korean soil and the tributary states of the US empire would have difficulty justifying the transfer of their citizens' tax dollars to US weapons manufacturers.

To be sure, a pretext for permanently deploying troops to a foreign country is helpful in eliciting the consent of the people affected, but this argument implicitly assumes that there are no pretexts other than defense of South Korea from North Korean aggression for stationing US military personnel on the peninsula. On the contrary, the United States stations troops in scores of countries, none of which are divided, and yet pretexts for extending the Pentagon's reach to all these countries have never been difficult to construct. A sufficient pretext is a reference to a threat of some kind. Japan isn't divided, and there is no independent Japanese state from which a dependent US ally must be defended, yet there are 54,000 US troops in Japan.[22] The pretext for their presence is the need of the United States to protect an ally from external threat. Were the intra-Korean threat to the ROK eliminated, Washington would simply justify the placement of US military personnel and equipment on the Korean peninsula as a necessity of maintaining the security of an important ally against potential threats from China, or even Russia. Hence, there exists sufficient material to construct more than one pretext for US military occupation of Korea.

There are two broad methods Washington has used to weaken and undermine the DPRK, with a view to eventually destroying it: isolation and unremitting military pressure. Both are measures of economic warfare. Both are intended to bring about the economic collapse of North Korea. Isolation is achieved through a network of sanctions whose purpose is to deny the DPRK vital economic inputs, forcing it to rely on more expensive surrogates, or to suffer crippling shortages. Unremitting military pressure—that is, the unceasing threat of attack—keeps the DPRK on a permanent war footing, diverting critical resources from its civilian economy to military preparedness. The goal is to place the DPRK on the horns of a dilemma: allocate expenditures to the military sufficient to deter an attack and bankrupt the economy, or allocate sufficient expenditures to the civilian economy to allow it to thrive (as much as is possible with restricted access to inputs) at the expense of self-defense. Neither choice is palatable, and both lead eventually to disaster. As we'll see, the DPRK decision to build a nuclear weapons capability is a solution to the dilemma with which the United States has presented Pyongyang. Unremitting US hostility is the distal cause of the DPRK's decision to develop nuclear weapons.

The history of US sanctions on the DPRK is as old as the DPRK itself. From the moment the DPRK was founded in 1948, Washington has tried to block Pyongyang's access to vital economic inputs in order to make the state fail. As a rival to Washington's puppet state in Korea, and hostile to the US project of turning the peninsula into a stationary US aircraft carrier, the DPRK had to be destroyed.

The United States has attempted to bring about the quietus of other communist states and has used economic warfare in an effort to achieve this goal. Washington's initial offensive against China, beginning in the late 1940s, was "conducted predominantly on the economic front." Washington sought to plague China with "'a general standard of life around and below subsistence level', 'economic backwardness', and a 'cultural lag'." The Truman administration declared that there must be "'a heavy and long protracted cost to the whole social structure.' A 'state of chaos' and 'catastrophic economic situation' must ultimately be created, leading China 'toward disaster', 'collapse'." Successive administrations pursued the same policy, expanding the embargo to include "medicine, tractors and fertilisers." Walt W. Rostow, an anti-communist economist and principal player in the 1960s US foreign policy establishment, applauded US economic warfare for having retarded China's economic development by decades. "Metaphorically speaking," remarked political scientist Edward Luttwak, "it might be said that a ban of Chinese imports is the nuclear weapon that America keeps pointed at China."[23]

Sanctions have effects equivalent to a nuclear attack. In 1999, the political scientists John Mueller and Karl Mueller wrote an important paper in *Foreign Affairs*, the journal of the Council on Foreign Relations, in which they argued that economic sanctions "may have contributed to more deaths during the post-Cold War era than all weapons of mass destruction throughout history."[24] The scholars tallied deaths due to the use of weapons of mass destruction as follows: "The atomic bombings of Hiroshima and Nagasaki together killed more than 100,000 people, and at a high estimate suggests that some 80,000 died from chemical weapons in World War I. If one adds the deaths from later uses of chemical weapons in war or warlike situations ... as well as deaths caused by the intentional or accidental use of biological weapons and ballistic missiles, the resulting total comes to well under 400,000."[25] By contrast, the Allied economic blockade of Germany during the Great War is estimated to have caused almost twice as many deaths through hunger and malnutrition[26] while "as many as 576,000 Iraqi children may have died" from food scarcity-related diseases caused "by economic sanctions imposed by the Security Council, according to two scientists who surveyed the country for the Food and Agriculture Organization," whose findings were reported in the *Lancet*, the journal of the British Medical Association.[27]

"So long as they can coordinate their efforts," the two political scientists wrote, "the big countries have at their disposal a credible, inexpensive and potent weapon for use against small and medium-sized foes. The dominant powers have shown that they can inflict enormous pain at remarkably little cost to themselves or the global economy. Indeed, in a matter of months or years whole economies can be devastated."[28] And part of the devastation can be a death toll which exceeds that producible by a nuclear attack.

Perhaps Cuba is most comparable to the DPRK as a target of US economic warfare. "Of all the methods devised to obtain a change of regime, none seemed as compelling as the use of political isolation and economic sanctions," wrote the historian Louis A. Perez Jr. "Officially designated as an 'economic denial program', sanctions expanded into a full-blown policy protocol designed to induce economic hardship in Cuba. It should not be supposed that the Cuban people were unintended 'collateral damage' of U.S. policy. On the contrary, the Cuban people were the target. Cubans were held responsible for, and made to bear the consequences of, the programs and policies of their government."[29]

Sanctions were designed to create economic chaos, in order to promote disaffection and "inflict adversity as a permanent condition of daily life." According to US assistant Secretary of State Thomas Mann, US economic warfare aimed to "exert a serious pressure on the Cuban economy and contribute to the growing dissatisfaction and unrest in the country." US President Dwight Eisenhower defined the aim of sanctions as the creation of "conditions which will bring home to the Cuban people the cost of Castro's policies and of his Soviet orientation." Eisenhower anticipated that "as the situation unfolds, we shall be obliged to take further economic measures which will have the effect of impressing on the Cuban people the cost of this communist orientation." The US president concluded that, "If they are hungry," Cubans "will throw Castro out."[30] Perez added:

> The intent was to "weaken [the Castro government] economically," explained one State Department briefing paper, to "promote internal dissension; erode its internal political support ... [and] seek to create conditions conducive to incipient rebellion." Sanctions were designed to create "the necessary preconditions for nationalist upheaval inside Cuba," the State Department Bureau of Intelligence and Research explained, to obtain the downfall of the Castro government "as a result of internal stresses and in response to forces largely, if not wholly, unattributable to the U.S." The idea was to use "economic pressures . . . in order to engender more public discomfort and discontent," explained Assistant Secretary Rubottom, in the form of "a relentless, firm pressure, [and] a steady turning of the screw." The "only foreseeable means of alienating internal support," Deputy Assistant Secretary of State Lester Mallory concluded in 1960, "is through disenchantment and disaffection based on economic dissatisfaction and hardship." Mallory recommended that "every possible means should be undertaken promptly to weaken the economic life of Cuba, . . . [to deny] money and supplies to Cuba, to decrease monetary and real wages, to bring about hunger, desperation and [the] overthrow of government."[31]

Washington has aimed its sanctions at governments which adopt alternative, state-owned, enterprise-dependent, economic models which compete with Washington's Wall Street-centric model of an open (to US exploitation) world economy. One of the objectives of carrying out economic warfare against competing economic models is to sabotage them, so that they appear to be inferior alternatives to Washington's preferred model. Essential to this approach is to conceal the damage Washington's economic warfare has wrought on an economy and to attribute the targeted state's economic travails to the adoption of the wrong economic model.

The experiment with socialism, it is said, showed that public ownership and planning of the economy simply doesn't work. Didn't socialism fail in the USSR and Eastern Europe? Not at all. If success is defined as full employment and an unremittingly growing economy, then Soviet socialism was an unqualified success.

From the moment in 1928 that the Soviet economy became publicly owned and planned (i.e., socialist), to the point in 1989 that it was steered by Mikhail Gorbachev in a free market direction, Soviet GDP per capita growth exceeded that of all other countries but Japan, South Korea, and Taiwan. GDP per person grew by a factor of 5.2, compared with 4.0 for Western Europe and 3.3 for the Western European offshoots (the USA, Canada, Australia, and New Zealand).[32] In other words, over the period in which its publicly owned planned economy was in place, the USSR's record in raising incomes was better than that of the major industrialized capitalist countries. The Soviet Union's robust growth over this period is all the more impressive considering that the period includes the war years when a major assault by Nazi Germany left a trail of utter destruction in its wake. The German invaders destroyed over 1,500 cities and towns, along with 70,000 villages, 31,000 factories, and nearly 100 million head of livestock.[33]

Soviet economic growth was highest until 1970, at which point expansion of the Soviet economy began to slow. However, even during this so-called (and misnamed) post-1970 period of stagnation, GDP per capita grew 27 percent.[34] And importantly, during the years of socialism, the Soviet economy never contracted. Contraction only came in the final years, when the Gorbachev government abandoned central planning and embraced markets as a method of regulating all economic activity.

In reality, the experience of the Soviet Union demonstrates that socialism did, indeed, work. However, the great powers went to extraordinary lengths to sabotage it so that it wouldn't. From its infancy, the Soviet Union was menaced by a program of sabotage no different from that which Washington has directed at the DPRK. In 1920, the Bolsheviks complained that "Russia, thanks to her Soviet form of economy, could supply Europe ... with double and triple the quantity of foodstuffs and raw materials that Tsarist Russia used to supply. Instead of this, Anglo-French imperialism has compelled the Toilers' Republic to devote all its forces to self-defense."[35] Throughout the Soviet Union's seven decades of existence, a substantial fraction of its budget was allocated to the military as an imperative of self-defense against aggressive capitalist powers, first imperial Britain and imperial France, followed by the Axis powers (especially Nazi Germany), and then the United States. In all these cases, the USSR had to play catch-up against hostile powers which had economies many times larger, and were therefore capable of fielding militaries many times stronger at a lighter cost burden relative to GDP. Without the crippling effects of incessant military pressure, the Soviet economy would very likely have posted even stronger growth.

North Korea finds itself in the same situation as a victim of military pressure imposed by a stronger foe. But there's a critical difference. The Soviet Union was a vast continental country containing almost all the inputs a modern industrial economy needed to thrive, including oceans of oil. It was therefore virtually invulnerable to blockade and could draw on its own natural resources to fuel its economy. In contrast, Cuba and the DPRK, small countries with limited resources, depend on trade to obtain vital economic inputs. Consequently, Washington is in a better position to create havoc on the Cuban and North Korean economies than it was on the Soviet economy, and to attribute the resulting chaos to socialism.

This point is "essential to the US purpose, for central to US objectives" is "the need to maintain the appearance that the collapse of" the DPRK or Cuba, should they collapse, is "the result of conditions from within" and "the product of government economic mismanagement ... thereby avoiding appearances of US involvement."[36] According to Perez:

> In Cuba, [the] "United States sought to produce disarray in the Cuban economy but in such a fashion as to lay responsibility directly on Fidel Castro. The goal of the United States ... was to make 'Castro's downfall seem to be the result of his own mistakes'. [The US ambassador] in Havana early stressed the importance of appearance: 'It is important that the inevitable downfall of the present Government not be attributed to any important extent to economic sanctions from the United States as a major factor.' The United States ... sought 'to make it clear that when Castro fell, his overthrow would be due to inside and not outside causes'! This was the purport of a lengthy memorandum by George Denney, Director of State Department Bureau of Intelligence

and Research. The idea was to eliminate Castro 'without resort to invasion or attributable acts of violence and violations of international law', specifically by 'creating the necessary preconditions for nationalist upheaval inside Cuba ... as a result of internal stresses and in response to forces largely, if not wholly, unattributable to the US'. Denney continued: If the Castro Communist experiment will appear to have failed not on its own merits but as a result of obvious or inadequately disguised US intervention, or as a consequence of the fraudulent invocation ... of a unilateral and lopsided Monroe Doctrine, the validity of Castro's revolutionary course might remain unquestioned. This Castro Communist experiment constitutes a genuine social revolution, albeit a perverted one. If it is interrupted by the force of the world's foremost 'imperialist' and 'capitalist' power in the absence of a major provocation, such action will discredit the US and tend to validate the uncompleted experiment ... Direct US assistance should be avoided ... Excessive US or even foreign assistance or involvement will become known and thus tend to sap nationalist initiative, lessen revolutionary motivation and appeal, and allow Castro convincingly to blame the US."[37]

An egregious example of blaming the target of sanctions for the sanctions' effects was provided in 2010 by Amnesty International. The Western human rights organization released a report that condemned the DPRK government for failing to meet "its obligations to respect, protect and fulfil the right to health of its citizens," citing "significant deprivation in [North Koreans'] enjoyment of the right to adequate care, in large part due to failed or counterproductive government policies." The report documented rundown healthcare facilities which operated "with frequent power cuts and no heat" and medical personnel who "often do not receive salaries, and many hospitals [that] function without medicines and essentials." Horrific stories were recounted of major operations carried out without anesthesia. Whether the report was accurate or not is difficult to determine, but if we assume, for the sake of argument, that it was, the assessment suffered from a glaring flaw: it made not a single reference, direct or indirect, to the US-led campaign of economic strangulation that has lasted the better part of a century and has been designed to make the DPRK—along with its healthcare system—fail.[38] The report's conclusion was tantamount to attributing the economic devastation caused by the Nazi assault on the Soviet Union to the alleged failures of Soviet policy, rather than the scorched earth policy of Nazi Germany, with the Nazi invasion treated as if it had never happened.

US sanctions against the DPRK have included the following:

- limits on the export of goods and services
- prohibition of most foreign aid and agricultural sales
- a ban on Export-Import Bank funding
- denial of favorable trade terms
- prohibition of imports from North Korea
- blocking of any loan or funding through international financial institutions
- limits on export licensing of food and medicine for export to North Korea
- a ban on government financing of food and medicine exports to North Korea
- prohibition on import and export transactions related to transportation
- a ban on dual-use exports (i.e., civilian goods that could be adapted to military purposes)
- prohibition on certain commercial banking transactions[39]

In recent years, US sanctions have been complemented by "efforts to freeze assets and cut off financial flows"[40] by blocking banks that deal with North Korean companies from access to the US banking system. The intended effect is to make the DPRK a banking pariah that no bank in the world will touch. Former US President George W. Bush was "determined to squeeze" North Korea "with every financial sanction possible" until its economy collapsed.[41] The Trump administration took up the same cudgel and wielded it with even fiercer determination.

Washington has also acted to deepen the bite of sanctions, pressing other countries, including the DPRK's chief trading partner, China, to join its campaign of economic warfare against a state it faults for maintaining a Marxist-Leninist system and non-market economy.[42] This has included the sponsoring of a United Nations Security Council resolution compelling all nations to refrain for exporting dual-use items to North Korea (a repeat of the sanctions regime that led to the crumbling of Iraq's healthcare system in the 1990s). Dual-use items are goods that have important civilian uses but might also be used for military purposes. In Arab nationalist Iraq, medical "diagnostic techniques that use radioactive particles, once common in [the country, were] banned under [UN] sanctions, and plastic bags needed for blood transfusions [were] restricted."[43] On October 14, 2006 the United Nations Security Council banned the export to the DPRK of any goods, including those used for civilian purposes, which could contribute to WMD-related programs—the very same sanctions that led, at minimum, to hundreds of thousands of Iraqi deaths in the 1990s when the export of potentially weapons-related material, also essential to the maintenance of sanitation, water treatment, and healthcare infrastructure, was held up or blocked.

Kaesong, a vast industrial park of South Korean factories situated near the armistice line (on the DPRK side) that employed North Korean workers, provides an example of how all-encompassing the dual-use sanctions net has been cast. "U.S. officials blocked the installation of a South Korean switchboard system at Kaesong on the ground that the equipment contained components that could have been adapted for military use. As a result, the 15 companies that operated at Kaesong shared a single phone line, and messages often had to be hand-delivered across the border."[44] While dual-use sanctions may appear to be targeted, just about any item required for the provision of basic healthcare, sanitation, and education—chlorine, syringes, x-ray equipment, medical isotopes, blood transfusion bags, even graphite for pencils—can be construed to have military uses and therefore banned for export. One Western official who worked on her country's North Korea desk spent much of her time reviewing material for export to the DPRK to determine whether it could be used for military purposes, including corrugated metal for roofing. Since virtually any item has potential military uses, virtually every export item was blocked.

The DPRK is so heavily sanctioned—the most sanctioned country on earth, according to George W. Bush—that for years US officials doubted that additional sanctions could make any difference. Obama, echoing his predecessor, called the DPRK "the most isolated nation on earth," and, furthermore, "doubted whether new sanctions would change its behavior."[45] The *New York Times* noted that North Korea "is under perhaps the heaviest sanctions on earth,"[46] while the *Wall Street Journal* added that "North Korea is already an isolated nation, so there isn't much more economic pressure the U.S. can bring to bear,"[47] while historian Bruce Cumings observed that the DPRK has "been isolated by the United States since the regime was formed in 1948."[48]

While economic warfare hasn't brought about the capitulation of Pyongyang that Washington has long sought, it's clear that the US-led campaign of economic warfare has set back the DPRK's economic development. According to a former DPRK diplomat, the decades since the dissolution of the socialist bloc, which North Korea relied on for trade, have been the most difficult:

> This had a major impact on our economy. And with the disappearance of the USSR, the US moved to a policy of intensification, believing that our days were numbered. The US intensified its economic blockade and its military threat. They stopped all financial transactions between the DPRK and the rest of the world. The US controls the flow of foreign currency: if they say that any bank will be the target of sanctions if it does business with the DPRK, then obviously that bank has to go along with them. The US issued such an ultimatum to all companies: if they do business with North Korea, they will be subject to sanctions by the US. This is still in place. The US government thought that if they cut economic relations between the DPRK and the rest of the world, we would have to submit to them. The only reason that we have been able to survive is the single-hearted unity of the people. The people united firmly around the leadership. We worked extremely hard to solve our problems by ourselves.[49]

In June 2017, the foreign ministry of the DPRK released a statement on US economic warfare. US sanctions, the ministry said, had "grown utterly vicious and barbaric" and represented an attempt to "obliterate the rights to existence and development of the state and people of the DPRK, destroy modern civilization and bring [North Korea] back into medieval darkness." The ministry cited a "prohibition on the export of underground resources including coal" and sanctions on dual-use items as measures that were "having adverse consequences for the people's livelihood and normal economic activities." So all-encompassing were sanctions that even the importation of "frozen chicken, cosmetics packaging and zipper tab production equipment and materials as well as frequency stabilizers and voltage regulators to be used at fishery stations" was blocked. UNICEF attempted to import "24.4 tons of malaria mosquito repellent" with no success. Over a dozen "mobile X-ray units and the reagent for diagnosis of tuberculosis" were held up for delivery by six months because they were designated as dual-use items. "In January 2017, a hundred thousand ampoules of ephedrine being imported by a health company of the DPRK" were blocked.[50] One DPRK source estimated that the damage done by economic sanctions and blockade to 2005 is astronomical.[51]

On top of economic warfare, North Korea has faced unceasing US military hostility. The US military has had a continuous presence on the Korean peninsula since 1945, and only for a brief period of roughly 12 months, from the summer of 1949 to the summer of 1950, have there been less than tens of thousands of US troops on Korean soil. Over the same period, the US has had an unceasing and major military presence in nearby Japan. US warships patrol the DPRK's maritime borders, and US warplanes, including B-2 (Swan of Death) strategic bombers fly menacingly close to its airspace, prowling at times only 12 nautical miles from the North Korean coastline. Washington kept battlefield nuclear weapons on the Korean peninsula from the late 1950s to the early 1990s and refuses to renounce the first strike use of strategic nuclear weapons against North Korea—and refused to do so even before Pyongyang acquired its own nuclear weapons capability! Indeed, US nuclear doctrine allows for the use of nuclear weapons in response to any North Korean attack, conventional or otherwise, against any country the United States deems to be an ally or partner.[52]

North Korea hasn't been the only country to face Washington's hostile treatment. What Felix Greene wrote in 1970 of China and Cuba remains true of North Korea today:

> The United States imposed a 100 percent embargo on trade with these countries; she employs great pressure to prevent her allies from trading with them; she arms and finances their enemies; she harasses their shipping; she threatens them with atomic missiles which she announces are pre-targeted and pre-programmed to destroy their major cities; her spy ships prowl just beyond these countries' legal territorial waters; her reconnaissance planes fly constantly over their territory. And having done all in their power to disrupt these countries' efforts to rebuild their societies by means of blockades to prevent essential goods from reaching them, any temporary difficulties and setbacks these countries may encounter are magnified and exaggerated and presented as proof that a socialist revolutionary government is 'unworkable'.[53]

Faced with much larger, hostile adversaries, Pyongyang has been forced to channel a crushingly large percentage of its GDP into defense. In absolute numbers, the DPRK's military expenditures are small—an estimated $3.4 billion to $9.5 billion per annum,[54] roughly on par, as already noted, with the budget of the New York City Police Department. In contrast, the ROK's military budget was $36 billion in 2017 and was scheduled to increase to $38 billion in 2018—four to eleven times larger than the DPRK's.[55] But as a percentage of its economy, North Korea's military outlays are colossal. Estimates vary, but Pyongyang's military expenditures are thought to fall somewhere between 15 and 25 percent of the DPRK's gross domestic product.[56] That puts North Korea in a class all its own. In 2015, the average country spent 2.2 percent of its GDP on its military. The United States spent 3.3 percent and the ROK 2.6 percent.[57] However, Pyongyang's large military expenditure relative to GDP is not out of the ordinary for a country at war. In World War II—a war in which the United States faced no existential threat—US military expense as a percentage of GDP reached as high as 38 percent.[58] Considering that the DPRK is in both a *de jure* and *de facto* state of (cold) war with the United States, South Korea, and other US satellites, and that the military threat to North Korea posed by these forces is existential, the country's significant military outlays as a percentage of the GDP are far from anomalous. But they are onerous. South Korea is able to spend a very modest percentage of its GDP on its military and still vastly outspend its northern neighbor in absolute terms because it has a much larger economy. The greater relative size of South Korea's economy is partly a function of differences in population size. South Korea has roughly twice the population of North Korea. Partly it's a corollary of decades of US-led economic warfare against the DPRK, which has stunted North Korea's economic development. And partly it's a consequence of Washington taking unusual steps to accelerate South Korea's economic growth so that it would outpace its northern rival.

According to Bruce Cumings, during the Cold War, the "United States was willing to indulge certain countries, especially places like [South] Korea sitting on the fault lines of the Cold War, so that they could become self-supporting and compete in world markets."[59] One of the ways Washington indulged the ROK was through direct injections of aid. "Official sources say that about $12 billion of the [US] treasury went to [South] Korea in the years 1945-1965"[60]—about $108 billion in today's dollars. The DPRK also received aid from the socialist bloc, but on nowhere near the same scale. In 1965, when South Korea's exports totaled only $200 million, Seoul received loans and grants from Japan of $500 million and direct investment from Japanese enterprises of $200 million—an injection of $700 million in total, more than three times the amount of the ROK's exports, about $5.4 billion in today's dollars.[61]

Seoul's deployment of hundreds of thousands troops to Vietnam on behalf of Washington's war of aggression on Ho Chi Minh's liberation forces netted the ROK billions of dollars in aid. Washington paid Seoul lucre of $7.5 million for every mercenary division it committed to the war. From 1965 to 1970, the South Korean mercenary army earned the state about $1 billion, equal to nearly $8 billion in 2018. Mercenary lucre accounted for an estimated 7 to 8 percent of South Korea's GDP and for almost one-fifth of its total foreign earnings.[62] Additionally, Vietnam became a bonanza for South Korean firms, upon whom Washington showered a wealth of war-related contracts, especially for steel and transportation equipment. As already noted, almost all of the ROK's steel production during this period was absorbed by the US war effort in Vietnam.[63]

At the same time, Washington allowed Seoul to pursue an economic development model that Obama would later decry as a dead-end. US policy turned a blind eye toward the ROK's pursuit of "a state-led neomercantalist program of protectionism at home and export-led growth abroad, which relied above all on the openness of the vast [US] market"—"the essence of the 'Asian development state'," as Bruce Cumings described it. The South Korean economy was to be an engine "of economic growth by any means necessary, because of the great value [it] had in providing an alternative model of development in the global struggle with communism."[64] And yet the model very much resembled the paradigm of state-directed economic development favored by the USSR and China.

When Park Chung-hee came to power in 1961, he immediately called for economic self-sufficiency[65] and implemented a program of import substitution—that is, replacement of foreign imports with domestic production. Keen to secure export markets for corporate America, Washington had traditionally looked unfavorably upon countries which substituted domestic goods for US exports as a development strategy, but equally keen to facilitate South Korea's economic development, the United States offered Park almost unqualified support for this otherwise routinely deplored policy.[66] Park also introduced a succession of five-year plans prepared by an Economic Planning Board,[67] recalling the five-year plans of the USSR, and multi-year plans of the DPRK. Moreover:

> [t]he government owned all the banks, so it could direct the life blood of business—credit. Some big projects were undertaken directly by state-owned enterprises—the steel maker, POSCO, being the best example—although the country had a pragmatic, rather than ideological, attitude to the issue of state ownership. If private enterprises worked well, that was fine; if they did not invest in important areas, the government had no qualms about setting up state-owned enterprises ... and if some private enterprises were mismanaged, the government often took them over, restructured them, and usually (but not always) sold them off again.[68]

Every measure of economic development Washington deplored, and punished countries for pursuing, Washington approved, in order to ensure that South Korea developed faster than its communist rival to the north. Chang Ha-Joon, author of *Bad Samaritans: The Myth of Free Trade and the Secret History of Capitalism*, added that:

> [The South] Korean government also had absolute control over scarce foreign exchange (violation of foreign exchange controls could be punished with the death penalty). When combined with a carefully designed list of priorities in the use of foreign exchange, it ensured that hard-earned foreign currencies were used for importing vital machinery and industrial inputs. The [South] Korean government heavily controlled foreign investment as well, welcoming it with open arms in certain sectors while shutting it out completely in others, according to the evolving national development plan. It also had a lax attitude towards foreign patents, encouraging 'reverse engineering' and overlooking 'pirating' of patented products.[69]

A revisionist retelling of the story of South Korea's economic take-off locates the cause of the ROK's robust growth in Seoul's acceptance and vigorous pursuit of the very same open-economy, pro-foreign investment, free-trade, free-enterprise model that today Washington insists every country adopt. And yet the truth is quite the opposite. The United States temporarily bestowed upon the ROK the dual advantages of significant economic aid accompanied by exemption from the stifling constraints on former colonial countries of Washington's open-economy model. The intended aim was to hothouse the South Korean economy. At the same time, the United States undertook to do whatever it could to cripple the economy of its puppet state's northern rival, both directly, through economic warfare and unceasing military threat, and indirectly, by seeking to weaken, undermine, and eventually destroy the socialist bloc on which the DPRK depended for trade. And, then, when these efforts had come to fruition, and the South Korean economy began to grow at a faster clip than that of North Korea, Washington masked the exogenous role its policy had played in the divergence and attributed the outcome to endogenous variables—the alleged failures and inadequacies of communism, on the one hand, and the merits of South Korea's capitalism, on the other.

Hence, owing to the United States nurturing the South Korean economy and sabotaging that of the DPRK, so that a yawning chasm opened up between the two of them, Seoul is able to (and does) fund its military on a far grander scale than is within the capability of its northern rival. With military expenditures of only 2.6 percent of its GDP the ROK is able to outspend the DPRK in absolute terms many times over. It is impossible for Pyongyang to match this level of expenditure. Indeed, despite allocating as much as one-quarter of its GDP to defense, North Korea is still vastly outspent by Seoul. Far from posing a military threat to the ROK, the DPRK is so militarily weak by comparison that it is forced to sacrifice its civilian economy in order to mount even a fragile defense. The process is self-amplifying. The more Pyongyang sacrifices its civilian economy to its military, the more the gulf widens between the two countries' economies. The only hope for the DPRK is to break the vicious cycle.

The vicious cycle is supported by incessant military pressure exerted by Washington and its auxiliary South Korean military on North Korea via annual large-scale war games, the largest on the planet, and Washington's unremitting threat of overwhelming attack.

The United States has carried out annual anti-DPRK war game exercises with South Korea since 1976, in the form of what today are called the Ulchi-Freedom Guardian exercises, conducted during the summer, and the Key Resolve exercises, conducted in the late winter and early spring.

The Key Resolve exercises of March and April 2016 were the largest ever, involving 300,000 South Korean troops and 17,000 US military personnel. The exercises were structured around a hypothetical invasion of North Korea for the purpose of "recovering" the entire territory of the peninsula. Troops rehearsed "decapitation"—which is to say, killing North Korean leaders—and seizing the DPRK's ballistic missiles and nuclear weapons arsenal.[70] In advance of the simulated invasion, the United States flew four advanced F-22 stealth fighter jets over South Korea.[71] Every element of the exercise, from the mobilization of hundreds of thousands of troops, to the Pentagon bringing advanced weaponry onto the peninsula, was intended to force the North Koreans to exhaust their limited resources by inducing them to react to the threat by pouring money into mobilization of their own forces to prepare for a possible attack.

In 2013, the White House approved a detailed plan, called 'the playbook,' to ratchet up tension with North Korea during that year's Key Resolve exercises. The plan called for low-altitude B-52 bomber flights over the Korean peninsula. These were carried out in early March. A few weeks later, two nuclear-capable B-2 stealth bombers dropped dummy payloads on a South Korean missile range. The flights were deliberately conducted in broad daylight at low altitude, according to a US defense official, to produce the intended minatory effect. "We could fly it at night, but the point was for them to see it."[72] A few days later, the Pentagon deployed two advanced F-22 warplanes to South Korea, also part of the 'play-book' plan to intimidate Pyongyang. The White House, according to the *Wall Street Journal*, knew that the North Koreans would react by threatening to retaliate against the United States and South Korea. Pentagon officials acknowledged that North Korean military officers are particularly agitated by bomber flights because of memories of the destruction wrought from the air during the Korean War.[73]

The summer 2017 Ulchi-Freedom Guardian exercises also involved a series of visits to the Korean peninsula by advanced US strategic bombers to practice "attack capabilities," accompanied by ROK and Japanese warplanes. At the same time, Washington directed a Navy aircraft carrier group to the region—all to North Korea's consternation, the *Wall Street Journal* noted.[74] The exercises involved 50,000 ROK soldiers, 17,500 US troops (of which 3,000 came from outside the peninsula) along with the participation of military personnel from seven US satellite countries (including Canada, Australia, New Zealand, Columbia, Denmark, the Netherlands, and the UK) In addition, almost half a million ROK public employees participated in the simulation.[75]

War game exercises are provocative for the obvious reason that the mobilization of large numbers of troops and equipment is indistinguishable from the marshaling of armed forces for an invasion. How can the DPRK military leadership know whether the arrival of a US Navy aircraft carrier group in nearby waters, flights by strategic bombers, and the mobilization of 350,000 troops, is a rehearsal for an invasion, or the start of one? These mobilizations, note the DPRK, may "go over to an actual war any time"[76] and are an opportunity for a preventive attack.[77] Consequently, twice a year (at minimum), the DPRK is forced onto a war footing to defend itself against a possible invasion, placing an enormous strain on its economy. At other times, as in 2017, US exercises become unremitting, with different mobilizations following in rapid succession, forcing the KPA to maintain an unflagging and exhausting state of readiness. While the United States and South Korea, with much larger economies, can easily afford biannual simulations of an attack, and can also readily afford to launch a string of successive troop and equipment mobilizations, for Pyongyang, the cost of mobilizing to deter an attack is crippling. As the *Wall Street Journal* noted:

> North Korea upped the tempo of its training flights sixfold, to 700 a day, on the first day of the 2013 U.S. and South Korean "Key Resolve" annual maneuvers. That naturally sent Seoul's analysts to their calculators, concluding triumphantly that the North was either draining its war reserve or starving its civilian economy of fuel ... When the U.S. and Japanese navies are operating in nearby waters, the North must keep its jets in the air and defenses mobilized. When U.S. and South Korean ... troops are on the move near its border, it must activate troops in response. ... The U.S. and its allies can maintain their mobilization virtually indefinitely. North Korea can't. Motor fuel is a sore point, but so are food, equipment, and sanitation and health care for troops in the field.[78]

In late October and early November of 2017, the Pentagon directed three US carrier strike groups to sail to the waters east of Korea, which Koreans know as the East Sea and the Japanese call the Sea of Japan. A US naval force this large hadn't been assembled in ten years, and if the North Koreans regarded the anomaly as a premonitory sign of an impending attack, it's likely that this was the reaction Washington intended to produce. In the midst of what would almost certainly look to North Korean military authorities to be the marshaling of a massive strike force for an attack, a formation of US B1-B strategic bombers took off from Anderson Air Force Base at Guam, passed over Okinawa, and headed toward Jeju Island, off the southern tip of Korea. From there the bombers turned north, picked up an escort of US and ROK jetfighters, and proceeded directly toward the DPRK. Almost certainly, alarm bells went off at KPA headquarters. We can assume the DPRK's aging jet fighters were scrambled, using up scarce aviation fuel. Before reaching the armistice line, the bombers quickly changed course, and diverted to a US firing range, where they dropped a dummy payload, and then headed home.[79] Later, the DPRK media referred to the bomber flight as a "surprise nuclear strike drill," but during the flight, North Korean generals would surely have wondered whether they were witnessing a drill or the start of a nuclear attack. the *Wall Street Journal* noted that US bombers had "buzzed" North Korea, an indisputable act of intimidation—and clearly a provocation—from a state that never tires of accusing North Korea of engaging in provocative acts. During the Reagan years, the United States had used a similar approach to unnerve the Soviets. "A squadron [of nuclear bombers] would fly straight at Soviet airspace, and [Soviet] radars would light up and units would go on alert. Then at the last minute the squadron would peel off and return home."[80]

The objective of anti-DPRK mobilizations by the United States, the ROK, and other US tributaries, is to exhaust the North Korean economy—to hobble it so badly that it fails, or to force the North Koreans to let down their guard. That's certainly the conclusion Pyongyang has drawn. The "U.S. seeks to steadily escalate tension on the Korean Peninsula," according to North Korea's official news agency, KCNA, "through ceaseless joint military exercises and thus make the DPRK exhausted and slacken its alertness."[81] The United States, says *Rodong Sinmun*, the newspaper of the ruling Workers' Party, "is plugging the DPRK into an arms race through ceaseless war drills and arms build-up in a sinister bid to throw hurdles in its efforts to develop its economy and improve the standard of its people's living and force them to live under a touch-and-go situation and thus seek an opportunity for a pre-emptive attack upon it."[82] It's difficult to argue with this assessment.

US officials regularly dismiss North Korean complaints that the US-led war games are provocations, by pointing out that the annual mobilizations for war are routine. But the recurring nature of the exercises hardly makes them less provocative—just routinely provocative. No mistake should be made that the exercises could ever be seen by any country against which they were directed as non-threatening, or even that Washington truly believes they can be sincerely characterized as such. This can be seen in the US reaction to far less menacing war games carried out by US adversaries. NATO officials argue that Russian exercises "right up against the borders, with a lot of troops," are "extraordinarily provocative"[83] and "destabilizing."[84] When Russia carried out war games in Belarus in the summer of 2017—which involved less than 40,000 troops and civilians,[85] a small fraction of the number of military and civilian personnel who took part in the 2016 Key Resolve exercises on the Korean peninsula—Russian President Vladimir Putin was accused of "saber-rattling" and the exercises were said to raise "fears of aggression."[86] NATO members, "particularly the Baltic States, worried that the drills were a precursor to a potential invasion of their territories."[87] Western analysts expressed fear that Russia's exercises heightened "the risk of an accident or miscalculation that could touch off a crisis."[88] Additionally, concerns were raised that an "error by an alliance or Russian soldier, such as misreading a drill as an aggressive act, could quickly escalate into a crisis if one side were to respond with force. An incident such as a crashed jet fighter could also raise questions about whether an accident or aggression by the other side occurred."[89]

All of these concerns are legitimate. But they apply just as strongly to US-ROK mobilizations, if not more so, considering that the US-led exercises are on an altogether larger scale, and therefore the possibility of error is all the greater. According to the *Hankyoreh*, a liberal South Korean newspaper, "The biggest concern among experts is that the growing scale of joint military exercises has increased the potential for misunderstanding by Pyongyang. Robert Litwak, director of international security studies for the Wilson Center, told the *Hankyoreh* in a March [2017] interview that exercises [may look] like a defensive maneuver for us, [but] from North Korea's perspective, they may think we're preparing an attack when you start bringing B2 fighters'."[90] And yet fostering the impression in Pyongyang that the United States and its Korean puppet state are preparing an attack is precisely the intention. The point isn't to practice the defense of South Korea against an attack from North Korea (which isn't going to happen anyway, since North Korea hasn't the resources to mount a successful invasion) but to keep Pyongyang off balance and pouring its limited resources into deterring an attack from the US-ROK (Canada, Australia, New Zealand, Columbia, Denmark, the Netherlands, and UK) side.

The United States also used a strategy of induced military overburden against the Soviet Union. The Reagan administration spent massively on an arms build-up in the 1980s, in an effort to force the Soviet Union to spend itself into bankruptcy in an effort to keep up.[91] As the Soviets struggled to keep pace, their more limited resources were diverted increasingly to arms spending. Improvements in living standards were slowed and investment and consumption expenditures were forced to take a back seat to military outlays. US cold warrior Robert McNamara explained the strategy:

> The Soviet Union came out of the Second World War with a brilliant military victory. With heavy casualty and high economic expenditure ... this country had three priorities for its plan after the war. 1. Renewing the country's infrastructure completely so the Soviet people could reach the promise of communism; 2. Rebuilding and renewing the country's defense in the face of the stalking capitalist world; 3. Gaining new friends in the world, especially in Eastern Europe and the Third World. ...
>
> If the United States succeeds in engaging the Soviet Union in an arms race, then all these plans would go out the window. ... Our goal was very simple: the second priority would, if possible, replace the first priority. In other words, first increasing the military expenditure and last, improving the people's standard of living ... and of course this would affect the third priority as well.

> What is the meaning of this? It means that if the Soviet Union is dragged into an arms race and a massive portion of its budget, 40 percent if possible, is allocated to this purpose, then a lesser amount would be left for improving the people's lives, and therefore, the dream of communism, which so many people are awaiting around the world, would be postponed and the friends of the Soviet Union and the supporters of the idea of communism would have to wait a long time. ... On the basis of this calculation, the arms race may even threaten Soviet ideology in Moscow.[92]

US military pressure, combined with economic strangulation, has indisputably threatened the citadel of Korea's movement for emancipation. But the DPRK still stands. The state has, in recent years, adopted a policy aimed at strengthening its ability to defend itself, while at the same time reducing the military drain on its civilian economy. The policy is called *byungjin* (parallel development.) It relies on nuclear weapons as a deterrent, allowing the DPRK to spend less on its armed forces, and more on its civilian economy. And the policy appears to be working. Astonishingly, despite the escalation of Washington's efforts in recent years to ruin North Korea, the country's economy grew by an estimated 3.9 percent in 2016[93]—more than either the US or South Korean economies grew. The deterrent value of nuclear arms affords North Korea the space it needs to rebalance it spending away from its military to economic growth. It is perhaps for this reason that the CIA concluded that no amount of pressure would force the DPRK to give up its nuclear program.[94] Nuclear weapons are the key to both the DPRK's survival and to its overcoming the obstacles to its economic development that the United States has placed in its way.

CHAPTER 14

Byungjin

"Defensive weapons are not provocative unless you are an aggressor." —James Mattis, US Defense Secretary[1]

During the Cold War, US nuclear doctrine allowed the Pentagon to use, or threaten to use, nuclear weapons in response to *any* attack against the United States, its allies, or its partners, even if the attack was carried out by conventional means by a non-nuclear weapons state. Moreover, the attack needn't have been even directed at the United States for US nuclear doctrine to authorize the use of the Pentagon's most lethal weapons.[2] In principle, the Pentagon could launch a nuclear strike on Country A for using a troop of Boy Scouts to attack Country B with pea-shooters. With regard to Korea, Washington could reach for its nuclear sword to annihilate the DPRK, were it to launch a general invasion across the DMZ in pursuit of its patriotic duty to reunify its country and eject a foreign occupation army.

The United States contemplated using nuclear weapons against North Korea during the Korean War, both initially, during the war for the south, and later, after the Chinese PVA routed US forces in the north.[3] When US president Dwight D. Eisenhower was ready to bring the stalemated war to an end, he backed up his demand for talks by secretly letting Pyongyang and Beijing know that unless they complied, he would order a nuclear strike.[4] By 1958, the United States had secretly deployed battlefield nuclear weapons to South Korea, where they would remain until 1991. For decades, Pentagon planners worked out scenarios in which nuclear weapons would be used to defeat DPRK forces in any war on the peninsula.[5] Washington was ever ready to be a nuclear bully because there was never any danger that the DPRK could reply in kind. US "generals who previously served in Korea told [Bruce Cumings] that they'd be willing to use nuclear weapons in the Korean but not the European theater because in the Korean theater [the DPRK] had no nuclear weapons,"[6] and therefore couldn't retaliate in kind.

The DPRK's first attempt to deter a US nuclear attack was, paradoxically, to join the Nuclear Non-Proliferation Treaty, which it did in 1985. The treaty, in force from March 5, 1970 onward, commits treaty members "to pursue negotiations in good faith on measures relating to ... nuclear disarmament." The treaty divides signatories into two categories: nuclear weapons and non-nuclear weapons states, based on whether they have "manufactured and exploded a nuclear weapon or other nuclear explosive device prior to 1 January, 1967." States with pre-1967 nuclear weapons are designated as nuclear weapons states, and include the United States, Russia, China, Britain, and France. Countries that had no nuclear weapons prior to 1967 are called non-nuclear weapons states, even if they have acquired nuclear weapons subsequent to that date.

The treaty requires that while they remain treaty signatories, non-nuclear weapons states refrain from manufacturing or otherwise acquiring nuclear weapons. In exchange for making this commitment, they are to receive technical advice, know-how, and other assistance from nuclear weapons states in developing peaceful applications of nuclear energy.

For their part, nuclear weapons states are constrained by two obligations: first, to help non-nuclear weapons states access nuclear technology for civilian purposes; and second, to pursue negotiations in good faith on measures relating to nuclear disarmament. The treaty's preamble obliges all states to forebear from using the threat of force in their relations with other countries. The preamble specifically recalls "that, in accordance with the Charter of the United Nations, states must refrain in their international relations from the threat or use of force against the territorial integrity or political independence of any state."

Have the nuclear weapons states fulfilled their treaty obligation to work toward disarmament? Given the scant progress these powers have made in bringing about a nuclear weapons-free world, one would be hard pressed to answer in the affirmative. Despite lofty rhetoric, none of the nuclear weapons states has taken any serious step toward eliminating their nuclear arsenals. The US Nuclear Posture Review of 2010, for instance, declares that the United States will never give up its nuclear weapons so long as nuclear weapons exist. That other nuclear weapons states hold the same view guarantees that disarmament will never happen.

Pessimism is also warranted by the reaction of the nuclear weapons states to the 2017 UN Prohibition on Nuclear Weapons. The United States, France, and Britain issued a statement condemning the treaty, on the ground that they—the most militarily consequential countries on the planet—uniquely needed nuclear weapons to defend themselves.[7] At the same time, they insisted that the DPRK, a military pipsqueak by comparison—which, given its New York City Police Department-sized armed forces might have the greatest need for nuclear weapons as a means of self-defense—should be forever denied them.

What's more, the prohibition against the use of military threat in international relations promulgated in the UN Charter, and referred to in the treaty's preamble, is routinely ignored by three of the nuclear weapons states, namely, the United States, Britain, and France. Rather than refraining, in their international relations, from the threat or use of force against the territorial integrity or political independence of any state, these states, led by Washington, are indefatigable in employing force, both actual and threatened, to bend other countries to their will.

In 1993, the US Strategic Command announced that it was retargeting some of its strategic nuclear weapons (i.e., hydrogen bombs) away from the former Soviet Union to North Korea. A month later, Pyongyang announced that it would withdraw from the NPT, signaling that if Washington was going to dangle a nuclear sword of

Damocles over its head, North Korea would take countermeasures.[8] The source of fissile material for the DPRK's nuclear weapons program would be a 30-megawatt nuclear reactor established at Yongbyon in 1987. Pyongyang had imported the reactor from the Soviet Union, intending to substitute nuclear power for coal and imported oil, relying on the DPRK's substantial uranium deposits. South Korea and Japan were building nuclear reactors too, and were also seeking to reduce dependency on oil imports.

Washington immediately set to work undermining Pyongyang's plans to build nuclear weapons. Just as Israel had launched a bombing raid to destroy the Osirak nuclear reactor in Iraq in 1981—an effort to prevent the Arab nationalist government from developing nuclear arms, which would have put it beyond the pale of US and Israeli bullying—the United States would dispatch bombers or launch cruise missiles to destroy the Yongbyon facility. Not only would the DPRK be prevented from acquiring the nuclear fuel it needed to make a nuclear device, Pyongyang's plans to redress its vulnerabilities in energy production would also be undermined, thus contributing to the achievement of the longstanding US foreign policy goal of bringing about the end of North Korea.

In the end, Washington chose not to destroy the Yongbyon facility—a decision that almost certainly would have led Pyongyang to shell Seoul, occasioning mass destruction and a major loss of life—when Jimmy Carter, then a former US president, flew to Pyongyang to work out a deal with Kim Il-sung. The deal, called the Agreed Framework, would see North Korea re-enter the NPT and shut down Yongbyon, in return for the US pledging to normalize relations, build two proliferation-safe light water reactors, and, while the reactors were under construction, provide shipments of fuel oil to meet the DPRK's energy requirements. While this seemed like a workable basis for a long-term agreement, the accord offered a respite only. Washington had no interest in a permanent *modus vivendi* with North Korea. US officials believed it was only a matter of a few years before the accumulated effects of its economic sanctions, Pyongyang's enormous defense expenditures relative to GDP, and the collapse of the DPRK's export markets, would bring the Korean experiment in anti-imperialist self-sufficiency crashing down. According to the CIA's projections, North Korea would throw in the towel by 2002.[9] If Washington could drag its feet, it wouldn't have to honor its side of the pact.

Washington's go-slow approach to the Agreed Framework hardly enamored Pyongyang to its decision to reverse its initial plan to withdraw from the NPT. It was clear from Washington's temporizing that it had no real intention of meeting its obligations under the agreement. This became unmistakable when the George W. Bush administration tore up the agreement and went on the offensive. First, it effectively declared war, designating North Korea part of an "Axis of Evil." Next, it put the DPRK on a list of seven countries deemed possible targets of a nuclear strike. The list also included Russia, China, Syria, Libya, Iran, and Iraq.[10] (Note, again, that all of these countries operated economies that failed to comply with the Washington-prescribed model of integration into a US-superintended global economy, open to US investors and businesses.) With the Bush administration renewing hostilities, North Korea gave notice that it would withdraw from the NPT. The "Bush administration's nuclear attack plan showed," Pyongyang said, "that the United States ... [was] pursuing world domination with force of arms and that the United States [was] not hesitant in launching a nuclear attack on any nation if it [was] regarded as an obstacle to this end."[11]

Echoing these concerns, a North Korean diplomat explained his country's decision to exit the NPT and embark on the development of nuclear weapons:

> The NPT clearly states that nuclear power states cannot use nuclear weapons for the purpose of threatening or endangering non-nuclear states. So the DPRK thought that if we joined the NPT, we would be able to get rid of the nuclear threat from the US. Therefore, we joined. However, the US never withdrew its right of pre-emptive nuclear strike. They always said that, once US interests are threatened, they always have the right to use their nuclear weapons for pre-emptive purposes.[12]

He added:

> The world situation changed again after 11 September 2001. After this, Bush said that if the US wants to protect its safety, then it must remove the 'Axis of Evil' countries from the earth. The three countries he listed as members of this 'Axis of Evil' were Iran, Iraq and North Korea. Having witnessed what happened in Afghanistan and Iraq, we came to realise that we couldn't put a stop to the threat from the US with conventional weapons alone. So we realised that we needed our own nuclear weapons in order to defend the DPRK and its people.[13]

The NPT allows states to exit the accord if they believe their continued participation is injurious to their highest interests. "Each Party shall in exercising its national sovereignty have the right to withdraw from the Treaty if it decides that extraordinary events, related to the subject matter of this Treaty, have jeopardized the supreme interests of its country." Clearly, Washington's overt hostility, the listing of North Korea as a target of a possible nuclear strike, and the Bush administration's virtual declaration of war, constituted "extraordinary events" which jeopardized the DPRK's "supreme interests."

After North Korea began to develop nuclear weapons, the United States amended its nuclear doctrine in an attempt to bring the DPRK back into the non-proliferation treaty. In 2010, the Obama administration declared that the United States would no longer use, or threaten to use, nuclear weapons against countries that did not possess them and were not seeking them. Hence, if the DPRK agreed to relinquish its nuclear weapons, and rejoin the NPT, Washington would forebear from future use of nuclear weapons against the DPRK. "This revised assurance" was "intended to underscore the security benefits of adhering to and fully complying with the NPT, and to persuade non-nuclear weapons states party to the Treaty to work with the United States and other interested parties to adopt effective measures to strengthen the non-proliferation regime," declared the revised nuclear protocol.[14] The offer was, however, too little, too late. And the United States' record in working out non-proliferation agreements with target countries, and then attacking them after they disarmed, was unpropitious.

On the day Baghdad fell to invading US forces, one of the Bush administration's chief war mongers, John Bolton, belligerently warned Iran, Syria, and the DPRK to "draw the appropriate lesson."[15] Three years later, on October 9, 2006, the DPRK announced to the world the lesson it had drawn. On that day, it detonated an atomic bomb. By 2017, North Korea had detonated five more nuclear devices.[16]

The lesson learned, namely that disarming is an invitation to an attack, was reinforced when NATO secretly armed Islamist militants and launched an air war to oust Muammar Gaddafi, after the Libyan leader, in a misguided attempt to curry favor with the West, dismantled his weapons of mass destruction, leaving his country vulnerable to attack. Saddam Hussein made the same blunder in Iraq a decade earlier. One DPRK diplomat asked:

> What happened to Libya? When Gaddafi wanted to improve Libya's relations with the US and UK, the imperialists said that in order to attract international investment he would have to give up his weapons programs. Gaddafi even said that he would visit the DPRK to convince us to give up our nuclear program. But once Libya dismantled all its nuclear programs and this was confirmed by Western intelligence, the West changed its tune.[17]

Rudiger Frank, a professor of East Asian Economy and Society at the University of Vienna, argues that three signal events underscored for Pyongyang that the decision it took to develop nuclear weapons was prudent:

> The first such instance was Gorbachev's foolish belief that his policies to end the arms race and confrontation with the West would be rewarded by respect for the Soviet Union. ... On the contrary, [the USSR] was destroyed piece by piece by Western support of anti-communist governments in its European satellites and independence movements in various (now former) Soviet Republics. In the end, the reformer was ousted, NATO was expanded, and his once mighty country was weakened and ridiculed. Others had an even less desirable fate, such as Romania's Ceausescu or East Germany's Honecker.
>
> The second instance was [Arab nationalist] Iraq. Humiliated after a quick defeat in the First Gulf War, [Saddam] accepted Western control

> over about half of his airspace in 1991 and had to suffer regular small-scale attacks on ground targets for more than a decade. Sanctions led to the 'oil for food' program of 1995. However, his compliance did not save [Saddam's government] from allegations of hiding weapons of mass destruction, and ultimately from complete annihilation in the Second Gulf War.
>
> Now, there is Libya's Gaddafi. It was not so long ago that it was popular in political circles to urge [the DPRK] to follow Gaddafi's example. On February 14, 2005, the conservative South Korean newspaper Chosun Ilbo even reported that then ROK Minister of Foreign Affairs and Trade, and ... UN Secretary General, Ban Ki Moon, was sent to Libya to urge Mr. Gaddafi to visit North Korea and persuade Kim Jong Il to abandon his nuclear weapons.[18]

The culmination of Gaddafi's attempts to ingratiate himself with the West was his murder at the hands of NATO's proxy jihadists, but not before one of their number sodomized him with a knife.

None of this was lost on the North Koreans. A February 21, 2013 commentary by the KCNA noted that, "The tragic consequences in those countries which abandoned halfway their nuclear programs, yielding to the high-handed practices and pressure of the U.S. in recent years, clearly prove that the DPRK was very far-sighted and just when it made the option. They also teach the truth that the U.S. nuclear blackmail should be countered with substantial counter-measures, not with compromise or retreat."[19] *Rodong Sinmun* observed that, "Had it not been the nuclear deterrence of our own, the U.S. would have already launched a war on the peninsula as it had done in Iraq and Libya and plunged it into a sorry plight as [it did Yugoslavia] at the end of the last century and Afghanistan early in this century."[20]

The DPRK says it developed nuclear weapons "to protect its sovereignty and vital rights from the U.S. nuclear threat and hostile policy which have lasted for more than half a century,"[21] and which culminated in the Bush administration's nuclear saber rattling and threat of war.

Compare North Korea's reasons for having nuclear weapons with those of Britain. The UK government's 2006 White Paper, "The Future of the United Kingdom's Nuclear Deterrent," states that

"The primary responsibility of any government is to ensure the safety and security of its citizens," and that for "50 years [Britain's] independent nuclear deterrent has provided the ultimate assurance of [the country's] national security." "The UK's nuclear weapons," the document declares, are designed "to deter and prevent nuclear blackmail and acts of aggression against our vital interests that cannot be countered by other means."[22]

Russia invokes the same rationale for maintaining its nuclear arsenal.[23] And, as we've already seen, the United States and France also say they need nuclear weapons to defend themselves.

The rationale of nuclear weapons states for maintaining a stock of nuclear weapons "applies with even greater force to weak states that may come under threat from stronger ones. The smaller and weaker the state, the greater the need for nuclear weapons to make potential aggressors think twice before threatening or invading them." Pointing specifically to Britain, researcher David Morrison argues that if "one of the strongest states in this world needs to have nuclear weapons in order to deter potential aggressors," then it follows that every state needs them. Why should smaller states be uniquely denied the means to deter and prevent nuclear blackmail and acts of aggression against their vital interests? Morrison caps his point by speculating that, "Had Iraq succeeded in developing nuclear weapons, the US/UK would not have invaded in March 2003 (and hundreds of thousands of Iraqis who died as a consequence would still be alive)."[24]

Of course, it's impossible to know how history would have unfolded, had Iraq been in a position to present the possibility of a nuclear counter-strike as a deterrent to Washington's drive to war; but the idea that nuclear weapons can deter aggression is not implausible. In 2010, General Kevin P. Chilton, at the time head of US Strategic Command, reminded *Washington Post* columnist Walter Pincus that, "Throughout the ... history of nuclear weapons, no nuclear power has been conquered or even put at risk of conquest."[25] Explaining the grim logic that compels threatened countries like North Korea to reach for a nuclear sword, Putin wrote in RIA Novosti on February 27, 2012: "If I have the A-bomb in my pocket, nobody will touch me because it's more trouble than it is worth. And those who don't have the bomb might" become victims of a US-led campaign of "'humanitarian intervention'. Whether we like it or not, foreign interference" by the United States and its satellites encourages states which resist integration into the US empire to acquire nuclear weapons as a means of safeguarding their liberty.[26] Echoing Putin's analysis, the chief of the Israeli army's planning division, Major General Amir Eshel, observed, "Who would have dared deal with Qaddafi or Saddam Hussein if they had a nuclear capability? No way."[27]

"It is ironic," noted Pincus, that the five permanent members of the United Nations Security Council, all of whom insist on non-proliferation (for other countries) "are all modernizing their stockpiles." The "United States has a multi-billion-dollar program to upgrade its three major nuclear warheads and a more costly effort to build new land, sea and air strategic delivery systems. France is modernizing its nuclear bombs and missiles as well as its strategic submarine ... Russia and China are modernizing, too."[28] The United States will "spend $80 billion ... to maintain and modernize the nation's nuclear arsenal,"[29] while ally Britain announced in 2012 "contract awards of $595 million to begin design of replacements for its four nuclear submarines that carry Trident sub-launched ballistic missiles," even though it was "in the midst of an austerity program that [included] cutting education, health and retirement programs."[30]

Not only is the United States modernizing its nuclear weapons arsenal, it is also developing new WMD. The Pentagon has been working on a precision-guided atom bomb designed, as the *New York Times* puts it, "with problems like North Korea in mind." The "bomb's explosive force can be dialed up or down depending on the target, to minimize collateral damage." Owing to the weapon's "smaller yields and better targeting," it is more tempting to use. The bomb, called the B61, "is the first of five new warhead types planned as part of an atomic revitalization estimated to cost up to $1 trillion over three decades. As a family, the weapons and their delivery systems move toward the small, the stealthy and the precise," making their use "more thinkable."[31]

The Pentagon is also at work on non-nuclear WMD "approaching the level of strategic nuclear arms in their strike capability."[32] The new class of weapons, termed "'Prompt Global Strike' could be fired from the United States and hit a target anywhere in less than an hour." The new weapons would "give the president a non-nuclear option for, say, a ... pre-emptive attack on ... North Korea," achieving the effects of a nuclear weapon without, it is hoped, "turning a conventional war into a nuclear one."[33]

Some blame the Bush administration's hostility toward North Korea for precipitating Pyongyang's decision to acquire nuclear weapons. If only Bush hadn't ripped up the Agreed Framework, they argue, North Korea wouldn't have gone down the nuclear path. This is plausible, but would a different administration have behaved differently? The answer, it seems, is: probably not.

US policy from the moment of the DPRK's birth has sought to bring about the demise of North Korea. This policy has remained intact, throughout a succession of Democratic and Republican administrations. A policy of permanent peaceful co-existence, and not just one that is tactical and temporary, is not in the cards. Imperialists, Mao once observed, will never lay down their butcher knives and become Buddhists. And the Wall Street politicos in Washington have never contemplated a conversion to pacifism. During the years of the Clinton administration, when the Agreed Framework was in place, US policy was as strongly focused on the goal of bringing about the death of the DPRK as it had ever been. But during those years, it appeared that the long sought-after dissolution of the patriot state was imminent, and that Washington could play along with the illusion that it had arrived at an *entente* with Pyongyang, while awaiting the inevitable. And the inevitability of a North Korean collapse, appeared, from Washington's point of view, to be beyond question. North Korea was reeling from the dissolution of the socialist bloc and the concomitant loss of important trading partners, and had been wracked by a series of natural disasters which left it food-insecure. Its economy was shrinking and its people were hungry. Moreover, the absorption of Communist East Germany into the US-led West Germany seemed to foretell of similar events unfolding on the Korean peninsula. The achievement of US policy goals vis-à-vis North Korea seemed like only a matter of waiting for a foreordained conclusion. Accordingly, Washington tarried, doing little to build the light-water reactors it had promised Pyongyang. But the CIA's prediction of an imminent North Korean collapse was wrong. By the time Bush arrived on the scene, it was clear that the DPRK was not about to follow East Germany into surrender. If US foreign policy imperatives were to be achieved, pressure on Pyongyang would have to be intensified.

Once it became clear to Pyongyang that Washington was feigning amicable cooperation, while clutching a knife behind its back, its motivation to remain in the NPT began to melt away. When Bush revealed the knife, and threatened to draw blood, the motivation disappeared altogether. Now, it made sense to exit the treaty and begin work on the development of nuclear weapons to deter US aggression, which, for Pyongyang, hardly seemed hypothetical.

Pyongyang, however, would use the ultimate weapon, not only to deter nuclear attacks, but to deter conventional attacks, as well. Obama's offer, made in his 2010 revision to US nuclear doctrine, to drop the provision that allowed the Pentagon to use nuclear weapons against non-nuclear weapons states, suffered from a serious flaw. It failed to prohibit the US military from using its formidable array of conventional arms to bring about the DPRK's demise. The United States had already turned North Korea into a charcoal briquette during the Korean War (to invoke language Colin Powell had used in a warning to the DPRK), incinerating territory north of the 38th parallel by dropping an ocean of incendiaries on people and buildings. In the space of more than half a century, US conventional military capabilities had advanced considerably. If the Pentagon could lay waste to North Korea once, it could do so again, except this time more rapidly, and with considerably less effort. The US threat lay, therefore, not with the United States' nuclear weapons arsenal alone, but also in its stock of conventional weapons, which is capable of transforming the territory of North Korea into a terrain of smoking ruins. When US leaders remind Pyongyang that the United States has within its grasp the power to make North Korea cease to exist, they are not necessarily referring to a US nuclear strike.

If the United States possesses the awesome power to completely destroy North Korea (for a second time) why doesn't it use it? The answer is because it cannot do so without incurring a considerable cost, and because there is a less costly alternative, which is therefore more attractive. Although North Korea was burned to the ground in the early 1950s, the United States failed to eliminate the DPRK as a state. North Koreans know the Korean War as the Great Fatherland Liberation War, to mark the liberation of northern Korea after its brief occupation by US, ROK, and other US imperial forces. Destroying a country's infrastructure, killing millions of its people, and driving the survivors into underground redoubts, may be within the grasp of the United States, but bringing about the surrender of a people is another matter. What's more, because Seoul, a city of some 25 million, is within range of North Korean artillery, a US-ROK attack on the DPRK would trigger a counterattack resulting in significant cost to Washington's puppet state in lost and crippled lives and damaged infrastructure. The more attractive option, from the US point of view, is the continued two-pronged campaign of warfare against the North Korean economy, in which DPRK industry is starved of inputs while the KPA is forced to draw resources from the civilian economy in order to deter possible attacks materializing from the planned and surprise US-led war games. Eventually, (Washington hopes), Pyongyang will realize that it's impossible to simultaneously meet its security obligations and economic goals, and give up.

In the meantime, attention can be drawn to the DPRK's precarious economic state as an object lesson to the rest of the world in the folly of pursuing socialist policies. The purported folly can be perceived on two levels, one which attributes North Korea's economic travails to endogenous factors, and the other which acknowledges the role of exogenous causes. On the first level, the endogenous one, the role of the United States in hobbling the DPRK economy is hidden, and the economic difficulties of North Korea are attributed to Pyongyang adopting "unsound" economic policies (state ownership and central planning) which are presented as inherently unworkable and "a dead end." This reinforces an ideological hegemony which comports with Wall Street's interests while fostering the belief among people who could benefit from socialism that public ownership of enterprises and central planning, with their attendant robust social welfare and full employment, while perhaps attractive in principle, are unworkable in practice, and that they lead inevitably to economic hardship, consumer goods shortages, and growing poverty, as proved by the DPRK (and its predecessor socialist bloc states and contemporary Cuba). After all, goes the argument, isn't capitalist South Korea many times richer than Communist North Korea? On the second level, the exogenous level, Washington's long campaign to weaken and undermine the North Korean economy is acknowledged and invoked to illustrate the folly of defying the US empire. A socialist path will only arouse the wrath of Washington's Wall Street politicos, this view warns, and therefore is best avoided in favor of more "realistic" alternatives. Of course, the only "realistic" alternative is submission.

For Pyongyang, nuclear weapons became a way to steer a course between the Scylla of stunted economic growth and the Charybdis of military vulnerability. The reasoning was that a nuclear counterstrike against the United States and its East Asian army in reserve raised the stakes sufficiently for Washington that it would never seriously contemplate an aggressive war against North Korea. As a consequence, Pyongyang could lighten the economic burden of funding its military. Rather than spending 15 to 25 percent of its GDP on self-defense, Pyongyang could bring the ratio down to a level more congruent with economic growth, confident that a modest nuclear weapons arsenal possessed a far greater deterrent capability than a massive and expensive army equipped with aging equipment.

It also solved the problem of the growing gulf between the conventional forces of the DPRK and those of its peninsular rival. South Korea's economy and military budget overshadowed North Korea's. The situation was unsustainable. Eventually, ROK military dominance would be so overwhelming that the DPRK's security situation would become intolerably precarious. William Perry, who served as the US Secretary of Defense in the Clinton administration, observed that Pyongyang believed "correctly that [DPRK] conventional capabilities [were] not as good as those of South Korea and the U.S., so they compensate[d] for this with their nuclear forces."[34] Indeed, the real choice the DPRK faced was between building a massive and expensive army equipped with obsolescent equipment increasingly incapable of deterring an ROK attack, or building nuclear weapons which raised the stakes of US aggression above the level the US empire was willing to pay.

The ratio of deterrence to cost vastly favored nuclear weapons over conventional military means, and for a country with a very limited budget, which ran the risk of bankrupting itself in the pursuit of self-defense, the acquisition of nuclear arms became a solution of considerable merit to an otherwise intractable problem. Pyongyang had no choice—other than capitulation and abandonment of Korea's struggle for freedom—but to develop nuclear arms. Of course, the nuclear weapons solution wasn't perfect. It failed to address the problem of the US-led campaign to blockade the DPRK's access to vital industrial inputs, but it did provide Pyongyang with a way to free itself from the horns of the dilemma on which it had been thrust by US-Korea policy that forced North Korea to pit spending on a large army against economic growth.

A formal linkage between the development of nuclear arms and economic advance was promulgated in May 2015. The DPRK government announced that it would pursue a "'two-track program' of building the economy and nuclear weapons," setting this as the country's 'permanent strategic course'."[35] The *New York Times* summed up the policy, called *byungjin*, by observing that in the DPRK's estimation only "a nuclear arsenal" would "make North Korea secure from American invasion and let it focus on growth."[36]

Building nuclear warheads, however, wasn't enough. North Korea also had to build the means of delivering them to their target. The most economical and realistic option was ballistic missiles, since the DPRK lacked the resources to build and operate a long-range strategic bomber force and didn't possess the forward operating bases on foreign soil that would place the bombers within range of the United States. On top of mastering ballistic missile technology, DPRK scientists and engineers had to figure out how to miniaturize the warheads to fit atop a missile. Plus, they had to develop heat-resistant shielding to prevent the warheads from burning up during re-entry into the earth's atmosphere. Washington did all it could to sabotage the development work, running "a highly secret cyber-war against [North Korea] for years, seeking to infect and disrupt its missile program."[37]

More importantly, however, Washington stepped up its program of economic warfare against the DPRK, shepherding a series of sanctions resolutions through the UN Security Council which declared North Korea's nuclear weapons and ballistic missile tests to represent threats to international peace and security. The United Nations Charter authorizes the Security Council to "determine the existence of any threat to the peace, breach of the peace, or act of aggression." Once it has identified a threat it is further authorized to "decide what measures shall be taken ... to maintain or restore international peace and security." The United States identified the DPRK's efforts to develop nuclear weapons and the means of delivering them as threats to international peace and security, and persuaded the members of the Security Council to go along, thereby successfully passing a number of resolutions that required all UN members to impose various punitive economic measures on North Korea.

Pyongyang objected on wholly reasonable grounds. To be sure, a first strike *use* of ballistic missiles to deliver a nuclear warhead against an adversary is a breach of international peace and security. However, *testing* a ballistic missile is not. Sending tanks across an international frontier to cause or threaten harm to an enemy is a breach of international peace and security. Putting tanks through their paces on a proving range is not. If the testing of weapons systems is a threat, then virtually every member of the United Nations—which is to say, any country which has ever tested a rifle, mortar, cannon, or fighter jet—has committed, or is currently committing, acts that violate the UN Charter. The development of the means of self-defense cannot be legitimately classified as a breach of international peace and security.

Did Pyongyang seek to develop nuclear weapons and delivery systems for self-defense rather than aggression? The evidence in the affirmative is overwhelming. The DPRK's principal adversary, the United States, has the means to annihilate the DPRK, both through conventional and nuclear means. Recognizing this, the DPRK would never launch a first strike, either against the United States or South Korea. When he was president, Bill Clinton said that if the DPRK leadership ever used nuclear weapons, "it would be the end of their country." Clinton went on to argue that it was therefore "pointless for [the North Koreans] to try to develop nuclear weapons."[38] However, the US president overlooked the value to the DPRK of a nuclear sword as a means of deterring US aggression. Wesley Clark, the US Army General who commanded the 1999 NATO war on Communist Yugoslavia, remarked that "The leaders of North Korea use bellicose language, but they know very well that they do not have a military option available. ... Were they to attack South Korea, their nation would be completely destroyed. It would literally cease to exist."[39] Neither do South Koreans have illusions that the DPRK's nuclear weapons are intended for aggression. "To South Koreans," observes the *New York Times*, "the idea that North Korea would fire a nuclear-armed ICBM at the United States without being attacked is absurd. They argue that [the DPRK leadership] knows the United States would retaliate by destroying the North and that they do not regard [it] as suicidal."[40]

Nor do Korea specialists believe that North Korea's nuclear arsenal was built with anything more than self-defense in mind. According to the Associated Press, they "generally accept Pyongyang's stated rationale that it sought its own bomb for defensive reasons."[41]

Pyongyang articulated the DPRK's nuclear posture in 2013. The patriot state defined nuclear weapons as serving "the purpose of deterring and repelling the aggression and attack of the enemy." Pyongyang declared that it would limit the use of its nuclear weapons to repulsion of an "invasion or attack from a hostile nuclear weapons state," and would prohibit their use against "non-nuclear states," except those which "join a hostile nuclear weapons state in its invasion and attack on the DPRK."[42]

Clark referred to North Korea's belligerent language. Bellicose language has been used by Pyongyang in response to US-ROK threats, often deliberately provoked, as in the 2013 playbook incident referred to earlier, in which the United States deliberately exacerbated tensions during that year's Key Resolve troop mobilizations, with the intention of provoking North Korea. In quieter moments, the DPRK media routinely refer to North Korea's nuclear weapons in pacific, self-defensive terms, for example: "It is natural for DPRK to bolster nuclear deterrent for self-defense"[43]; "DPRK's nuclear force is treasured sword to safeguard peace"[44]; and "DPRK's nuclear force deters U.S. nuclear war."[45] In fact, Pyongyang has declared repeatedly that its nuclear weapons deter war on the peninsula, believing that in the absence of a nuclear deterrent, the United States would eventually take advantage of North Korea's obsolescing conventional military equipment, and its diminishing conventional military strength, to launch an attack.

The UN Charter, argued DPRK foreign minister Ri Yong Ho in 2017, "recognizes the right to self-defense of every state." And there exists no international law which prohibits the testing of ballistic missiles. If such a prohibition existed, every permanent member of the UN Security Council would be in violation of the law, since all these countries, possess and have tested, ballistic missiles. Neither is the DPRK prevented by law from possessing and testing nuclear weapons. Pyongyang withdrew legally from the NPT, and did so, on the perfectly legitimate ground that the treaty prevented it from developing a credible deterrent to the unceasing threat of war posed by the United States. Given that the open hostilities from 1950 to 1953 were ended by a cease-fire alone, and not a peace treaty, the United States is technically in a state of war with North Korea. And Washington's Wall Street politicos evince not the slightest interest in bringing the state of war to an end. Repeatedly, Pyongyang has petitioned Washington to negotiate a peace treaty, and repeatedly its petitions have been rebuffed. At one point, Colin Powell, at the time US secretary of state, greeted yet another North Korean entreaty for peace, with this peremptory dismissal: "We don't do non-aggression pacts or treaties, things of that nature."[46] David Straub, who had been director of the US State Department's Korea desk from 2002 to 2004, explained why Washington has no interest in arriving at a peace treaty with the DPRK: "North Korea's closed economic and social system means the country has virtually nothing of value to offer the United States."[47] Plus, North Korea poses not the slightest threat to the United States, so Washington has no incentive to work out an *entente*.

Ri pointed out that "there is no provision either in the UN Charter and or in any other international code which stipulates that ... nuclear and ballistic rocket activity poses a threat to ... international peace and security," adding that "those countries that had begun [the] same activities far ahead of the DPRK have never been called into question at the UN Security Council." Ri drew the conclusion that "the UN Security Council is the place where [guilt] is decided not on the basis of justice but by the criterion [of] whether one has ... veto power or not."[48] The North Korean foreign minister submitted a formal request to the UN Secretariat for an explanation of "what ground and with what authority the Security Council adopted" resolutions "prohibiting [the] nuclear and ballistic rocket activities of the DPRK." He asked, "If the Security Council has such ground and authority, why is it that it does not take issue with those countries which conduct the same nuclear and ballistic rocket activities."[49] The DPRK has also challenged the Security Council's authority to deny the DPRK access to nuclear weapons by pointing out that if it had this authority there would be no need for the Nuclear Non-Proliferation Treaty; the Security Council would simply issue a ukase limiting possession of nuclear arms to its own permanent members.

International law, however, rests on a foundation of treaties. Countries agree to be bound by the terms of treaties into which they voluntarily enter. The United States, Britain, and France cannot be bound by the UN Prohibition on Nuclear Weapons because they have refused to join the treaty. No international body can lawfully compel these countries to abide by the terms of a treaty they refuse to be part of. Likewise, no international body can lawfully order the DPRK to abide by the terms of the NPT, since North Korea is no longer a signatory. Nor is any international body authorized to compel the DPRK to refrain from the testing of ballistic missiles; no treaty exists banning their testing or use. Ri submitted his request to the Security Council in 2016 for an explanation of the legal basis on which it has criminalized the DPRK's self-defensive pursuit of nuclear arms and the means of delivering them. A year later he still hadn't received a reply. It's likely he never will, since the Security Council's actions are *ultra vires*, beyond its authority, and therefore are not legally defensible.

The DPRK's nuclear and ballistic tests are provocative only in the sense of provoking consternation in Washington that its options in bringing about the demise of North Korea had been attenuated by Pyongyang's development of nuclear arms. David E. Sanger, a *New York Times* reporter who is close to the US foreign policy establishment through his membership in the Council on Foreign Relations, revealed why Washington was alarmed by North Korea's nuclear and ballistic missile testing. "The fear," wrote Sanger, "is not that [North Korea] would launch a pre-emptive attack on the [United States]; that would be suicidal, and if [North Korea] has demonstrated anything ... [it] is all about survival." Washington was alarmed, Sanger corrected, because the DPRK had "the ability to strike back." In other words, nuclear weapons gave Pyongyang a way to defend itself.[50] As one North Korean put it, "The army and the people of the DPRK are no longer what they used to be in the past when they had to counter US [nuclear arms] with rifles."[51] That, wrote Sanger, made North Korea "dangerous."[52]

But if the Security Council can construe the testing of weapons as a threat to international peace and security because Washington and Seoul regard these activities as provocations, then a much stronger case can be made for sanctioning the United States and South Korea, along with other members of the US empire, Canada, Great Britain, France, Australia, New Zealand, and the Netherlands, for regularly carrying out war games on a colossal scale, which have the effect of provoking the DPRK and would provoke any country in North Korea's position. Indeed, that the regular mobilization of troops and weapons systems is provocative, apart from this being virtually axiomatic, is evidenced by the United States' own reaction to Russian war games along Russia's border with NATO countries which Washington has characterized as provocative and destabilizing. Western sources have described Russian troop maneuvers as "belligerent actions" and "an exercise in intimidation that" recall "the most ominous days of the Cold War," which "could lead to unintended confrontations"[53]—threats, in their view, to international peace and security. The case to be made that the Ulchi Freedom Guardian and Key Resolve exercises threaten international peace and security is all the stronger considering that these exercises are the underlying cause of the DPRK's nuclear and ballistic missile testing activities, which the Security Council deplores as threats to international order. The only order the DPRK's activities threaten, however, is the global economic order that Washington's Wall Street politicos maintain by using, or threatening to use, military force, including nuclear arms, against countries determined to exercise sovereignty.

CONCLUSION

The First Real Holy War

In his 1900 pan-Africanist statement, W.E.B. Dubois wrote that "The problem of the twentieth century" is that of white supremacy—the "tacit but clear modern philosophy which assigns to the white race alone the hegemony of the world and assumes that other races ... will either be content to serve the interests of the whites or die out before their all-conquering march."[1] This can be re-stated for the current century: the problem of the twenty-first century is the problem of US supremacy—the tacit but clear modern philosophy which assigns to the United States hegemony over the world and assumes that other countries will either be content to serve the interests of the United States' dominant economic class or die out before its all-conquering march.

Korean patriots, who have long struggled for freedom, will not die out before US supremacy's all-conquering march. Korea remains divided, its southern half under the control of a US-puppet state. Tens of thousands of US troops continue to occupy the country, successors to a preceding Japanese occupation. And the US empire—unprecedented in scope and reach, as Zbigniew Brzezinski described it—remains undiminished in its resolve to smash the anti-imperialist patriot state based at Pyongyang—one of the few top-to-bottom alternatives to capitalism and the interests of the Wall Street politicos. For decades, Washington has waited for the DPRK to collapse, certain its efforts to bring about the end of North Korea would pay off. But the patriot state endures. Kim Il-sung recognized that Korea's fight for freedom might last hundreds of years. But it would succeed. "India won its independence from England after 200 years of colonial enslavement," he observed. "The Philippines and Indonesia won their independence after 300 years. Algeria after 130 years. Sri Lanka after 150 years and Vietnam after nearly 100 years."[2] It may take 200 years, maybe 300, but Koreans will one day be free. And one day, all of us, too, will be free from US supremacy's all-conquering march. The path to freedom is being blazed by Koreans, Cubans, Venezuelans, Syrians, Chinese, Zimbabweans, and others who stand in a direct line of descent from the democratic revolution inaugurated in France in 1789, pushed forward by the Bolsheviks in Russia in 1917, and advanced by the national liberation struggles of the twentieth century.

On September 1, 1920, the communist movement, which had inspired Kim Il-sung and countless other Koreans, issued a manifesto at the close of a congress of peoples of the East, held at Baku.[3] The congress had observed that the Western empires had handed over Korea—"that flourishing land with a thousand-years-old culture ... to the Japanese imperialists for them to tear to pieces, and [the Japanese] are now with fire and sword making the Korean people submit to" exploitation by Japanese masters. Harking to the "fraudulent" holy war which governments "under the green banner of the Prophet" had, during the Great War, used to mobilize Muslims to serve "only the interests of ... self-seeking rulers," the congress called for "the first real holy war"—a war to be waged under a red banner "for the ending of the division of mankind into oppressor peoples and oppressed peoples, for complete equality of all peoples and races, whatever language they speak, whatever the color of their skin and whatever the religion they profess." This would be a war, the manifesto declared, "to end the division of countries into advanced and backward, dependent and independent, metropolitan and colonial." It would be a "holy war for the liberation of all mankind ... for the ending of all forms of oppression of one people by another and of all forms of exploitation of man by man." Koreans joined the holy war when it was proclaimed at Baku—indeed, before that. And they have never disengaged from it. Koreans, of both the north and south, forever united as one people despite the political division forced upon them by Washington, continue their fight for freedom against the successor to the Japanese occupation, the United States, the "last powerful imperialist predator" which has "spread its dark wings over" the whole world.

Notes

Introduction – One Country—Two States

1. William R. Polk, "How history explains the Korean crisis," *Consortiumnews.com*, August 28, 2017. https://consortiumnews.com/2017/08/28/how-history-explains-the-korean-crisis/.
2. Bruce Cumings, *The Korean War: A History.* (New York: Modern Library, 2010), 243.
3. Robert L Worden, ed. *North Korea: A Country Study.* (Library of Congress, 2008), 204. http://www.loc.gov/catdir/toc/ecip0822/2008028547.html.
4. "DPRK's nuclear force is treasured sword to safeguard peace," *Rodong Sinmun*, August 16, 2017.
5. Louise Young. *Japan's Total Empire: Manchuria and the Culture of Wartime Imperialism.* (Berkeley: University of California Press,1998), 3-4.
6. Bruce Cumings, *Korea's Place in the Sun: A Modern History.* (New York: W.W. Norton & Company, 2005), 153.
7. "Defense intelligence director says N. Korea would win in a one-on-one war," *The Hankyoreh*, November 6, 2013.
8. "President Moon rebukes Defense Ministry for its 'lack of confidence'," *The Hankyoreh*, August 29, 2017.

Chapter 1 – The Empire of Japan

1. Bertolt Brech,. *War Primer.* (New York: Verso, 2017), 44.
2. Young, p. 23.
3. James Macdonald, *When Globalization Fails: The Rise and Fall of Pax Americana.* (New York: Farrar, Straus and Giroux, 2015), 124.
4. Macdonald, 124; S.C.M. Paine. *The Japanese Empire: Grand Strategy from the Meiji Restoration to the Pacific War.* (Cambridge: Cambridge University Press, 2017), 96.
5. Paine, *The Japanese Empire*, 2.
6. Macdonald, 124.
7. Paine, 2017, 54.

8. David Fromkin, *A Peace to End All Peace: The Fall of the Ottoman Empire and the Creation of the Modern Middle East.* (New York: Holt Paperbacks, 1989), 475.
9. Paine, *The Japanese Empire,* 10.
10. Israel Eptsein, *The Unfinished Revolution in China.* (Boston: Little, Brown & Company, 1947), 28.
11. Young, 23.
12. Paine, *The Japanese Empire,* 82.
13. Ibid., 22.
14. Ibid., 22.
15. Ibid., 45.
16. Ibid., 46.
17. Ibid., 51.
18. Ibid., 51.
19. Bruce Cumings, *Korea's Place in the Sun: A Modern History.* (New York: W.W. Norton & Company, 2005), 141.
20. Paine, *The Japanese Empire,* 79-80.
21. Kim Il Sung, *With the Century.* (Korean Friendship Association, 2003).
22. Cumings, *Korea's Place,* 143.
23. Anna Louise Strong, *In North Korea: First Eye-Witness Report.* (Soviet Russia Today, 1949), 27-28.
24. Paine, *The Japanese Empire,* 80.
25. Cumings, *Korea's Place,* 146.
26. Ibid., 145.
27. Frank Baldwin, ed., *Without Parallel: The American-Korean Relationship Since 1945.* (New York: Pantheon Books, 1975), 5.
28. Kim, *With the Century.*
29. Paine, *The Japanese Empire,* 82.
30. Cumings, *Korea's Place,* 182.
31. Young, 28.
32. Strong, 27.
33. Henry Heller, *The Cold War and the New Imperialism: A Global History, 1945-2005.* (New York: Monthly Review Press, 2006), 68.
34. Strong, 37.
35. Ibid.
36. Cumings, *Korea's Place,* 169.
37. Ibid., 178.
38. Ibid., 176.
39. Ibid., 175.
40. Ibid., 177.
41. Ibid., 183.
42. Cumings, *The Korean War,* 39.
43. Michael Schaller, "America's Favorite War Criminal: Kishi Nobusuke and the Transformation of U.S.-Japan Relations," Japan Policy Research Institute, JPRI Working Paper No. 11. (July 1995).

44. Ibid.
45. Ibid.
46. Bruce Cumings, "A Murderous History of Korea," *London Review of Books*, Vol. 39, No. 10, (May 18, 2017).
47. Cumings, *The Korean War*, 41.
48. Ibid., 41.
49. Ibid., 42.
50. Ibid.
51. Ibid., 147.
52. Ibid., 154-155.
53. Paine, *The Japanese Empire*, 92.
54. Kim, *With the Century*.
55. Ibid.
56. Ibid.
57. Paine, *The Japanese Empire*, 92.
58. Stephen Kinzer, "Wilson perfectly embodies U.S. hypocrisy. That's why we should remember him." *Politico Magazine*, December 6, 2015. https://www.politico.com/magazine/story/2015/12/woodrow-wilson-center-princeton-foreign-policy-213419#ixzz3tb4S5BjY
59. Ibid.
60. Fromkin, 295; Kinzer.
61. Kinzer.
62. Kim, *With the Century*.
63. Ibid.
64. Ibid.
65. Ibid.
66. Ibid.
67. Ibid.
68. V.I. Lenin, "The Tasks of the Russian Social-Democratic Labour Party in the Russian Revolution." *Lenin Collected Works*. (Progress Publishers, Vol. 23, 1964), 355-361.
69. Kim, *With the Century*.
70. David A. Andelman, *A Shattered Peace: Versailles 1919 and the Price We Pay Today*. (Hoboken: John Wiley & Sons, 2008), 126.
71. Ho Chi Minh, "The path which led me to Leninism," *Selected Works of Ho Chi Minh Vol. 4*, (Foreign Languages Publishing House, 1960).
72. Domenico Losurdo, *Class Struggle: A Political and Philosophical History*. (Basingstoke: Palgrave MacMillan, 2016), 139.
73. V.I. Lenin, "National and colonial questions," *Lenin's Collected Works, 2nd English Edition*. (Progress Publishers, Moscow, Vol. 32, 1965), 144-151.
74. Ho.
75. Kim Il Sung, "For a free and peaceful new world," (Pyongyang: Foreign Languages Publishing House, April 29, 1991).

76. Address Before a Joint Session of the Congress on the Persian Gulf Crisis and the Federal Budget Deficit by George H. W. Bush, September 11, 1990.
77. Damian Paletta and Julian E. Barnes, "Yemen unrest spells setback for U.S.," *The Wall Street Journal*, January 23, 2017.
78. Minutes of the Second Congress of the Communist International, Seventh Session, July 30, https://www.marxists.org/history/international/comintern/2nd-congress/ch07.htm .
79. Paine, *The Japanese Empire*, 111.
80. Jean-Paul Sartre, Preface to *The Wretched of the Earth* by Frantz Franon. (New York: Grove Press, 1963.), 21.
81. Sidney and Beatrice Webb. *Soviet Communism: A New Civilization*. 3rd ed. (London: Longmans, Green and Co, 1944), xxi – xxiii.
82. Jon Letman, "USAG Humphreys: The Story Behind America's Biggest Overseas Base," *The Diplomat*, November 6, 2017. https://thediplomat.com/2017/11/camp-humphreys-the-story-behind-americas-biggest-overseas-base/.

Chapter 2 – Imperialism

1. V.I. Lenin, *Imperialism: The Highest Stage of Capitalism*. (New York: International Publishers, 2000), 8.
2. https://www.upi.com/Haig-Syria-should-be-next-target/83271010433391/
3. Julian E. Barnes, "Nato plans to create two new commands amid Russian tensions," *The Wall Street Journal*, October 24, 2017.
4. De Borchgrave.
5. Carol E. Lee, "On final Asia trip, Obama faces tests to U.S. power," *The Wall Street Journal*, September 7, 2016; *The Wall Street Journal*, June 23, 2015.
6. Jeffrey D. Sachs, "The fatal expense of American imperialism," *The Boston Globe*, October 30, 2016.
7. David Vine, "The United States probably has more foreign military bases than any other people, nation, or empire in history," *The Nation* (New York, NY), September 14, 2015.
8. Ibid.
9. Charles W. Mills, *The Racial Contract*. (Ithaca: Cornell University Press, 1997), 18-19.
10. Ibid., 18.
11. Ibid.
12. Michael M. Phillips, "New ways the U.S. projects power around the globe: Commandoes," *The Wall Street Journal*, April 24, 2015.
13. Zbigniew Brzezinski, *The Grand Chessboard: American Primacy and its Geostrategic Imperatives*. (New York: Basic Books, 1997). See Chapter 1, titled "A Hegemony of a New Type."
14. Domenico Losurdo, "Uri Avnery between US international dictatorship and Israel's extrajudicial killings," *Voltairenet.org*, November 18, 2011.
15. Brzezinski, 23.
16. Ibid., 23-24.

17. Ibid., 25.
18. Ibid., 25.
19. Ibid., 27.
20. Bruce Cumings. *Korea's Place in the Sun: A Modern History.* New York: W.W. Norton & Company, 2005, 332.
21. Quoted in Lenin, *Imperialism*, 79.
22. Macdonald, p. 97.
23. Ibid., 124.
24. Ibid., 98.
25. Ibid., 98.
26. Ibid., 113.
27. Ibid., 114.
28. Young, 26.
29. Ibid., 15.
30. Macdonald, 114.
31. Young, 40.
32. Cumings, 332.
33. Macdonald, 114.
34. Ibid., 114-115.
35. Ibid., 130.
36. Hjalmar Schacht, "Germany's Colonial Demands, *Foreign Affairs* 15, no. 2, (1937).
37. This is the thesis propounded by Lenin in *Imperialism: The Highest Stage of Capitalism.*
38. Lenin, *Imperialism*, 11.
39. Ibid., 13.
40. Ibid., 96.
41. Ibid., 8.
42. Kim, *With the Century.*
43. Ibid.

Chapter 3 – The Patriot

1. Cumings, *The Korean War*, 46.
2. Cumings, "A Murderous History."
3. Kim, *With the Century.*
4. Ibid.
5. Strong, 22.
6. Strong, 22.
7. Bruce Cumings, *North Korea: Another Country.* (New York: The New Press, 2004), 111.
8. Ibid., 159.
9. Ibid., 105.
10. Ibid., 115.
11. Cumings, "A Murderous History."

12. Cumings, *North Korea*, 121.
13. Ibid., 108.
14. Ibid., 115-116.
15. Ibid., 120.
16. Ibid., 116.
17. Ibid., 108.
18. Ibid., 108.
19. Ibid., 121.
20. Ibid., 121-122.
21. Ibid., 105.
22. Macdonald, 126.
23. Ibid.
24. Ibid., 128.
25. Ibid.
26. Ibid., 151.
27. Ibid., 153.
28. Ibid., 151-152.
29. Ibid., 152.
30. Ibid., 153.
31. Ibid., 154.
32. Ibid., 156.
33. Ibid., 151-152.

Chapter 4 – The US Occupation

1. Kim Il-sung, "On the establishment of the Workers' Party of north Korea and the question founding the Workers' Party of South Korea," *Kim Il Sung: Selected Works I,* 1946), 102-120. https://www.marxists.org/archive/kim-il-sung/1946/09/26.htm
2. Cumings, *Korea's Place*, 187.
3. Cumings, *The Korean War*, 243.
4. Kim, 1991.
5. Kim, *With the Century.*
6. Cumings, *Korea's Place*, 187.
7. Ibid.
8. Mills, 25-26.
9. Nelson Mandela, "Statement from the dock at the opening of the Rivonia Trial, Pretoria Supreme Court, April 20, 1964."
10. Arno J Mayer, *Why Did the Heavens Not Darken? The 'Final Solution' in History.* (New York: Verso, 2012), 97.
11. Robert O. Paxton, *The Anatomy of Fascism.* (New York: Alfred A Knopf, 2004), 22.
12. Jacques R. Pauwels, *The Great Class War: 1914-1918.* (Toronto: James Lorimer & Company, 2016), 57.
13. Milena Rampoldi, "A conversation with Marxist philosopher Thomas Metscher," *Marxism-Leninism Today,* https://mltoday.com/article/2666-a-conversation-with-marxist-philosopher-thomas-metscher/31

14. Paine, *The Japanese Empire*, 111.
15. Cumings, *Korea's Place*, 187-188.
16. Ibid., 188.
17. Ibid.
18. Ibid., 190.
19. Heller, 69.
20. Cumings, *Korea's Place*, 186.
21. Strong, 16-17.
22. Kim Il Sung, "On eliminating dogmatism and formalism and establishing Juche in ideological work," *Kim Il Sung: Selected Works* 582-606, December 28, 1955. https://www.marxists.org/archive/kim-il-sung/1955/12/28.htm
23. The Research Institute of History, Academy of Science of the Democratic People's Republic of Korea. *History of the Just Fatherland Liberation War of the Korean People*. (Pyongyang: Foreign Languages Publishing House, 1981), 2.
24. Strong, 16-17.
25. Ibid., 7.
26. Epstein, *The Unfinished Revolution*, 3.
27. Melvyn P Leffler, *The Specter of Communism: The United States and the Origins of the Cold War, 1917-1953*. (New York: Hill and Wang, 1994), 100.
28. Strong, 30.
29. Cumings, *Korea's Place*, 182.
30. Cumings, *The Korean War*, 111.
31. Cumings, "A Murderous History."
32. Cumings, *Korea's Place*, 355.
33. Ibid., 358.
34. Ibid., 212.
35. Ibid., 201.
36. Ibid., 197.
37. Ibid., 193.
38. Ibid., 194.
39. Ibid., 193.
40. Ibid., 198.
41. Ibid., 198.
42. Ibid., 199.

Chapter 5 – The Patriot State

1. Cumings, *Korea's Place*, 204.
2. Ibid., 199.
3. Baldwin, 34.
4. Cumings, *Korea's Place*, 199.
5. Ibid., 209.
6. Kim, "On eliminating dogmatism."
7. Strong, 14.
8. Ibid., 18.
9. Cumings, *Korea's Place*, 195.

10. Worden, p. 41.
11. Ibid.
12. Leffler, 97.
13. Baldwin, 9.
14. Louis A. Perez Jr, "Fidel Castro: A life—and death—in context," *TRTWorld*, November 29, 2016. https://www.trtworld.com/opinion/fidel-castro-a-life-and-death-in-context-3925.
15. Strong, 29.
16. Kim Il Sung, "On the establishment of the Workers' Party of north Korea and the question founding the Workers' Party of South Korea," Kim Il Sung: Selected Works I, September 26, 1946, pp. 102-120. https://www.marxists.org/archive/kim-il-sung/1946/09/26.htm
17. Strong, pp. 30-31.
18. Cumings, *Korea's Place*, 151.
19. Strong, 39.
20. Ibid., 40.
21. Kim, "On the establishment."
22. Strong, p. 37.
23. Kim, "On the establishment."
24. Ibid.
25. Strong, 37; Cumings, *Korea's Place*, 228.
26. Joan Robinson, "Korean Miracle." *Monthly Review* 16, no. 9, (1965): 541-549.
27. Robinson.
28. Robinson.

Chapter 6 – The War Against Communists of the South

1. Cumings, *Korea's Place*, 371.
2. Ibid., 201-202.
3. Ibid., 200.
4. Ibid., 194.
5. Ibid., 201.
6. Worden, *North Korea*, 34.
7. Cumings, *Korea's Place*, 200.
8. Ibid., 201.
9. Ibid., 201.
10. Young, *Japan's Total Empire*, 28.
11. Strong, 7.
12. Heller, *The Cold War*, 70.
13. Cumings, *Korea's Place*, 192.
14. Ibid., 221.
15. Strong, 15.
16. Cumings, *Korea's Place*, 223.
17. Ibid.,. 223.
18. Ibid., 208.

19. Ibid., 209.
20. Ibid., 202-203.
21. Strong, 13.
22. Ibid.,14.
23. Cumings, "A Murderous History."
24. Brzezinski, 25.
25. Polk.
26. Cumings, *Korea's Place*, 195.

Chapter 7 – Suppressing a Worldwide Movement for Liberty, Equality and the Unity of Humankind

1. Baldwin, 7.
2. Leffler, 30.
3. Leffler, 31.
4. Steven Hahn, *A Nation Without Borders: The United States and its World in an Age of Civil Wars, 1830-1910*. (New York: Viking, 2016).
5. Brzezinski, 4.
6. Leffler, 55.
7. Ibid., 56-57.
8. Ibid., 50.
9. Ibid., 57.
10. Ibid.
11. Ibid., 58.
12. Ibid., 59.
13. Ibid., 61.
14. Ibid., 63.
15. Ibid., 63.
16. Ibid., 85.
17. Ibid., 87-88.
18. Macdonald, 178-179.
19. Paine, *The Japanese Empire*, 111.
20. Macdonald, 178-179.
21. Leffler, 88.
22. Ibid.
23. Cumings, *Korea's Place*, 201.
24. Leffler, 88.
25. Ibid., 89.
26. Cumings, *Korea's Place*, 201.

Chapter 8 – The Political Partition of Korea

1. Strong, 8.
2. Cumings, *Korea's Place*, 211.
3. Strong, 9.
4. Ibid.

5. Ibid.
6. Cumings, *Korea's Place*, 211-212.
7. Ibid.
8. Strong, 3.
9. Ibid., 6.
10. Cumings, *Korea's Place*, 212.
11. Ibid.
12. Ibid., 222.
13. Ibid.
14. Kim, *With the Century*.
15. Kim Il Sung, "Answers to the Questions Raised by the Iraqi Journalists' Delegation," Pyongyang, 1971. https://www.marxists.org/archive/kim-il-sung/1971/x01/x01.htm
16. Cumings, *Korea's Place*, 243.
17. CIA, "Consequence of US troop withdrawal from Korea in spring, 1949," February 28, 1949.
18. Cumings, 2005, 246.
19. Choe Sang-Hun, "South Korea admits civilian massacre during war," *The New York Times*, November 27, 2009.
20. Diane Kraft, "South Korea's National Security Law: A Tool of Oppression in an Insecure World," *Wisconsin International Law Journal* 24, no. 2, (2006).
21. Cumings, *Korea's Place*, 348.
22. Kraft.

Chapter 9 – The Campaign of 1950-1953

1. Bertolt Brecht, *War Primer*. (New York: Verso, 2017), 24.
2. Cumings, *The Korean War*, 23.
3. Richard Stokes, British minister of works, 1950-51, quoted in Cumings, *The Korean War*, 64.
4. Polk.
5. Israel Epstein in *Gazette and Daily*, (York, PA). June 8, 1948, quoted by Strong, 6.
6. Cumings, *The Korean War*, 40 and 65.
7. Ibid., 44-45.
8. Kim, 1971.
9. Cumings, *The Korean War*, xviii.
10. Cumings, *Korea's Place*, 238.
11. Baldwin, 34.
12. Cumings, *Korea's Place*, 199.
13. Worden, 43.
14. Ibid.; Heller, 71.
15. Cumings, *Korea's Place*, 247.
16. Heller, 71.
17. CIA, "Consequence of US troop withdrawal from Korea in spring, 1949," February 28, 1949 . https://www.cia.gov/library/readingroom/docs/DOC_0000258388.pdf

18. Cumings, "A Murderous History."
19. Cumings, *Korea's Place*, 223.
20. Research Institute of History, Academy of Science of the Democratic People's Republic of Korea. *History of the Just Fatherland Liberation War of the Korean People*. Foreign Language Publishing House, 1981. 28.
21. Cumings, *Korea's Place*, 265.
22. Ibid., 263.
23. Polk.
24. Baldwin, 12.
25. Ibid.
26. Cumings, *Korea's Place*, 269.
27. Ibid., 270.
28. Timur Kuran, "What kills inequality: Redistribution's violent history," *Foreign Affairs*, August 15, 2017.
29. Choe Sang-Hun, "Korea investigates atrocities in race against time," *The New York Times*, September 4, 2009.
30. Jae-Soon Chang, "Hidden history: Families talk of Korean War executions, say US shares blame in deaths," Associated Press, May 18, 2008.
31. Cumings, "A Murderous History."
32. Cumings, *The Korean War*, 83.
33. Ibid., 83.
34. Ibid.
35. Choe, November 27, 2009.
36. Chang , May 18, 2008.
37. See for example: Nikolaus Wachsmann, *KL: A History of the Nazi Concentration Camps*. (New York: Farrar, Straus and Giroux, 2015).
38. Cumings, Korea's Place, 332.
39. Heller, 71; Worden, 44.
40. Cumings, *The Korean War*, xviii.
41. Leffler, 105.
42. Polk.
43. Ibid.
44. Ibid.
45. Cumings, Korea's Place, 294.
46. Charles Armstrong, "The Destruction and Reconstruction of North Korea, 1950-1960," *The Asia-Pacific Journal*, Japan Focus, Volume 7, March 16, 2009.
47. Robinson.
48. Armstrong.
49. Ibid.
50. Blaine Harden, "The U.S. war crime North Korea won't forget," *The Washington Post*, March 24, 2015.
51. Armstrong.
52. Cumings, *The Korean War*, 239.
53. Armstrong.
54. Ibid.

55. Iain Marlow, "South Korea's chaebol problem," *The Globe and Mail* (Toronto, ON), April 27, 2015; Armstrong.
56. Armstrong.
57. Cumings, *The Korean War*, 243.
58. Medhi Hasan, "Why Do North Koreans Hate Us? One Reason—They Remember the Korean War," *The Intercept*, May 3, 2017. https://theintercept.com/2017/05/03/why-do-north-koreans-hate-us-one-reason-they-remember-the-korean-war/.
59. Quoted in Domenico Losurdo, *Non-Violence: A History Beyond the Myth*, (Landham: Lexington Books, 2015), 216.
60. Bruce Cumings, "Latest North Korean provocations stem from missed US opportunities for demilitarization," *Democracy Now!*, May 29, 2009. https://www.democracynow.org/2009/5/29/north_korea.
61. Adam Johnson, "CNN celebrates 'joy" of McCain a day after his genocidal threat," *FAIR.org*, September 12, 2017. https://fair.org/home/cnn-celebrates-joy-of-mccain-a-day-after-his-genocidal-threat/.
62. Mark Landler, Choe Sang-hun and Helene Cooper, "North Korea fires a ballistic missile, in a further challenge to Trump," *The New York Times*, November 28, 2017.
63. Cumings, *The Korean War*, 239.

Chapter 10 – The Anti-Communist Police State

1. Cumings, *Korea's Place*, 208.
2. Ibid., 350.
3. Robinson.
4. Cumings, *Korea's Place*, 365.
5. Cumings, *The Korean War*, 46.
6. Choe Sang-hun, "An artist is rebuked for casting South Korea's leader in an unflattering light," *The New York Times*, August 30, 2014.
7. Mayer, 97.
8. *Newsweek*, September 23, 1974, 51-52.
9. Kinzer.
10. See: Reg Whitaker, Gregory S. Kealey, and Andrew Parnaby, *Secret Service: Political Policing in Canada from the Fenians to Fortress America*. (Toronto: University of Toronto Press, 2012).
11. Choe Sang-hun, "Leftist leaders accused of trying to overthrow South Korean government," *The New York Times*, August 28, 2013.
12. Choe, August 28, 2013.
13. Amnesty International recommends that "South Korea abolish or substantially amend the NSL in line with the country's international human rights obligations and commitments." See: "The National Security Law: Curtailing freedom of expression, and association in the name of security in the Republic of Korea," 2012. https://www.amnestyusa.org/reports/the-national-security-law-curtailing-freedom-of-expression-and-association-in-the-name-of-security-in-the-republic-of-korea/

14. Human Rights Watch says that "The law clearly violates South Korea's international human-rights obligations" KaySeok, "South Korea: Abolish or Fix National Security Law," *Joongang Daily*, September 17, 2010.
15. "National Security Law again being used in communist witch hunts," *The Hankyoreh*, January 13, 2015.
16. Kraft.
17. Kraft.
18. "Man acquitted, 30 years later for 'subversive books' on capitalism and revolution," *The Hankyoreh*, November 26, 2014.
19. Choe Sang-hun, "South Korean law casts wide net, snarling satirists in hunt for spies," *The New York Times*, January 7, 2012.
20. "Military expands book blacklist," *The Hankyoreh*, July 31, 2008.
21. Choe Sang-hun, "North Korean takes to Twitter and YouTube," *The New York Times*, August 17, 2010.
22. Choe Sang-hun, "Korea policing the Net. Twist? It's south Korea," *The New York Times*, August 12, 2012.
23. Choe Sang-hun, "South Korean indicated over Twitter posts from North," *The New York Times*, February 2, 2012.
24. Choe Sang-hun, "South Korean law casts wide net, snarling satirists in hunt for spies," *The New York Times*, January 7, 2012.
25. "South Korea Police State: National Intelligence Service (NIS) Arrests Rep. Lee Seok-ki: Did ROK Lawmaker Really Try to Overthrow the Government?" *Global Research News*, October 1, 2013. https://www.globalresearch.ca/south-korea-police-police-national-intelligence-service-nis-arrests-rep-lee-seok-ki-did-rok-lawmaker-really-try-to-overthrow-the-government/5358043.
26. Choe Sang-hun, "Leftist leader accused of trying to overthrow South Korean government," *The New York Times*, August 28, 2013.
27. Jamie Doucette and Se-Woong Koo, "Distorting Democracy: Politics by Public Security in Contemporary South Korea [UPDATE]", *The Asia-Pacific Journal*: Japan Focus, February 20, 2014.
28. Kraft.
29. Kraft.
30. Kraft.
31. Nicholas Kristof, "Free in Seoul After 44 Years, and Still Defiant," *The New York Times*, August 20, 1995.
32. Kristof.
33. Kristof.
34. Kristof.
35. Kristof.
36. Kristof.
37. Kristof.
38. Kristof.
39. Kristof.
40. Polk.

41. Cumings, 2005, p. 370.
42. Cumings, 2005, p. 371.
43. Cumings, 2005, p. 372.
44. Cumings, 2005, p. 371; Matthew Burns, George E. Ogle B.D. '54: Defying injustice in Korea," *Duke Magazine*, August 1, 2003.
45. Cumings, 2005, p. 400.
46. "Pan-Africanism and Communism: An Interview with Hakim Adi," *Review of African Political Economy*, http://roape.net/2017/01/26/pan-africanism-communism-interview-hakim-adi/
47. Cumings, 2005, p. 349.
48. Cumings, 2005, p. 507; Worden, 2008, p. 220.
49. Letman.
50. Kim, 1991.
51. Cumings, 2005, p. 349.
52. Cumings, 2005, p. 350.
53. Cumings, 2005, p. 351.
54. Cumings, 2005, p. 351.
55. Cumings, 2005, p. 353.
56. Cumings, 2005, p. 334.
57. Kraft.
58. Cumings, 2005, p. 363.
59. Cumings, 2005, p. 363.
60. Cumings, 2005, p. 378.
61. Cumings, 2005, p. 379.
62. Cumings, 2005, p. 379.
63. Cumings, 2005, p. 380.
64. Cumings, 2005, p. 386.
65. Cumings, 2005, p. 381.
66. Cumings, 2005, p. 382.
67. Cumings, 2005, p. 382.
68. Tim Shorrock, "The Gwangju uprising and American hypocrisy: One reporter's quest for truth and justice in Korea," *The Nation*, June 5, 2015.
69. Cumings, 2005, p. 382.
70. Cumings, 2005, p. 384.
71. Cumings, 2005, p. 384.

Chapter 11 – Washington's Power Projection Platform in the Pacific

1. Tim Beal, "A Korean Tragedy," *The Asia-Pacific Journal* / Japan Focus, Volume 15, Issue 16, no. 2, (2017).
2. "The Limits of Power: Andrew Bacevich on the End of American Exceptionalism," *Democracy Now!*, August 20, 2008. https://www.democracynow.org/2008/8/20/the_limits_of_power_andrew_bacevich.
3. Choe Sang-hun, "South Korea delays shift in control of military," *The New York Times*, October 24, 2014.

4. Gordon Lubold and Jonathan Cheng, "Seoul presses US to hand over wartime command of South Korea military," *The Wall Street Journal*, October 26, 2017.
5. "Defense budget projected to rise 6.9% from last year's total," *The Hankyoreh*, August 30, 2017.
6. Alastair Gale and Chieko Tsuneoka, "Japan to increase military spending for fifth year in a row," *The Wall Street Journal*, December 21, 2016.
7. "Debate over size of North Korea's army reignites," *The Hankyoreh*, December 25, 2015.
8. Choe Sang-hun, "Behind North Korea's bluster, some see caution," *The New York Times*, September 26, 2017.
9. "Moon says dialogue with N. Korea 'impossible,' warns of destruction 'beyond recovery'," *Yonhap*, September 15, 2017.
10. "President Moon rebukes Defense Ministry for its 'lack of confidence'," *The Hankyoreh*, August 29, 2017.
11. Letman.
12. Cumings, *Korea's Place*, 255.
13. Ibid., 321.
14. Baldwin, 20.
15. Cumings, *Korea's Place*, 322.
16. Baldwin, 29.
17. David Axe, "South Korea's Secret War," *The Diplomat*, April 27, 2010. https://thediplomat.com/2010/04/south-koreas-secret-war/.
18. Polk.
19. Bruce Cumings, "Saber rattling won't fix North Korea threat," *Global Times*, September 18, 2017.
20. Cumings, *Korea's Place*, 245.
21. Baldwin, 18.
22. Letman.
23. Anna Fifield, "As North Korea intensifies its missile program, the U.S. opens an $11 billion base in the South," *The Washington Post*, July 29, 2017.
24. Kim, 1971.
25. Cumings, *Korea's Place*, 506.

Chapter 12 – US Supremacy's All-Conquering March

1. Graham E. Fuller, *A World Without Islam*. (Boston: Back Bay Books, 2010), 252-253.
2. Letter of outgoing US President Barack Obama to incoming President Donald Trump. http://edition.cnn.com/2017/09/03/politics/obama-trump-letter-inauguration-day/index.html
3. John McCain, "John McCain: Why We Must Support Human Rights," *The New York Times*, May 8, 2017.
4. Sartre, 26.
5. Martin Gilens and Benjamin I. Page, "Testing theories of American Politics: Elites, Interest Groups, and Average Citizens," *Perspectives on Politics* 12, no. 3 (2014).

6. See: Laurence H. Shoup, *Wall Street's Think Tank: The Council on foreign Relations and the Empire of Neoliberal Geopolitics, 1976-2014*. (New York: Monthly Review Press, 2015) and Laurence H. Shoup & William Minter, *Imperial Brain Trust: The Council on Foreign Relations & United States Foreign Policy*. Authors' Choice Press, 2004.
7. Leffler, 96.
8. Ibid., 64.
9. Ibid., 69.
10. US National Security Strategy, 2015.
11. Ibid.
12. "U.S. envoy urges no cut in U.N. funding," The Associated Press, January 13, 2017.
13. US National Security Strategy, 2015.
14. Felicia Schwartz, "U.S. to reduce staffing at embassy in Cuba in response to mysterious attacks," *The Wall Street Journal*, September 29, 2017.
15. Michael M. Grynbaum, "An 'apprentice' role for Trump opens door wide for questions," *The New York Times*, December 9, 2016.
16. Mark Landler, "Trump National Security team gets a slow start," *The New York Times*, January 18, 2017.
17. William J. Clinton, Inaugural Address. January 20, 1997.
18. Michael R. Gordon, Helene Cooper and Eric Schmitt, "Trump will call for a Pentagon plan to hit ISIS harder, official say," *The New York Times*, January 26, 2017.
19. Sohrab Ahmari, "A noble responsibility," *The Wall Street Journal*, May 6, 2013.
20. Solomon Hughes, "Trump warns McCain: 'I fight back'," *The Wall Street Journal*, October 17, 2017.
21. National Military Strategy of the United States, 2015.
22. Maxwell Watts, "U.S. allies in Asia are anxious, Pacific Fleet commander says," *The Wall Street Journal*, May 8, 2017.
23. James Stavridis, "Growing threat to the U.S. at sea," *The Wall Street Journal*, June 2, 2017.
24. Posture statement of 19th Chairman of the Joint Chiefs of Staff before the 115th Congress Senate Armed Services Budget Hearing, June 13, 2017.
25. Transcript: President Obama's speed outlining strategy to defeat Islamic state, *The Washington Post*, September 10, 2014.
26. US National Security Strategy, 2015.
27. Ibid.
28. Obama address to the United Nations General Assembly, 2016.
29. Paine, *The Japanese Empire*, 22.
30. Ibid., 103.
31. Christopher Marquis, "Absent From the Korea Talks: Bush's Hard-Liner," *The New York Times*, September 3, 2003.
32. Richard N. Haass, "Time to end the North Korean threat," *The Wall Street Journal*, December 23, 2014.

33. Statement by the President on the Trans-Pacific Partnership," The White House, Office of the Press Secretary, October 5, 2015.
34. See Assistant Secretary of State for Europe and Eurasian Affairs, Victoria Nuland's December 13, 2013 address to the US-Ukraine Foundation. https://www.youtube.com/watch?v=U2fYcHLouXY)
35. Losurdo, *Non-Violence: A History Beyond the Myth*. Lanham: Lexington Books, 2015. 2015, 28.
36. David Olusoga, *The World's War*. (London: Head of Zeus, 2014).

Chapter 13 – Sabotaging an Alternative to the US-Led Global Economic Order

1. Domenico Losurdo, "Beyond Mere Sentiment," *Revista Opera*, November 6, 2017.
2. Constitution of the Republic of Korea.
3. The Socialist Constitution of the Democratic People's Republic of Korea.
4. Ibid.
5. Ibid.
6. Address of Ri Yong-ho to the United Nations General Assembly, September 23, 2017.
7. The Socialist Constitution of the Democratic People's Republic of Korea.
8. Constitution of the Republic of Korea.
9. The Socialist Constitution of the Democratic People's Republic of Korea.
10. Ibid.
11. "Koreans' average work hours still second-longest in OECD," *The Korea Herald*, November 2, 2015.
12. Ahn Ju-yeop, quoted in *The Korea Herald*, November 2, 2015.
13. *Korea Herald*, November 2, 2015.
14. Ibid.
15. The Socialist Constitution of the Democratic People's Republic of Korea.
16. Constitution of the Republic of Korea.
17. Republic of Korea: Laws Governing Exploitative Labor Report, https://www.dol.gov/ilab/reports/pdf/southkorea_CL.pdf)
18. The Socialist Constitution of the Democratic People's Republic of Korea.
19. V.I. Lenin, *The State and Revolution*. (London: Penguin Books, 1992), 85.
20. The Socialist Constitution of the Democratic People's Republic of Korea.
21. Mark Landler and Julie Herschfeld Davis, "Trump tells Japan it can protect itself by buying US arms," *The New York Times*, November 8, 2017.
22. Motoko Rich, "A pacifist Japan starts to embrace the military," *The New York Times*, August 29, 2017.
23. Losurdo, *Class Struggle*, 288.
24. John Mueller and Karl Mueller, "Sanctions of Mass Destruction," *Foreign Affairs* (New York: NY), May/June 1999.
25. Ibid.
26. Ibid.

27. Barbara Crossette, "Iraq sanctions kill children, UN reports," *The New York Times*, December 1, 1995.
28. Mueller and Mueller.
29. Louis A Perez Jr, "Change through impoverishment: A half-century of Cuba-US relations," *nacla.org*, December 14, 2015. https://nacla.org/news/2015/12/13/change-through-impoverishment-half-century-cuba-us-relations.
30. Ibid.
31. Ibid.
32. See: Allen, Robert C., *Farm to Factory: A Reinterpretation of the Soviet Industrial Revolution*, (Princeton: Princeton University Press, 2003); David M. Kotz, "Socialism and Capitalism: Lessons from the Demise of State Socialism in the Soviet Union and China," *Socialism and Radical Political Economy: Essays in Honor of Howard Sherman*, ed. Robert Pollin, (Cheltenham and Northampton: Edward Elgar, 2000), 300-317; Kotz, David M. Kotz, "Socialism and Global Neoliberal Capitalism" Presentation, The Works of Karl Marx and Challenges for the XXI Century, Havana, Cuba, May 5-8, 2003; David M Kotz, "What Economic Structure for Socialism?" Presentation, The Works of Karl Marx and Challenges for the XXI Century, Havana, May 5-8, 2008; David M Kotz, "The Demise of the Soviet Union and the International Socialist Movement Today." Presentation, International Symposium on the 20th Anniversary of the Former Soviet Union and its Impact, Beijing, China, April 23, 2011; David Kotz and Fred Weir, *Revolution From Above: The Demise of the Soviet System*, Routledge, 1997.
33. Leffler.
34. "Socialism and Capitalism: Lessons from the Demise of State Socialism in the Soviet Union and China," in *Socialism and Radical Political Economy: Essays in Honor of Howard Sherman*, ed. Robert Pollin, Cheltenham and Northampton: Edward Elgar, 2000, 300-317; David M. Kotz, "Socialism and Capitalism: Lessons from the Demise of State Socialism in the Soviet Union and China," *Socialism and Radical Political Economy: Essays in Honor of Howard Sherman*, ed. Robert Pollin, (Cheltenham and Northampton: Edward Elgar, 2000), 300-317; Kotz, David M. Kotz, "Socialism and Global Neoliberal Capitalism" Presentation, The Works of Karl Marx and Challenges for the XXI Century, Havana, Cuba, May 5-8, 2003; David M Kotz, "What Economic Structure for Socialism?" Presentation, The Works of Karl Marx and Challenges for the XXI Century, Havana, May 5-8, 2008; David M Kotz, "The Demise of the Soviet Union and the International Socialist Movement Today." Presentation, International Symposium on the 20th Anniversary of the Former Soviet Union and its Impact, Beijing, China, April 23, 2011; David Kotz and Fred Weir, *Revolution From Above: The Demise of the Soviet System*, Routledge, 1997.
35. Manifesto, Second Congress of the Communist International, II. The Economic Situation, August 1920.
36. Louis A Perez Jr, "Fear and loathing of Fidel Castro: Sources of US policy toward Cuba," *Journal of Latin American Studies*, 34, (2002): 237-254.

37. Perez Jr, 2002.
38. Amnesty International, "The crumbling state of health care in North Korea", July 2010. http://www.amnesty.org/en/library/asset/ASA24/001/2010/en/13a097fc-4bda-4119-aae5-73e0dd446193/asa240012010en.pdf
39. Dianne E. Rennack, "North Korea: Economic sanctions", Congressional Research Service, October 17, 2006. http://www.au.af.mil/au/awc/awcgate/crs/rl31696.pdf
40. Mark Landler, "Envoy to coordinate North Korea sanctions," *The New York Times*, June 27, 2009.
41. David E. Sanger, "U.S. to roll out tepid welcome for president of South Korea," *The New York Times*, September 14, 2006.
42. According to Rennack, the following US sanctions have been imposed on North Korea for reasons listed as either "communism," "non-market economy," or "communism and market disruption": prohibition on foreign aid; prohibition on Export-Import Bank funding; limits on the exports or goods and services; denial of favorable trade terms.
43. Mueller and Mueller.
44. *The Washington Post*, November 16, 2005.
45. Alistair Gale and Kwanwod Jun, "North Korea says its successfully conducted hydrogen-bomb test," *The Wall Street Journal*, January 6, 2016.
46. David E. Sanger, Nicole Perlroth and Eric Schmitt, "U.S. asks China to help rein in Korean hackers," *The New York Times*, December 20, 2014.
47. Danny Yadron, Devlin Barret and Julian E. Barnes, "U.S. Struggles for Response to Sony Hack," *The Wall Street Journal*, December 18, 2014.
48. "North Korea warns of new tests as nuclear standoff intensifies," *Democracy Now!*, October 11, 2006. https://www.democracynow.org/2006/10/11/north_korea_warns_of_new_tests.
49. Yongho Tahe, Minister of the Embassy of the Democratic People's Republic of Korea in London, "Understanding and defending North Korea," *invent-the-future.org*, November 15, 2013.
50. "Press statement of DPRK foreign ministry," KCNA, June 16, 2017.
51. Tim Beal, "The Korean peninsula within the framework of US global hegemony," *The Asia-Pacific Journal*/ Pacific Focus, Volume 14, Issue 22, no. 3, November 2016.
52. Nuclear Posture Review, 2010.
53. Felix Greene, *The Enemy: What Every American Should Know about Imperialism*. (New York: Vintage, 1970), 292.
54. Alastair Gale and Chieko Tsuneoka, "Japan to increase military spending for fifth year in a row," *The Wall Street Journal*, December 21, 2016.
55. "Defense budget projected to rise 6.9% from last year's total," *The Hankyoreh*, August 30, 2017.
56. Holman W. Jenkins Jr., "Nukes won't save North Korea," *The Wall Street Journal*, August 1, 2017; Cumings, *Korea's Place*, 444; Gale and Tsuneoka.
57. The World Bank, https://data.worldbank.org/indicator/MS.MIL.XPND.GD.ZS

58. S.C.M. Paine, *The Wars for Asia, 1911-1949*. (Cambridge: Cambridge University Press, 2012), 52.
59. Cumings, *Korea's Place*, 305.
60. Ibid., 306.
61. Ibid., 321.
62. Ibid.
63. Ibid., 322.
64. Ibid., 332.
65. Ibid., 353.
66. Ibid., 305.
67. Ibid., 314.
68. Chang Ha-Joon, *Bad Samaritans: The Myth of Free Trade and the Secret History of Capitalism*. (London: Bloomsbury Press, 2008), 14.
69. Chang, 14.
70. Alastair Gale, "South Korea accuses North of hacking as tensions escalate," *The Wall Street Journal*, March 7, 2016; "Korea-US drills to maps out N.K. end-game scenario," *The Korea Herald*, February 18, 2016.
71. Gale.
72. Jay Solomon, Julian E. Barnes and Alastair Gale, "North Korea warned,"*The Wall Street Journal*, March 29, 2013.
73. Julian E. Barnes, "U.S. pledges further show of force in Korea," *The Wall Street Journal*, March 29, 2013.
74. Jonathan Cheng, "North Korea compares Donald Trump to Adolph Hitler," *The Wall Street Journal*, June 27, 2017.
75. "U.S. will be to blame for consequences from joint military drill: KPA Panmunjom Mission," *Rodong Sinmun*, August 23, 2017; Jonathan Cheng, "War games begin as U.S., South Korea brace for North's fury," *The Wall Street Journal*, August 20, 2017; Choe Sang-Hun, "South Korea faces an uncomfortable reality: A nuclear neighbor," *The New York Times*, August 21, 2017; "Number of American troops participating in Ulchi Freedom Guardian exercise to decrease," *The Hankyoreh*, August 19, 2017.
76. "KCNA commentary lays bare U.S. scenario for invading DPRK," KCNA, September 8, 2015.
77. "US-S. Korean Ulji Freedom Guardian joint military drills under fire," *Rodong Sinmun*, August 14, 2015.
78. Holoman W. Jenkins, Jr., "Nukes won't save North Korea," *The Wall Street Journal*, August 1, 2017.
79. "US surprise nuclear strike drill in S. Korea," KCNA, November 2, 2017; Jonathan Cheng, "U.S. bombers buzz North Korea as Trump's Asia trip looms," *The Wall Street Journal*, November 2, 2017.
80. Peter Schweizer, *Victory: The Reagan Administration's Secret Strategy that Hastened the Collapse of the Soviet Union*. (New York: The Atlantic Monthly Press, 1994), 8-9.
81. "KCNA commentary lays bare U.S. scenario for invading DPRK," KCNA, September 8, 2015.

82. "US-S. Korean Ulji Freedom Guardian joint military drills under fire," Rodong Sinmun, August 14, 2015.
83. Julian E. Barnes and Anton Trolanovski, "Nato sets forces to counter Russia," *The Wall Street Journal*, April 30, 2016.
84. Gregory L. White and Olga Razumovskaya, "Vladimir Putin appears in public for first time after 10-day absence," *The Wall Street Journal*, March 16, 2015.
85. Emily Ferris, "The True Purpose of Russia's Zapad Military Exercises: Why Moscow Wanted to Send a Message to Minsk," *Foreign Affairs* (New York, NY), October 4, 2017.
86. Michael R. Gordon and Eric Schmitt, "Russia's military drills near NATO border raise fears of aggression," *The New York Times*, July 31, 2017.
87. Ferris.
88. Nathan Hodge, "Russia says war games are 'purely defensive'," *The Wall Street Journal*, August 29, 2017.
89. Julian E. Barnes, "Planned Russian exercises in September sow NATO worries," *The Wall Street Journal*, March 28, 2017.
90. "US experts argue in favor of scaling down S. Korea-US military exercises," *The Hankyoreh*, June 20, 2017.
91. Sean Gervasi, "A full court press: The destabilization of the Soviet Union," *Covert Action Quarterly*, (1990), 21-26; 14.
92. Robert McNamara, quoted in Bahman Azad, *Heroic Struggle, Bitter Defeat: Factors Contributing to the Dismantling of the Socialist State in the USSR*, (New York: International Publishers, 2000), 138.
93. Rick Gladstone and David E. Sanger, "Security Council tightens economic vice on North Korea, blocking fuel, ships and workers," *The New York Times*, December 22, 2017.
94. Gladstone and Sanger.

Chapter 14 – *Byungjin*

1. Michael R. Gordon, "Jim Mattis, in Ukraine, says U.S. is thinking of sending weapons," *The New York Times*, August 24, 2017.
2. *Nuclear Posture Review*.
3. Ramzy Austin, "When the US last faced an emerging nuclear threat in East Asia," *The New York Times*, August 10, 2017.
4. Julie Hirschfeld Davis, "With North, past presidents preferred words over 'fire'," *The New York Times*, August 9, 2017.
5. Bruce Cumings, "Saber rattling won't fix North Korea threat," *Global Times*, September 18, 2017.
6. Ibid.
7. Joint Press Statement from the Permanent Representatives to the United Nations of the United States, United Kingdom and France following the adoption of a treaty banning nuclear weapons, 7 July 2017.
8. Cumings, *Korea's Place*, 488-489.
9. Mark Mazzetti, "In '97, U.S. Panel Predicted a North Korea Collapse in 5 Years," *The New York Times*, October 27, 2006.

10. "Report: Nuclear weapons policy review names potential targets," *CNN.com*, March 10, 2002. http://www.cnn.com/2002/US/03/09/nuclear.weapons/.
11. KCNA, January 22, 2003.
12. Yongho Thae.
13. Yongho Thae.
14. *Nuclear Posture Review.*
15. "U.S. Tells Iran, Syria, N. Korea 'Learn from Iraq,'" *Reuters* (London, England), April 9, 2003.
16. Alastair Gale, "North Korea's relentless march to nuclear prowess," *The Wall Street Journal*, September 3, 2017.
17. Yongho Thae.
18. Rudiger Frank, "Libyan lessons for North Korea: A case of déjà vu", *38 North.org*, March 21, 2011. http://www.38north.org/2011/03/libyan-lessons-for-north-korea/.
19. "Nuclear test part of DPRK's substantial countermeasures to defend its sovereignty," KCNA, February 21, 2013.
20. "Gone are the days of US nuclear blackmail," *Rodong Sinmun*, February 22, 2013.
21. "FM spokesman slams U.S. for deliberately linking negotiations with Iran over nuclear issue with DPRK," *Rodong Sinmun*, July 22, 2015.
22. Quoted in David Morrison, "Britain's 'dependent' nuclear deterrent," http://www.david-morrison.org.uk/nuclear-weapons/deterrent-dependent.htm .
23. Peter Nicholas and William Boston, "Obama's nuclear proffer gets Russian rebuff," *The Wall Street Journal*, June 19, 2013.
24. Morrison.
25. Walter Pincus, "As missions are added, Stratcom commander keeps focus on deterrence," *The Washington Post*, March 30, 2010.
26. Quoted in Morrison.
27. Ethan Bronner, "Israel sense bluffing in Iran's threats of retaliation", *The New York Times*, January 26, 2012.
28. Walter Pincus, "Nuclear weapons just don't make sense," *The Washington Post*, May 23, 2012.
29. Peter Baker, "Obama expands modernization of nuclear arsenal," *The New York Times*, May 13, 2010.
30. Pincus, May 23, 2012.
31. William J. Broad and David E. Sanger, "As U.S. modernizes nuclear weapons, 'smaller' leaves some uneasy," *The New York Times*, January 11, 2015.
32. Peter Nicholas and William Boston, "Obama's nuclear proffer gets Russian rebuff," *The Wall Street Journal*, June 19, 2013.
33. David E. Sanger and Thom Shanker, "White House is rethinking nuclear policy," *The New York Times*, February 28, 2010.
34. "Former US Secretary of Defense favors 'three nos' on North Korean nukes," *The Hankyoreh*, October 3, 2016.
35. "How much will new UN sanctions affect North Korea's coal exports to

China?" *The Hankyoreh*, December 1, 2016.
36. Choe Sang-hun, "As economy grows, North Korea's grip on society is tested," *The New York Times*, April 30, 2017.
37. Bruce Cumings, "This is what's really behind North Korea's nuclear provocations," March 23, 2017d.
38. Gwen Ifill, "Clinton Ends Asia Trip at Korea's Demilitarized Zone," *The New York Times*, July 12, 1993.
39. Quoted in Domenico Losurdo. *Non-Violence: A History Beyond the Myth*. Lanham: Lexington Books, 2015. 216.
40. Choe Sang-Hun, "South Korea faces an uncomfortable reality: A nuclear neighbor," *The New York Times*, August 21, 2017.
41. Charles J. Hanley and Randy Hershaft, "U.S. often weighed N. Korea nuke option," The Associated Press, October 11, 2010.
42. "Law on consolidating position of nuclear weapons state adopted," *Rodong Sinmun*, April 2, 2013.
43. *Rodong Sinmun*, May 12, 2017.
44. *Rodong Sinmun*, August 16, 2017.
45. KCNA, August 13, 2017.
46. "Beijing to host North Korea talks," *The New York Times*, August 14, 2003.
47. Kim Hyun, US "Has No Intention to Build Close Ties with N Korea: Ex-official," *Yonhap News*, September 2, 2009.
48. "Statement by H.E. Mr. Ri Yong Ho, Minister of Foreign Affairs of The Democratic People's Republic of Korea at the General Debate of the 71st Session of The United Nations General Assembly," September 23, 2016.
49. "Statement by H.E. Mr. Ri Yong Ho, Minister of Foreign Affairs of The Democratic People's Republic of Korea at the General Debate of the 71st Session of The United Nations General Assembly," September 23, 2016.
50. David E. Sanger, "What can Trump do about North Korea? His options are few and risky," *The New York Times*, July 4, 2017.
51. *Rodong Sinmun*, August 17, 2015.
52. Sanger, July 4, 2017.
53. Eric Schmitt, "Vast exercise demonstrated Russia's growing military prowess," *The New York Times*, October 1, 2017.

Conclusion – The First Real Holy War

1. Mills, 117.
2. Kim, With the Century.
3. Manifesto of the Congress to the Peoples of the East, Baku, September 1, 1920.

BIBLIOGRAPHY

Allen, Robert C. *Farm to Factory: A Reinterpretation of the Soviet Industrial Revolution*. Princeton: Princeton University Press, 2003.

Andelman, David, A. *A Shattered Peace: Versailles 1919 and the Price We Pay Today*. Hoboken: John Wiley & Sons, 2008.

Azad, Bahman. *Heroic Struggle, Bitter Defeat: Factors Contributing to the Dismantling of the Socialist State in the USSR*. New York: International Publishers, 2000.

Baldwin, Frank, ed. *Without Parallel: The American-Korean Relationship Since 1945*. New York: Pantheon Books, 1975.

Beal, Tim. *North Korea: The Struggle Against American Power*. London: Pluto Press, 2005.

— *Crisis in Korea: America, China and the Risk of War*. London: Pluto Press, 2011.

Brzezinski, Zbigniew. *The Grand Chessboard: American Primacy and its Geostrategic Imperatives*. New York: Basic Books, 1997.

Chang, Ha-Joon. *Bad Samaritans: The Myth of Free Trade and the Secret History of Capitalism*. London: Bloomsbury Press, 2008.

Cumings, Bruce. *North Korea: Another Country*. New York: The New Press, 2004

— *Korea's Place in the Sun: A Modern History*. New York: W.W. Norton & Company, 2005

— *The Korean War: A History*. New York: Modern Library, 2010.

Deane, Hugh. *The Korean War: 1945-1953*. San Francisco: China Books & Periodicals, 1999.

Epstein, Israel. *The Unfinished Revolution in China*. Boston: Little, Brown & Company, 1947.

Fanon, Franz. *The Wretched of the Earth.* New York: Grove Press, 1963.

Fromkin, David. *A Peace to End All Peace: The Fall of the Ottoman Empire and the Creation of the Modern Middle East.* New York: Holt Paperbacks, 1989.

Fuller, Graham E. *A World Without Islam.* Boston: Back Bay Books, 2010.

Greene, Felix. *The Enemy: What Every American Should Know About Imperialism.* New York Vintage, 1970.

Hahn, Steven. *A Nation Without Borders: The United States and its World in an Age of Civil Wars, 1830-1910.* New York: Viking, 2016.

Heller, Henry. *The Cold War and the New Imperialism: A Global History, 1945-2005.* New York: Monthly Review Press, 2006.

Kim Il Sung. *With the Century.* Korean Friendship Association, 2003.

Kotz, David with Fred Weir. *Revolution From Above: The Demise of the Soviet System.* London: Routledge, 1997.

Leffler, Melvyn P. The *Specter of Communism: The United States and the Origins of the Cold War, 1917-1953.* New York: Hill and Wang, 1994.

Lenin, V.I. *The State and Revolution.* London: Penguin Books, 1992.

— *Imperialism: The Highest Stage of Capitalism.* New York: International Publishers, 2000.

Losurdo, Domenico. *Non-Violence: A History Beyond the Myth.* Lanham: Lexington Books, 2015.

— *War and Revolution. Rethinking the Twentieth Century.* New York: Verso, 2015.

— *Class Struggle: A Political and Philosophical History.* Basingstoke: Palgrave MacMillan, 2016.

Macdonald, James. *When Globalization Fails: The Rise and Fall of Pax Americana.* New York: Farrar, Straus and Giroux, 2015.

Mayer, Arno J. *Why Did the Heavens Not Darken? The 'Final Solution' in History.* New York: Verso, 2012.

Mills, Charles W. *The Racial Contract.* Ithaca: Cornell University Press, 1997.

Olusoga, David. *The World's War.* London: Head of Zeus, 2014.

Paine, S.C.M. *The Wars for Asia, 1911-1949.* Cambridge: Cambridge University Press, 2012.

— *The Japanese Empire: Grand Strategy from the Meiji Restoration to the Pacific War.* Cambridge: Cambridge University Press, 2017.

Pauwels, Jacques, R. *The Myth of the Good War: American in the Second World War*. Toronto: James Lorimer & Company, 2002.

— *The Great Class War: 1914-1918*. Toronto: James Lorimer & Company, 2016.

Paxton, Robert O. *The Anatomy of Fascism*. New York: Alfred A Knopf, 2004.

Research Institute of History, Academy of Science of the Democratic People's Republic of Korea. *History of the Just Fatherland Liberation War of the Korean People*. Pyongyang: Foreign Languages Publishing House, 1981.

Scheidel, Walter. *The Great Leveler: Violence and the History of Inequality from the Stone Age to the Twenty-First Century*. Princeton: Princeton University Press, 2017.

Schweizer, Peter. *Victory: The Reagan Administration's Secret Strategy that Hastened the Collapse of the Soviet Union*. New York: The Atlantic Monthly Press, 1994.

Shoup, Laurence H. & William Minter. *Imperial Brain Trust: The Council on Foreign Relations & United States Foreign Policy*. Authors' Choice Press, 2004.

Shoup, Laurence H. *Wall Street's Think Tank: The Council on foreign Relations and the Empire of Neoliberal Geopolitics, 1976-2014*. New York: Monthly Review Press, 2015.

Stone, I.F. *The Hidden History of the Korean War*. New York: Monthly Review Press, 1952.

Strong, Anna Louise. *In North Korea: First Eye-Witness Report*. Soviet Russia Today, 1949.

Wachsmann, Nikolaus. *KL: A History of the Nazi Concentration Camps*. New York: Farrar, Straus and Giroux, 2015.

Webb, Sidney and Beatrice. *Soviet Communism: A New Civilization*. 3rd. ed. London: Longmans, Green and Co, 1944.

Whitaker, Reg, Gregory S. Kealey, and Andrew Parnaby. *Secret Service: Political Policing in Canada from the Fenians to Fortress America*. Toronto: University of Toronto Press, 2012.

Worden, Robert L, ed. *North Korea: A Country Study*. Book. From Library of Congress, 2008. http://www.loc.gov/catdir/toc/ecip0822/2008028547.html.

Young, Louise. *Japan's Total Empire: Manchuria and the Culture of Wartime Imperialism*. Berkeley: University of California Press, 1998.

Index

Page references in *italics* indicate an illustration.

ALSO AVAILABLE FROM BARAKA BOOKS

The Einstein File
The FBI's Secret War on the World's Most Famous Scientist
Fred Jerome (Forewords by Ajamu Baraka and David Suzuki)

Slouching Towards Sirte
NATO's War on Libya and Africa
Maximilian C. Forte

Rwanda and the New Scramble for Africa
From Tragedy to Useful Imperial Fiction
Robin Philpot

The Question of Separatism
Quebec and the Struggle over Sovereignty
Jane Jacobs

The Complete Muhammad Ali
Ishmael Reed

Justice Belied
The Unbalanced Scales of International Criminal Justice
John Philpot & Sébastien Chartrand, Editors

Songs Upon the Rivers
The Buried History of the French-speaking Canadiens and Métis
From the Great Lakes and the Mississippi across to the Pacific
Robert Foxcurran, Michel Bouchard, and Sébastien Malette

Rebel Priest in the Time of Tyrants
Mission to Haiti, Ecuador and Chile
Claude Lacaille

Scandinavian Common Sense
Policies to Tackle Social Inequalities in Health
Marie-France Raynault & Dominique Côté

FSC
www.fsc.org
MIX
Paper
FSC® C100212

Printed by Imprimerie Gauvin
Gatineau, Québec